S0-BIH-160

STUDY GUIDE

FUNDAMENTALS OF FINANCIAL MANAGEMENT

Sixth Edition

STUDY GUIDE

FUNDAMENTALS OF FINANCIAL MANAGEMENT

Sixth Edition

Eugene F. Brigham
Dana A. Aberwald
University of Florida

THE DRYDEN PRESS
A Harcourt Brace Jovanovich College Publisher
Fort Worth Philadelphia San Diego New York Orlando Austin
San Antonio Toronto Montreal London Sydney Tokyo

ISBN 0-03-055029-7
Printed in the United States of America
123-066-987654321

Copyright © 1992, 1989, 1986 by The Dryden Press

All rights reserved. No part of this publication may be reproduced
or transmitted in any form or by any means, electronic or
mechanical, including photocopy, recording, or any information
storage and retrieval system, without permission in writing from
the publisher.

Requests for permission to make copies of any part of the work
should be mailed to: Permissions Department, Harcourt Brace
Jovanovich, Publishers, 8th Floor, Orlando, Florida 32887.

Address orders:
The Dryden Press
Orlando, FL 32887

Address editorial correspondence:
The Dryden Press
301 Commerce Street, Suite 3700
Fort Worth, TX 76102

The Dryden Press
Harcourt Brace Jovanovich

PREFACE

This *Study Guide* is designed primarily to help you develop a working knowledge of the concepts and principles of financial management. Additionally, it will familiarize you with the types of true/false and multiple choice test questions that are being used with increasing frequency in introductory finance courses.

The *Study Guide* follows the outline of *Fundamentals of Financial Management*. You should read carefully the next section, "How To Use This *Study Guide*," to familiarize yourself with its specific contents and to gain some insights into how it can be used most effectively.

We would like to thank Lou Gapenski, West Ludwig, Bob Karp, and Carol Stanton for their considerable assistance in the preparation of this edition, and Bob LeClair for his helpful ideas in prior editions which we carried over to this one.

We have tried to make the *Study Guide* as clear and error-free as possible. However, some mistakes may have crept in, and there are almost certainly some sections that could be clarified. Any suggestions for improving the *Study Guide* would be greatly appreciated and should be addressed to us. Since instructors almost never read study guides, we address this call for help to students!

Eugene F. Brigham
Dana A. Aberwald
College of Business Administration
University of Florida
Gainesville, FL 32611-2017

December 1991

HOW TO USE THIS STUDY GUIDE

Different people will tend to use the *Study Guide* in somewhat different ways. This is natural, because both introductory finance courses and individual students' needs vary widely. However, the tips contained in this section should help all students use the *Study Guide* more effectively, regardless of these differences.

Each chapter contains (1) an overview, (2) an outline, (3) definitional self-test questions, (4) conceptual self-test questions, (5) self-test problems, and (6) answers and solutions to the self-test questions and problems. You should begin your study by reading the overview; it will give you an idea of what is contained in the chapter and how this material fits into the overall scheme of things in financial management.

Next, read over the outline to get a better fix on the specific topics covered in the chapter. It is important to realize that the outline does not list every facet of every topic covered in the textbook—the *Study Guide* is intended to highlight and summarize the textbook, not to supplant it. Also, note that appendix material is clearly marked as such within the outline. Thus, if your instructor does not assign a particular appendix, you may not want to study that portion of the outline.

The definitional self-test questions are intended to test your knowledge of, and also to reinforce your ability to work with, the terms and concepts introduced in the chapter. If you do not understand the definitions thoroughly, review the outline prior to going on to the conceptual questions and problems.

The conceptual self-test questions focus on the same kinds of ideas that the textbook end-of-chapter questions address, but in the *Study Guide* the questions are set out in a true/false or multiple choice format. Thus, for many students these questions can be used to practice for the types of tests that are being used with increasing frequency. However, regardless of the types of tests you must take, working through the conceptual questions will help drive home the key concepts of financial management.

The numeric problems are also written in a multiple choice format. Generally, the problems are arranged in order of increasing difficulty. Also, note that some of the *Study Guide* problems are convoluted in the sense that information normally available to financial managers is withheld, and information normally unknown is given. Such problems are designed to test your knowledge of a subject, and you must work "backwards" to solve them. Furthermore, such problems are included in the *Study Guide* in part because they provide a good test of how well you understand the material, and in part because you may well be seeing similar problems on your exams.

Finally, each *Study Guide* chapter provides the answers and solutions to the self-test questions and problems. The rationale behind a question's correct answer is explained where necessary, but the problem solutions are always complete. Note that the problems in the early chapters generally provide both "table-based" and "financial calculator" solutions. In later chapters, only calculator solutions are shown. You should not be concerned if your answer differs from ours by a small amount which is caused by rounding errors.

Of course, each student must decide how to incorporate the *Study Guide* in his or her overall study program. Many students begin an assignment by reading the *Study Guide* overview and outline to get the "big picture," then read the chapter in the textbook. Naturally, the *Study Guide* overview and outline is also used extensively to review for exams. Most students work the textbook questions and problems, using the latter as a self-test and review tool. However, if you are stumped by a text problem, try the *Study Guide* problems first, because their detailed solutions can get you over stumbling blocks.

CONTENTS OF THE STUDY GUIDE

CHAPTER

CHAPTER 1
AN OVERVIEW OF FINANCIAL MANAGEMENT

OVERVIEW

This chapter provides an overview of financial management and should give you a better understanding of the following: (1) what forces will affect financial management in the future, (2) how businesses are organized, (3) how finance fits into the structure of a firm's organization, (4) how financial managers relate to their counterparts in other departments, and (5) what the goals of a firm are and how financial managers can contribute to the attainment of these goals.

OUTLINE

I. **Finance consists of three interrelated areas: money and capital markets, investments, and financial management. Career opportunities within each field are varied and numerous, but financial managers must have a knowledge of all three areas.**

   A. Many finance majors go to work for financial institutions, including banks, insurance companies, savings and loans, and credit unions. The bank officer trainee is the most common initial job in this area.

   B. Finance graduates who go into investments generally work for a brokerage house in sales or as a security analyst; for a bank, a mutual fund, or an insurance company in the management of their investment portfolios; or for a financial consulting firm, advising individual investors or pension funds on how to invest their funds.

   C. Financial management, the broadest of the three areas, and the one with the greatest number of job opportunities, is important to all types of businesses. The types of jobs one encounters in this area range from decisions regarding plant expansions to the choice of stocks or bonds to finance expansion.

II. **The two most important trends for financial management during the 1990s are likely to be the continued globalization of business and the increased use of computer technology.**

   A. Three factors have made the trend toward globalization mandatory for many businesses.
      1. Transportation and communications improvements have lowered shipping costs, lowered trade barriers, and increased competition.
      2. Due to increased technology, higher development costs have resulted, necessitating increased unit sales.

© 1992 The Dryden Press
All rights reserved.

3. Competitive pressures have forced companies to shift manufacturing operations to lower-cost countries.

B. Continued advances in computer technology are revolutionizing the way financial decisions are made. Thus, the new generation of financial managers will need stronger computer and quantitative skills than were required in the past.

III. **Historical trends discussed above have greatly increased the importance of financial management. Today the financial manager must make decisions in a much more coordinated manner, and he or she generally has direct responsibility for the control process. Because there are financial implications in virtually all business decisions, nonfinancial executives simply must know enough finance to work these implications into their own specialized analyses.**

IV. **The financial manager's task is to acquire and use funds so as to maximize the value of the firm. Some specific activities follow.**

A. Financial managers use *forecasting and planning* to shape the firm's future position.

B. Financial managers make *major investment and financing decisions*.

C. Financial managers *coordinate and control* when interacting with other executives so that the firm operates as efficiently as possible.

D. The financial manager must *deal with the capital markets*.

V. **The three main forms of business organization are the sole proprietorship, the partnership, and the corporation. About 80 percent of businesses operate as sole proprietorships, but when based on dollar value of sales, 80 percent of all business is conducted by corporations.**

A. A *sole proprietorship* is a business owned by one individual.
   1. Advantages are: (a) it is easily and inexpensively formed and is subject to few government regulations, and (b) it pays no corporate income taxes (however, all business earnings are taxed as personal income to the owner).
   2. Disadvantages are: (a) it is limited in its ability to raise large sums of capital, (b) the proprietor has unlimited personal liability for business debts, and (c) it has a life limited to the life of the individual who created it.

B. A *partnership* exists when two or more persons associate to conduct a noncorporate business.
   1. Its major advantage is its low cost and ease of formation.
   2. Disadvantages are: (a) unlimited liability, (b) limited life, (c) difficulty in transferring ownership, and (d) difficulty of raising large amounts of capital.

© 1992 The Dryden Press
All rights reserved.

C. A *corporation* is a legal entity created by a state, and it is separate and distinct from its owners and managers.
   1. Advantages are: (a) unlimited life, (b) ownership which is easily transferred through the exchange of stock, and (c) limited liability. Because of these three factors, it is much easier for corporations to raise money in the capital markets.
   2. Disadvantages are: (a) corporate earnings are subject to double taxation and (b) setting up a corporation and filing required state and federal reports are more complex than for a sole proprietorship or partnership.
   3. A charter must be filed with the state where the firm is headquartered, and bylaws which govern the management of the company must be prepared.

D. The value of any business, other than a very small one, will probably be maximized if it is organized as a corporation.

VI. **Maximizing the price of the firm's common stock is the most important goal of most corporations.**

A. Other objectives, such as personal satisfaction, employee welfare, and the good of the community, also have an influence, but for publicly-owned companies they are less important than stock price maximization.

B. Hostile takeovers and proxy fights have also stimulated management to maximize share price.

C. Social responsibility raises the question of whether businesses should operate strictly in their stockholders' best interests or also be responsible for the welfare of their employees, customers, and the communities in which they operate.
   1. Any voluntary socially responsible acts that raise costs will be difficult, if not impossible, in industries that are subject to keen competition.
   2. Even firms with above-average profits will be constrained in exercising social responsibility by capital market forces, because investors will normally prefer a firm that concentrates on profits over one excessively devoted to social action.
   3. Socially responsible actions that increase costs may have to be put on a mandatory, rather than a voluntary, basis to insure that the burden falls uniformly on all businesses.
   4. Industry and government must cooperate in establishing rules for fair hiring, product safety, environmental protection, and other programs that affect all businesses.

D. The same actions that maximize stock price also benefit society.

VII. **Business ethics can be thought of as a company's attitude and conduct toward its employees, customers, community, and stockholders. Most firms today have in place strong codes of ethical behavior; however, it is imperative that top management be openly committed to ethical behavior and that they communicate this commitment through their own personal actions as well as company policies.**

© 1992 The Dryden Press
All rights reserved.

VIII. **An agency relationship exists when one or more persons (the principals) hire another person (the agent) to act on their behalf, delegating decision-making authority to that agent. Agency relationships exist (1) between stockholders and managers and (2) between stockholders and creditors (debtholders).**

    A. A potential *agency problem* exists whenever a manager owns less than 100 percent of the firm's common stock.

       1. Since the firm's earnings do not go solely to the manager, he or she may not concentrate exclusively on maximizing shareholder wealth.

       2. Another potential conflict between management and stockholders arises in a leveraged buyout because management might attempt to *minimize* the firm's stock price just prior to the buyout. However, the Securities and Exchange Commission (SEC) now requires disclosure of material information relating to proposed deals where a conflict of interest exists.

       3. Several mechanisms are used to cause managers to act in shareholders' best interests: (a) the threat of firing, (b) the threat of takeover, and (c) the proper structuring of managerial incentives.

    B. Another agency problem involves conflicts between stockholders and creditors (debtholders). Conflicts arise if (1) management, acting for its stockholders, takes on projects that have greater risk than was anticipated by creditors or (2) the firm increases its level of debt higher than was anticipated. Both of these actions decrease the value of the debt outstanding. It is in the firm's best interest to deal fairly with its creditors in order to assure future access to debt markets at reasonable interest costs.

IX. **The financial manager can affect the firm's stock price by influencing the following factors: (1) projected earnings per share, (2) timing of the earnings stream, (3) riskiness of these projected earnings, (4) use of debt, and (5) dividend policy. Every significant corporate decision should be analyzed in terms of its effects on these factors and, through them, on the price of the firm's stock.**

X. **Although managerial actions affect the value of a firm's stock, external factors also influence stock prices. Included among them are legal constraints, the general level of economic activity, the tax laws, and conditions in the stock market.**

SELF-TEST QUESTIONS

Definitional

1. Finance consists of three interrelated areas: (1) _____ ___ _____ _____, which deals with many of the topics covered in macroeconomics, (2) _____, which focuses on the decisions of individuals and financial institutions as they choose securities for their investment portfolios, and (3) _____ _____ or "business finance."

©1992 The Dryden Press
All rights reserved.

2. In the 1990s, two of the most important trends are likely to be the continued _____ of business and the increased use of _____ _____.

3. Sole proprietorships are easily formed, but often have difficulty raising _____, they subject proprietors to unlimited _____, and they have a limited _____.

4. Partnership profits are taxed as _____ income in proportion to each partner's proportionate ownership.

5. A partnership is dissolved upon the withdrawal or _____ of any one of the partners. In addition, the difficulty in _____ ownership is a major disadvantage of the partnership form of business organization.

6. A _____ is a legal entity created by a state, and it is separate from its owners and managers.

7. The concept of _____ means that a firm's stockholders are not personally liable for the debts of the business.

8. Modern financial theory operates on the assumption that the goal of management is the _____ of shareholder _____. This goal is accomplished if the firm's _____ _____ is maximized.

9. Socially responsible activities that increase a firm's costs will be most difficult in those industries where _____ is most intense.

10. Firms with above-average profit levels will find social actions _____ by capital market factors.

11. An _____ relationship exists when one or more persons (the principals) hire another person (the agent) to act on their behalf.

12. Potential agency problems exist between a firm's shareholders and its _____ and also between shareholders and _____.

13. A firm's stock price depends on several factors. Among the most important of these are the level of projected _____ _____ _____ and the riskiness of these projections.

Conceptual

14. The primary objective of the firm is to maximize EPS.

   a. True   b. False

©1992 The Dryden Press
All rights reserved.

15. The types of actions that help a firm maximize stock price are generally not directly beneficial to society at large.

   a. True   b. False

16. There are factors that influence stock price over which managers have virtually no control.

   a. True   b. False

17. Which of the following factors affect stock price?

   a. Level of projected earnings per share.
   b. Riskiness of projected earnings per share.
   c. Timing of the earnings stream.
   d. The manner of financing the firm.
   e. All of the above factors.

18. Which of the following factors tend to encourage management to pursue stock price maximization as a goal?

   a. Shareholders link management's compensation to company performance.
   b. Managers' reactions to the threat of tender offers and proxy fights.
   c. Managers do not have goals other than stock price maximization.
   d. Statements a and b are both correct.
   e. Statements a, b, and c are all correct.

ANSWERS TO SELF-TEST QUESTIONS

1. money and capital markets; investments; financial management
2. globalization; computer technology
3. capital; liability; life
4. personal
5. death; transferring
6. corporation
7. limited liability
8. maximization; wealth; stock price
9. competition
10. constrained
11. agency
12. managers; creditors (or debtholders)
13. earnings per share

14. b. An increase in earnings per share will not necessarily increase stock price. For example, if the increase in earnings per share is accompanied by an increase in the riskiness of the firm, stock price might fall. *The primary objective is the maximization of stock price.*

15. b. The actions that maximize stock price generally also benefit society by promoting efficient, low-cost operations; encouraging the development of new technology, products, and jobs; and requiring efficient and courteous service.

©1992 The Dryden Press
All rights reserved.

16. a. Managers have no control over factors such as (1) external constraints (for example, antitrust laws and environmental regulations), (2) the general level of economic activity, (3) taxes, and (4) conditions in the stock market, all of which affect the price of the firm's stock.

17. e. The firm's stock price is dependent on all the factors mentioned. One additional factor not mentioned is dividend policy.

18. d. Mechanisms which tend to force managers to act in the shareholders' best interests include (1) the threat of firing, (2) the threat of takeover, and (3) the proper structuring of managerial incentives.

©1992 The Dryden Press
All rights reserved.

CHAPTER 2
ANALYSIS OF FINANCIAL STATEMENTS

OVERVIEW

Financial analysis is designed to determine the relative strengths and weaknesses of a company. Investors need this information to estimate both future cash flows from the firm and the riskiness of those flows. Financial managers need the information provided by analysis both to evaluate the firm's past performance and to map future plans. Financial analysis concentrates on *financial statement analysis*, which highlights the key aspects of a firm's operation. Financial statement analysis involves a study of the relationships between income statement and balance sheet accounts, how these relationships change over time (or trend analysis), and how a particular firm compares with other firms in its industry. Although financial analysis has limitations, when used with care and judgment, it can provide some very useful insights into the operations of a company.

OUTLINE

I.   **A firm's annual report to shareholders presents two important types of information. The first is a verbal statement of the company's recent operations and its expectations for the coming year. The second is a set of quantitative financial statements which report what actually happened to earnings and dividends over the past few years.**

    A. The *income statement* summarizes the firm's revenues and expenses over the past year. Earnings per share (EPS) is called "the bottom line," denoting that of all the items on the income statement, EPS is the most important.

    B. The *balance sheet* shows the firm's assets and the claims against those assets. It portrays the financial condition at a point in time.
        1. Assets, found on the left-hand side of the balance sheet, are typically shown in the order of their liquidity. Claims, found on the right-hand side, are generally listed in the order in which they must be paid.
        2. Only cash represents actual money. Noncash assets should produce cash flows eventually, but they do not represent cash in hand.
        3. Claims against the assets consist of liabilities and common stockholders' equity, or net worth. Thus, Assets − Liabilities − Preferred stock = Common stockholders' equity.
        4. The common equity section of the balance sheet is divided into three accounts: common stock, paid-in capital, and retained earnings. Common stock and paid-in capital accounts arise from the issuance of stock to raise capital. Retained earnings are built up over time as the firm "saves" a part of its earnings rather than paying all earnings out as dividends.

2-1

©1992 The Dryden Press
All rights reserved.

5. Different methods, such as FIFO and LIFO, can be used to determine the value of inventory. These methods, in turn, affect the reported cost of goods sold, profits, and EPS.
6. Companies often use the most accelerated permissible method to calculate depreciation for tax purposes, but use straight line depreciation, which results in a lower expense, for stockholder reporting.

C. The balance sheet may be thought of as a snapshot of the firm's financial position *at a point in time* (for example, end of year), while the income statement reports on operations *over a period of time* (for example, one calendar year).

D. The *statement of retained earnings* reports changes in the equity accounts between balance sheet dates.
1. The balance sheet account "retained earnings" represents a claim against assets, not assets per se.
2. Retained earnings as reported on the balance sheet do not represent cash and are not "available" for the payment of dividends or anything else. Retained earnings represent funds which have already been reinvested in operating assets of the firm.

E. In finance the emphasis is on the *cash flows* which the company is expected to generate. The firm's net income is important, but cash flows are even more important because dividends must be paid in cash, and cash is also necessary to purchase the assets required to continue operations.
1. A firm's cash flows are generally equal to cash from sales, minus cash operating costs, minus interest charges, and minus taxes.
2. Depreciation is a noncash charge, so it must be added back to net income to obtain an estimate of the cash flow from operations.
3. A stock's value is based on the *present value of the cash flows* which investors expect it to provide in the future. The cash flow provided by the stock itself is the expected future dividend stream, and that expected dividend stream provides the fundamental basis for the stock's value. There are two classes of cash flows:
   a. Operating cash flows arise from normal operations, and they are the difference between sales revenues and cash expenses, including taxes paid.
   b. Other cash flows arise from the issuance of stock, from borrowing, or from the sale of fixed assets.

F. To understand how timing of cash flows influences the financial statements, one must understand the *cash flow cycle* within a firm. It shows the way in which actual net cash, as opposed to accounting net income, flows into or out of the firm during some specified period.

G. The *statement of cash flows* reports the impact of a firm's operating, investing, and financing activities on cash flows over an accounting period.

©1992 The Dryden Press
All rights reserved.

H. Most annual reports today also give a summary of earnings and dividends over the last few years.

    1. Normally, dividends are smaller than earnings, although in any given year the opposite can be true.

    2. The percentage of earnings paid out as dividends is called the *dividend payout ratio.*

II. Financial statements are used to help predict the firm's future earnings and dividends. From an investor's standpoint, predicting the future is what financial statement analysis is all about. From management's standpoint, financial statement analysis is useful both as a way to anticipate future conditions and, more importantly, as a starting point for planning actions that will influence the future course of events. An analysis of the firm's ratios is the first step in a financial analysis.

    A. *Liquidity ratios* are used to measure a firm's ability to meet its current obligations as they come due.

        1. The *current ratio* measures the extent to which the claims of short-term creditors are covered by short-term assets. It is determined by dividing current assets by current liabilities.

        2. The *quick,* or *acid test, ratio* is calculated by deducting inventories from current assets and then dividing the remainder by current liabilities. Inventories are excluded because it may be difficult to liquidate them at their full book value.

    B. *Asset management ratios* measure how effectively a firm is managing its assets, and whether or not the level of those assets is properly related to the level of operations as measured by sales.

        1. The *inventory turnover ratio* is defined as sales divided by inventories. It is often necessary to use the average inventory figure rather than the year-end figure, especially if a firm's business is highly seasonal.

        2. The *days sales outstanding (DSO)* is used to appraise accounts receivable, and it is computed by dividing average daily sales into accounts receivable to find the number of days' sales tied up in receivables. Thus, the DSO represents the average length of time that the firm must wait after making a sale before receiving cash.

        3. The *fixed assets turnover ratio* is the ratio of sales to net fixed assets. It measures how effectively the firm uses its plant and equipment.

        4. The *total assets turnover ratio* is calculated by dividing sales by total assets. It measures the utilization of all the firm's assets.

    C. *Debt management ratios* measure the extent to which a firm is using debt financing, or *financial leverage*, and the degree of safety afforded to creditors.

        1. The *debt ratio*, or ratio of total debt to total assets, measures the proportion of funds provided by creditors. The lower the ratio, the greater the protection afforded creditors in the event of liquidation.

        2. The *times-interest-earned (TIE) ratio* is determined by dividing earnings before interest and taxes (EBIT) by the interest charges. The TIE measures the

© 1992 The Dryden Press
All rights reserved.

extent to which operating income can decline before the firm is unable to meet its annual interest costs.

3. The *fixed charge coverage ratio* is similar to the TIE ratio, but it is more inclusive because it recognizes that many firms lease assets and incur long-term obligations under lease contracts and sinking funds.

D. *Profitability ratios* show the combined effects of liquidity, asset management, and debt management on operating results.

1. The *profit margin on sales* is calculated by dividing net income by sales.

2. The *basic earning power (BEP) ratio* is calculated by dividing the earnings before interest and taxes (EBIT) by total assets. It shows the raw earning power of the firm's assets, before the influence of taxes and leverage.

3. The *return on total assets (ROA)* is the ratio of net income to total assets after interest and taxes.

4. The *return on common equity (ROE)* measures the rate of return on the stockholders' investment. It is equal to net income divided by common equity.

E. *Market value ratios* relate the firm's stock price to its earnings and book value per share, and thus give management an indication of what investors think of the company's past performance and future prospects.

1. The *price/earnings (P/E) ratio*, or price per share divided by earnings per share, shows how much investors are willing to pay per dollar of reported profits. P/E ratios are higher for firms with high growth prospects, other things held constant, but they are lower for riskier firms.

2. The *market/book ratio*, defined as market price per share divided by book value per share, gives another indication of how investors regard the company. Higher ratios are generally associated with firms that have a high rate of return on common equity.

III. It is important to analyze trends in ratios as well as their absolute levels. Trend analysis can provide clues as to whether the firm's financial situation is improving or deteriorating.

IV. A modified Du Pont chart shows the relationships between return on investment, assets turnover, and the profit margin.

A. The profit margin times the total assets turnover is called the Du Pont equation. This equation gives the rate of return on assets (ROA): ROA = Profit margin × Total assets turnover.

B. The ROA times the equity multiplier (assets divided by common equity) yields the return on equity (ROE). This equation is referred to as the extended Du Pont equation: ROE = Profit margin × Total assets turnover × Equity multiplier.

©1992 The Dryden Press
All rights reserved.

V.   Comparative ratio analysis is useful in comparing a firm's ratios with those of other firms in the same industry. Sources for such ratios include Dun & Bradstreet, Robert Morris Associates, and the U.S. Commerce Department.

VI. There are some inherent problems and limitations to ratio analysis that necessitate care and judgment.

   A.   Ratios are often not useful for analyzing the operations of large firms which operate in many different industries because comparative ratios are not meaningful.

   B.   The use of industry averages may not provide a very challenging target for high-level performance.

   C.   Inflation affects depreciation charges, inventory costs, and therefore the value of both balance sheet items and net income. For this reason, the analysis of a firm over time, or a comparative analysis of firms of different ages, can be misleading.

   D.   Ratios may be distorted by seasonal factors, or manipulated by management to give the impression of a sound financial condition (window dressing).

   E.   Different operating policies, such as the decision to lease rather than to buy equipment, can distort comparisons.

   F.   Many ratios can be interpreted in different ways, and whether a particular ratio is good or bad should be based upon a complete financial analysis rather than the level of a single ratio at a single point in time.

VII. In Appendix 2A the actual preparation of the Statement of Cash Flows is discussed. Changes in each balance sheet account are identified as sources or uses of funds. Each balance sheet change is then classified as resulting from operations, long-term investments, or financing activities.

SELF-TEST QUESTIONS

Definitional

1.   Of all its communications with shareholders, a firm's _____ report is generally the most important.

2.   The income statement reports the results of operations during the past year, the most important item being _____ _____ _____.

3.   The _____ _____ lists the firm's assets as well as claims against those assets.

©1992 The Dryden Press
All rights reserved.

4. Typically, assets are listed in order of their _____, while liabilities are listed in the order in which they must be paid.

5. Assets − Liabilities − Preferred stock = _____ worth, or _____ _____ equity.

6. The three accounts which normally make up the common equity section of the balance sheet are common stock, _____ - ___ capital, and _____ _____ .

7. _____ _____ as reported on the balance sheet represent income earned by the firm in past years that has not been paid out as dividends.

8. Retained earnings are generally reinvested in _____ _____ and are not held in the form of cash.

9. The _____ _____ _____ is designed to show how the firm's operations have affected its cash position.

10. The three major categories of the Statement of Cash Flows are cash flows associated with _____ activities, _____ - _____ _____ activities, and _____ activities.

11. The current ratio and acid-test ratio are examples of _____ ratios. They measure a firm's ability to meet its _____ - _____ obligations.

12. The days sales outstanding (DSO) ratio is found by dividing average sales per day into accounts _____ . The DSO is the length of time that a firm must wait after making a sale before it receives _____ .

13. Debt management ratios are used to evaluate a firm's use of financial _____ .

14. The debt ratio, which is the ratio of _____ _____ to _____ _____, measures the proportion of funds supplied by creditors.

15. The _____ - _____ - _____ ratio is calculated by dividing earnings before interest and taxes by the amount of interest charges.

16. The combined effects of liquidity, asset management, and debt management are measured by _____ ratios.

17. Dividing net income by sales gives the _____ _____ on sales.

18. The _____ / _____ ratio measures how much investors are willing to pay for each dollar of a firm's current income.

19. Firms with higher rates of return on stockholders' equity tend to sell at relatively high ratios of _____ price to _____ value.

©1992 The Dryden Press
All rights reserved.

20. Individual ratios are of little value in analyzing a company's financial condition. More important are the _____ of a ratio over time and the comparison of the company's ratios to _____ average ratios.

21. A ___ _____ chart shows the relationships among return on investment, total assets turnover, and profit margin, and how they combine to produce return on equity.

22. Return on assets is a function of two variables, the profit _____ and _____ _____ turnover.

23. The trend of a particular ratio over time or a _____ ratio analysis gives a good indication of a firm's actual financial situation with regard to that ratio.

Conceptual

24. The equity multiplier can be expressed as 1 − (Debt/Assets).

   a. True   b. False

25. International Appliances Inc. has a current ratio of 0.5. Which of the following actions would improve (increase) this ratio?

   a. Use cash to pay off current liabilities.
   b. Collect some of the current accounts receivable.
   c. Use cash to pay off some long-term debt.
   d. Purchase additional inventory on credit (accounts payable).
   e. Sell some of the existing inventory at cost.

26. A high quick ratio is *always* a good indication of a well-managed liquidity position.

   a. True   b. False

27. Which of the following statements is most *correct*?

   a. Having a high current ratio and a high quick ratio is always a good indication that a firm is managing its liquidity position well.
   b. A decline in the inventory turnover ratio suggests that the firm's liquidity position is improving.
   c. If a firm's times-interest-earned ratio is relatively high, then this is one indication that the firm should be able to meet its debt obligations.
   d. Since ROA measures the firm's effective utilization of assets (without considering how these assets are financed), two firms with the same EBIT must have the same ROA.
   e. If, through specific managerial actions, a firm has been able to increase its ROA, then, because of the fixed mathematical relationship between ROA and ROE, it must also have increased its ROE.

©1992 The Dryden Press
All rights reserved.

28. Which of the following statements is most *correct*?

a. Suppose two firms with the same amount of assets pay the same interest rate on their debt and earn the same rate of return on their assets, and that ROA is positive. However, one firm has a higher debt ratio. Under these conditions, the firm with the higher debt ratio will also have a higher rate of return on common equity.

b. One of the problems of ratio analysis is that the relationships are subject to manipulation. For example, we know that if we use some cash to pay off some of our current liabilities, the current ratio will always increase, especially if the current ratio is weak initially, for example, below 1.0.

c. Generally, firms with high profit margins have high asset turnover ratios, and firms with low profit margins have low turnover ratios; this result is exactly as predicted by the extended Du Pont equation.

d. Firms A and B have identical earnings and identical dividend payout ratios. If Firm A's growth rate is higher than Firm B's, then Firm A's P/E ratio must be greater than Firm B's P/E ratio.

e. Each of the above statements is false.

SELF-TEST PROBLEMS

(The following financial statements apply to the next six problems.)

Roberts Manufacturing Balance Sheet
December 31, 1991
(Dollars in Thousands)

Cash	$ 200	Accounts payable	$ 205
Receivables	245	Notes payable	425
Inventory	625	Other current liabilities	115
Total current assets	$1,070	Total current liabilities	$ 745
Net fixed assets	1,200	Long-term debt	420
		Common equity	1,105
Total assets	$2,270	Total liabilities and equity	$2,270

©1992 The Dryden Press
All rights reserved.

Roberts Manufacturing
Income Statement for Year Ended December 31, 1991
(Dollars in Thousands)

Sales		$2,400
Cost of goods sold:		
Materials	$1,000	
Labor	600	
Heat, light, and power	89	
Indirect labor	65	
Depreciation	80	1,834
Gross profit		$ 566
Selling expenses		175
General and administrative expenses		216
Earnings before interest and taxes		$ 175
Less interest expense		35
Earnings before taxes		$ 140
Less taxes (at 40%)		56
Net income		$ 84

1. Calculate the liquidity ratios, that is, the current ratio and the quick ratio.

   a. 1.20; 0.60   **b.** 1.20; 0.80   **c.** 1.44; 0.60   **d.** 1.44; 0.80   **e.** 1.60; 0.60

2. Calculate the asset management ratios, that is, the inventory turnover ratio, fixed assets turnover, total assets turnover, and days sales outstanding.

   a. 3.84; 2.00; 1.06; 36.75 days   **b.** 3.84; 2.00; 1.06; 35.25 days
   c. 3.84; 2.00; 1.06; 34.10 days   **d.** 3.84; 2.00; 1.24; 34.10 days
   e. 3.84; 2.20; 1.48; 34.10 days

3. Calculate the debt management ratios, that is, the debt and times-interest-earned ratios.

   a. 0.39; 3.16   **b.** 0.39; 5.00   **c.** 0.51; 3.16   **d.** 0.51; 5.00   **e.** 0.73; 3.16

4. Calculate the profitability ratios, that is, the profit margin on sales, return on total assets, return on common equity, and basic earning power of assets.

   a. 3.50%; 4.25%; 7.60%; 8.00%   **b.** 3.50%; 3.70%; 7.60%; 7.71%
   c. 3.70%; 3.50%; 7.60%; 7.71%   **d.** 3.70%; 3.50%; 8.00%; 8.00%
   e. 4.25%; 3.70%; 7.60%; 8.00%

©1992 The Dryden Press
All rights reserved.

5. Calculate the market value ratios, that is, the price/earnings ratio and the market/book value ratio. Roberts had an average of 10,000 shares outstanding during 1991, and the stock price on December 31, 1991, was $40.00.

   a. 4.21; 0.36   b. 3.20; 1.54   c. 3.20; 0.36   d. 4.76; 1.54   e. 4.76; 0.36

6. Use the extended Du Pont equation to determine Roberts' return on equity.

   a. 6.90%   b. 7.24%   c. 7.47%   d. 7.60%   e. 8.41%

7. Lewis Inc. has sales of $2 million per year, all of which are credit sales. Its days sales outstanding is 42 days. What is its average accounts receivable balance?

   a. $233,333   b. $266,667   c. $333,333   d. $350,000   e. $366,667

8. A firm has total interest charges of $20,000 per year, sales of $2 million, a tax rate of 40 percent, and a profit margin of 6 percent. What is the firm's times-interest-earned ratio?

   a. 10   b. 11   c. 12   d. 13   e. 14

9. A fire has destroyed many of the financial records at Anderson Associates. You are assigned to piece together information to prepare a financial report. You have found that the firm's return on equity is 12 percent, and its debt ratio is 0.40. What is its return on assets?

   a. 4.90%   b. 5.35%   c. 6.60%   d. 7.20%   e. 8.40%

10. Rowe and Company has a debt ratio of 0.50, a total assets turnover of 0.25, and a profit margin of 10 percent. The president is unhappy with the current return on equity, and he thinks it could be doubled. This could be accomplished (1) by increasing the profit margin to 14 percent and (2) by increasing debt utilization. Total assets turnover will not change. What new debt ratio, along with the 14 percent profit margin, is required to double the return on equity?

   a. 0.55   b. 0.60   c. 0.65   d. 0.70   e. 0.75

11. Altman Corporation has $1,000,000 of debt outstanding, and it pays an interest rate of 12 percent annually. Altman's annual sales are $4 million; its average tax rate is 25 percent; and its net profit margin on sales is 10 percent. If the company does not maintain a TIE ratio of at least 5 times, its bank will refuse to renew the loan, and bankruptcy will result. What is Altman's TIE ratio?

   a. 3.33   b. 4.44   c. 2.50   d. 4.00   e. 5.44

©1992 The Dryden Press
All rights reserved.

12. Pinkerton Packaging's ROE last year was 2.5 percent, but its management has developed a new operating plan designed to improve things. The new plan calls for a total debt ratio of 50 percent, which will result in interest charges of $240 per year. Management projects an EBIT of $800 on sales of $8,000, and it expects to have a total assets turnover ratio of 1.6. Under these conditions, what return on equity will Pinkerton earn?

    a. 12.50%   **b.** 13.44%   **c.** 13.00%   **d.** 14.02%   **e.** 14.57%

Appendix 2A

(The following balance sheets apply to the next two problems.)

American Products Corporation
Balance Sheets
(Dollars in Millions)

	December 31, 1991	December 31, 1990
Cash	$ 21	$ 45
Marketable securities	0	33
Net receivables	90	66
Inventories	225	159
Total current assets	$336	$303
Gross fixed assets	450	225
Less accumulated depreciation	(123)	(78)
Net fixed assets	$327	$147
Total assets	$663	$450
Accounts payable	$ 54	$ 45
Notes payable	9	45
Other current liabilities	45	21
Long-term debt	78	24
Common stock	192	114
Retained earnings	285	201
Total liabilities and equity	$663	$450

During 1991, the company earned $114 million after taxes, of which $30 million were paid out as dividends.

2A-1. Looking only at the balance sheet accounts, what are the total sources of funds (which must equal the total uses of funds) for 1991 (dollars in millions)?

    a. $213   **b.** $286   **c.** $351   **d.** $428   **e.** $531

©1992 The Dryden Press
All rights reserved.

2A-2. What are the cash flows from operations for 1991 (dollars in millions)?

    a. -$123   **b.** $102   **c.** $123   **d.** -$57   **e.** -$102

ANSWERS TO SELF-TEST QUESTIONS

1. annual
2. earnings per share
3. balance sheet
4. liquidity
5. Net; Common stockholders'
6. paid-in; retained earnings
7. Retained earnings
8. operating assets
9. Statement of Cash Flows
10. operating; long-term investing; financing
11. liquidity; short-term (or current)
12. receivable; cash
13. leverage
14. total debt; total assets
15. times-interest-earned
16. profitability
17. profit margin
18. price/earnings
19. market; book
20. trend; industry
21. Du Pont
22. margin; total assets
23. comparative

24. b. 1 – (Debt/Assets) = Equity/Assets. The equity multiplier is equal to Assets/Equity.

25. d. This question is best analyzed using numbers. For example, assume current assets = $50 and current liabilities = $100; thus, the current ratio = 0.5. For Answer a, assume $5 in cash is used to pay off $5 in current liabilities. The new current ratio would be $45/$95 = 0.47. For Answer d, assume a $10 purchase of inventory on credit (accounts payable). The new current ratio would be $60/$110 = 0.55, which is an increase over the old current ratio of 0.5.

26. b. Excess cash resulting from poor management could produce a high quick ratio. Similarly, if accounts receivable are not collected promptly, this could also lead to a high quick ratio.

27. c. Excess cash resulting from poor management could produce high current and quick ratios. A decline in the inventory turnover ratio suggests that either sales have decreased or inventory has increased—which suggests that the firm's liquidity position is *not* improving. ROA = Net income/Total assets and EBIT does not equal net income. Two firms with the same EBIT could have different financing and different taxes resulting in different net incomes. Also, two firms with the same EBIT do not necessarily have the same total assets; thus statement d is false. ROE = ROA × Assets/Equity. If ROA increases because total assets decrease then the equity multiplier decreases, and depending on which effect is greater, ROE may or may not increase. Statement c is correct; the TIE ratio is used to measure whether the firm can meet its debt obligation, and a high TIE ratio would indicate this is so.

©1992 The Dryden Press
All rights reserved.

28. a. Ratio analysis is subject to manipulation; however, if the current ratio is less than 1.0 and we use cash to pay off some current liabilities, the current ratio will decrease, *not* increase. Statement c is just the reverse of what actually occurs. Firms with high profit margins have low turnover ratios and vice versa. Statement d is false; it does not necessarily follow that if a firm's growth rate is higher that its stock price will be higher. Statement a is correct. From the information given in statement a one can determine that the two firms' net incomes are equal; thus, the firm with the higher debt ratio (lower equity ratio) will indeed have a higher ROE.

SOLUTIONS TO SELF-TEST PROBLEMS

1. c. $\text{Current ratio} = \dfrac{\text{Current assets}}{\text{Current liabilities}} = \dfrac{\$1,070}{\$745} = 1.44.$

$\text{Quick ratio} = \dfrac{\text{Current assets} - \text{Inventory}}{\text{Current liabilities}} = \dfrac{\$1,070 - \$625}{\$745} = 0.60.$

2. a. $\text{Inventory turnover} = \dfrac{\text{Sales}}{\text{Inventories}} = \dfrac{\$2,400}{\$625} = 3.84.$

$\text{Fixed assets turnover} = \dfrac{\text{Sales}}{\text{Fixed assets}} = \dfrac{\$2,400}{\$1,200} = 2.00.$

$\text{Total assets turnover} = \dfrac{\text{Sales}}{\text{Total assets}} = \dfrac{\$2,400}{\$2,270} = 1.06.$

$\text{DSO} = \dfrac{\text{Accounts receivable}}{\text{Sales}/360} = \dfrac{\$245}{\$2,400/360} = 36.75 \text{ days}.$

3. d. $\text{Debt ratio} = \text{Total debt}/\text{Total assets} = \$1,165/\$2,270 = 0.51.$

$\text{TIE ratio} = \text{EBIT}/\text{INT} = \$175/\$35 = 5.00.$

4. b. $\text{Profit margin} = \dfrac{\text{Net income}}{\text{Sales}} = \dfrac{\$84}{\$2,400} = 0.0350 = 3.50\%.$

$\text{ROA} = \dfrac{\text{Net income}}{\text{Total assets}} = \dfrac{\$84}{\$2,270} = 0.0370 = 3.70\%.$

©1992 The Dryden Press
All rights reserved.

$$\text{ROE} = \frac{\text{Net income}}{\text{Common equity}} = \frac{\$84}{\$1,105} = 0.0760 = 7.60\%.$$

$$\text{BEP} = \frac{\text{EBIT}}{\text{Total assets}} = \frac{\$175}{\$2,270} = 0.0771 = 7.71\%.$$

5. e. $\text{EPS} = \dfrac{\text{Net income}}{\text{Number of shares outstanding}} = \dfrac{\$84,000}{10,000} = \$8.40.$

$$\text{P/E ratio} = \frac{\text{Price}}{\text{EPS}} = \frac{\$40.00}{\$8.40} = 4.76.$$

$$\text{Market/Book value} = \frac{\text{Market price}}{\text{Book value}} = \frac{\$40(10,000)}{\$1,105,000} = 0.36.$$

6. d. $\text{ROE} = \text{Profit margin} \times \text{Total assets turnover} \times \text{Equity multiplier}$

$$= \frac{\$84}{\$2,400} \times \frac{\$2,400}{\$2,270} \times \frac{\$2,270}{\$1,105} = 0.035 \times 1.057 \times 2.054 = 0.0760 = 7.60\%.$$

7. a. $\text{DSO} = \dfrac{\text{Accounts receivable}}{\text{Sales}/360}$

$42 \text{ days} = \dfrac{\text{Accounts receivable}}{\$2,000,000/360}$

$\text{AR} = \$233,333.$

8. b. Net income = \$2,000,000(0.06) = \$120,000.
Earnings before taxes = \$120,000/(1 - 0.4) = \$200,000.
EBIT = \$200,000 + \$20,000 = \$220,000.
TIE = EBIT/INT = \$220,000/\$20,000 = 11.

9. d. If Total debt/Total assets = 0.40, then Total equity/Total assets = 0.60, and the equity multiplier (Assets/Equity) = 1/0.60 = 1.667.

$$\frac{\text{NI}}{\text{E}} = \frac{\text{NI}}{\text{A}} \times \frac{\text{A}}{\text{E}}$$

ROE = ROA × EM
12% = ROA × 1.667
ROA = 7.20%.

©1992 The Dryden Press
All rights reserved.

10. c. If Total debt/Total assets = 0.50, then Total equity/Total assets = 0.50, and the equity multiplier (assets/equity) = 1/0.50 = 2.0.

ROE = PM × Total assets turnover × EM.

Before: ROE = 10% × 0.25 × 2.00 = 5.00%.
After: 10.00% = 14% × 0.25 × EM; thus EM = 2.8571.

$$\text{Equity multiplier} = \frac{\text{Assets}}{\text{Equity}}$$
$$2.8571 = \frac{1}{\text{Equity}}$$
$$0.35 = \text{Equity.}$$

Debt = Assets - Equity = 100% - 35% = 65%.

11. e. TIE = EBIT/INT, so find EBIT and INT.

Interest = $1,000,000(0.12) = $120,000.

Net income = $4,000,000(0.10) = $400,000.

Pre-tax income = $400,000/(1 − T) = $400,000(0.75) = $533,333.

EBIT = $533,333 + $120,000 = $653,333.

TIE = $653,333/$120,000 = 5.44×.

12. b. ROE = Profit margin × Total asset turnover × Equity multiplier
= NI/Sales × Sales/TA × TA/Equity.

Now we need to determine the inputs for the equation from the data that were given. On the left we set up an income statement, and we put numbers in it on the right:

Sales (given)	$8,000
− Cost	NA
EBIT (given)	800
− Interest (given)	240
EBT	560
− Taxes (40%)	224
Net income	$ 336

Now we can use some ratios to get some more data:

Turnover = 1.6 = S/TA.

©1992 The Dryden Press
All rights reserved.

D/A = 50%, so E/A = 50%, and therefore TA/E = 1/(E/A) = 1/0.5 = 2.00.

Now we can complete the Du Pont equation to determine ROE:

ROE = $336/$8,000 × 1.6 × 2.0 = 13.44%.

Appendix 2A

2A-1. c. Total sources and uses of funds = $351 million.

(In millions)	Change Sources	Uses
Cash	$ 24	
Marketable securities	33	
Net receivables		$ 24
Inventories		66
Gross fixed assets		225
Accumulated depreciation	45	
Accounts payable	9	
Notes payable		36
Other current liabilities	24	
Long-term debt	54	
Common stock	78	
Retained earnings	84	
	$351	$351

Note that accumulated depreciation is a contra-asset account, and an increase is a source of funds. Also note that no total lines such as total current assets can be used to determine sources and uses since to do so would be to "double count."

2A-2. b. Cash flows from operations (in millions of dollars):

Operating activities:	
Net income	$114
Other additions (sources of cash):	
Depreciation	45
Increase in accounts payable	9
Increase in other current liabilities	24
Subtractions (uses of cash):	
Increase in accounts receivable	(24)
Increase in inventories	(66)
Net cash flows from operations	$102

©1992 The Dryden Press
All rights reserved.

CHAPTER 3
THE FINANCIAL ENVIRONMENT: MARKETS, INSTITUTIONS, INTEREST RATES, AND TAXES

OVERVIEW

It is critical that financial managers understand the environment and markets within which they operate. In this chapter, we examine the markets where capital is raised, securities are traded, and stock prices are established. We examine the institutions that operate in these markets, and hence through which securities transactions are conducted. In the process, we shall see how money costs are determined, and we shall explore the principal factors that determine both the general level of interest rates in the economy and the interest rate on a particular debt security. We also examine the federal income tax system and its effect on financial management.

OUTLINE

I. **Financial markets bring together people and organizations wanting to borrow money with those having surplus funds.**

 A. There are many different financial markets in a developed economy, each dealing with a different type of instrument, serving a different set of customers, or operating in a different part of the country.

 B. The major types of financial markets include the following:
 1. *Money markets* are the markets for short-term debt securities, those securities that mature in less than one year.
 2. *Capital markets* are the markets for long-term debt and corporate stocks.
 3. *Primary markets* are the markets in which corporations sell newly issued securities to raise capital.
 4. *Secondary markets* are the markets in which existing, outstanding securities are bought and sold.

II. **Transfer of capital between savers and borrowers takes place in three different ways.**

 A. *Direct transfers* of money and securities occur when a business sells its stock or bonds directly to savers, without going through any type of financial institution.

 B. Transfer through an *investment banking house* occurs when a brokerage firm, such as Merrill Lynch, serves as a middleman. These middlemen help corporations design securities that will be attractive to investors, buy these securities from the corporations, and then resell them to savers in the primary markets.

©1992 The Dryden Press
All rights reserved.

C. Transfer through a *financial intermediary* occurs when a bank or mutual fund obtains funds from savers, issues its own securities in exchange, and then uses these funds to purchase other securities.
  1. Some major classes of intermediaries include commercial banks, savings and loan (S&L) associations, mutual savings banks, credit unions, pension funds, life insurance companies, and mutual funds.
  2. Ongoing regulatory changes have resulted in a blurring of distinctions between the different types of financial institutions. As a result, in the U.S. the trend has been toward huge *financial service corporations*, which own any number of financial intermediaries with national and even global operations.

III. **The stock market is one of the most important markets to financial managers, because it is here that the price of each stock, and hence the value of all publicly-owned firms, is established. There are two basic types of stock markets:**

  A. The *organized exchanges*, typified by the New York Stock Exchange (NYSE) and the American Stock Exchange (AMEX), are tangible, physical entities.

  B. The *over-the-counter (OTC) market* is, basically, all the dealers, brokers, and communications facilities that provide for security transactions not conducted on the organized exchanges.

IV. **Capital in a free economy is allocated through the price system. The interest rate is the price paid to borrow capital.**

  A. The level of *interest rates* is determined by the supply of, and demand for, investment capital.
  1. The demand for investment capital is determined by production opportunities available, and the rates of return producers can expect to earn on invested capital.
  2. The supply of investment capital depends on consumers' time preferences for current versus future consumption.
  3. Two additional factors affecting the level of interest rates are risk and inflation. The higher the perceived risk, the higher the required rate of return, and the higher the expected rate of inflation, the larger the required return.

V. **The quoted (or nominal) interest rate on a debt security, k, is composed of a real risk-free rate of interest, k*, plus several premiums that reflect inflation, the riskiness of the security, and the security's marketability: k = k* + IP + DRP + LP + MRP.**

  A. The *real risk-free rate of interest* (k*) is the interest rate that would exist on a riskless security if no inflation were expected, and it may be thought of as the rate of interest that would exist on short-term U.S. Treasury securities in an inflation-free world.

3-2

©1992 The Dryden Press
All rights reserved.

B. The *quoted,* or *nominal, risk-free rate of interest* (k_{RF}) is the real risk-free rate plus a premium for expected inflation: $k_{RF} = k^* + IP$. The actual rate of interest on short-term Treasury bills is normally used to measure k_{RF}, although the rate on long-term Treasury bonds is also used.

C. The *inflation premium (IP)*, which is the average inflation rate expected over the life of the security, compensates investors for the expected loss of purchasing power.

D. The *default risk premium (DRP)* compensates investors for the risk that a borrower will default and hence not pay the interest or principal on a loan.

E. A security which can be sold and quickly converted into cash at a fair price is said to be *liquid.* A *liquidity premium (LP)* is also added to the real rate for securities that are not liquid.

F. Long-term securities are more price sensitive to interest rate changes than are short-term securities. Therefore, a *maturity risk premium (MRP)* is added to longer-term securities to compensate investors for interest rate risk.

VI. **The term structure of interest rates is the relationship between yield to maturity and time to maturity for bonds of a given default risk class.**

A. When plotted, this relationship produces a *yield curve.*

B. Yield curves have different shapes depending on expected inflation rates and supply and demand conditions.
  1. The "normal" yield curve is upward sloping, because investors charge higher rates on longer term bonds, even when inflation is expected to remain constant.
  2. An inverted, or downward sloping, yield curve signifies that investors expect inflation to decrease.

VII. **Three theories have been proposed to explain the shape of the yield curve, or the term structure of interest rates.**

A. The *market segmentation theory* states that the slope of the yield curve depends on supply and demand conditions in the long-term and short-term markets. Under this theory, the curve could, at any time, be either upward or downward sloping.

B. The *liquidity preference theory* states that the yield curve tends to be upward sloping because investors prefer short-term to long-term securities due to the interest rate risk associated with long-term securities.

C. The *expectations theory* states that the yield curve depends upon expectations about future inflation rates. If the rate of inflation is expected to decline, the curve will

3-3

©1992 The Dryden Press
All rights reserved.

be downward sloping, and if the rate of inflation is expected to increase, the curve will be upward sloping.

    D. All three theories have merit; that is, actual yield curves are influenced by all three sets of factors.

VIII. Other factors that influence both the general level of interest rates and the shape of the yield curve include: (1) Federal Reserve policy, (2) federal budget deficits, (3) foreign trade balance, and (4) business activity.

IX. The level of interest rates also has a significant effect on stock prices.

    A. Since interest is a cost to companies, interest rates have a direct effect on corporate profits.

    B. Stocks and bonds compete in the marketplace for investor's capital. Therefore, a rise in interest rates will increase the rate of return on bonds, causing investors to transfer funds from the stock market to the bond market. The resultant selling of stocks lowers stock prices.

X. Interest rate movements have a significant impact on business decisions.

    A. Wrong decisions, such as using short-term debt to finance long-term projects just before interest rates rise, can be very costly.

    B. It is extremely difficult, if not impossible, to predict future interest rate levels.

    C. Sound financial policy calls for using a mix of long-term and short-term debt, and equity, so that the firm can survive in almost any interest rate environment.

XI. Individuals pay taxes on wages and salaries, on investment income (dividends, interest, and profits from the sale of securities), and on the profits of proprietorships and partnerships.

    A. U.S. income taxes are *progressive*; that is, the higher the income, the larger the percentage paid in taxes. Marginal tax rates begin at 15 percent, rise to 28 and then to 31 percent.

    B. Since dividends are paid from corporate income that has already been taxed (at rates going up as high as 31 percent), there is double taxation of corporate income. Interest on most state and local government securities, which are often called "municipals," is not subject to federal income taxes. This creates a strong incentive for individuals in high tax brackets to purchase such securities.

    C. Gains and losses on the sale of capital assets such as stocks, bonds, and real estate have historically received special tax treatment. Currently, all capital gains income

©1992 The Dryden Press
All rights reserved.

is taxed as if it were ordinary income, with a maximum tax rate capped at 28 percent.

XII. **Corporations pay taxes on profits.**

A. Corporate tax rates are as follows: 15 percent on the first $50,000 of taxable income, 25 percent on the next $25,000, 34 percent on the next $25,000, 39 percent on income between $100,000 and $335,000, and 34 percent for income greater than $335,000.

B. Interest and dividend income received by a corporation are taxed.
   1. Interest is taxed as ordinary income at regular corporate tax rates.
   2. However, 70 percent of the dividends received by one corporation from another is excluded from taxable income. The remaining 30 percent is taxed at the ordinary rate. Thus, the effective tax rate on dividends received by a 34 percent marginal tax bracket corporation is 0.30(34%) = 10.2%.

C. The tax system favors debt financing over equity financing.
   1. Interest paid is a tax-deductible business expense.
   2. Dividends on common and preferred stock are not deductible. Thus, a 40 percent federal-plus-state tax bracket corporation must earn $1/(1.0 − 0.40) = $1/0.60 = $1.67 before taxes to pay $1 of dividends, but only $1 of pretax income is required to pay $1 of interest.

D. Before 1987, long-term corporate capital gains were taxed at lower rates than ordinary income. However, at present long-term capital gains are taxed as ordinary income.

E. Ordinary corporate operating losses can be carried back to each of the preceding 3 years and forward for the next 15 years in the future to offset taxable income in those years. The purpose of permitting this loss treatment is to avoid penalizing corporations whose incomes fluctuate substantially from year to year.

F. The Internal Revenue Code imposes a penalty on corporations that improperly accumulate earnings if the purpose of the accumulation is to enable stockholders to avoid personal income tax on dividends.

G. If a corporation owns 80 percent or more of another corporation's stock, it can aggregate profits and losses and file a consolidated tax return. Thus, losses in one area can offset profits in another.

H. Small businesses which meet certain restrictions may be set up as *S corporations* which receive benefits of the corporate form—especially limited liability—yet are taxed as proprietorships or partnerships rather than as corporations.

©1992 The Dryden Press
All rights reserved.

SELF-TEST QUESTIONS

Definitional

1. Markets for short-term debt securities are called _____ markets, while markets for long-term debt and equity are called _____ markets.

2. Firms raise capital by selling newly issued securities in the _____ markets, while existing, outstanding securities are traded in the _____ markets.

3. An institution which issues its own securities in exchange for funds and then uses these funds to purchase other securities is called a financial _____.

4. An _____ _____ firm facilitates the transfer of capital between savers and borrowers by acting as a middleman.

5. The two basic types of stock markets are the _____ _____, such as the NYSE, and the _____-___-_____ market.

6. The risk that a borrower will not pay the interest or principal on a loan is _____ risk.

7. _____ _____ _____ bonds have zero default risk.

8. An _____ premium is added to the real risk-free rate to protect investors against loss of purchasing power.

9. The nominal rate of interest is determined by adding an _____ premium plus a _____ risk premium plus a _____ premium plus a _____ risk premium to the real risk-free rate of return.

10. The relationship between yield to maturity and term to maturity for bonds in a given default risk class is called the _____ _____ of interest rates, while the resulting plotted curve is the _____ curve.

11. The "normal" yield curve has an _____ slope.

12. Three theories have been proposed to explain the term structure of interest rates. They are the market _____ theory, the _____ preference theory, and the _____ theory.

13. Because interest rates fluctuate, a sound financial policy calls for using a mix of _____-_____ and _____-_____ debt, and _____.

14. A _____ tax system is one in which tax rates are higher at higher levels of income.

©1992 The Dryden Press
All rights reserved.

15. A progressive tax structure, which when combined with inflation increases the government's share of GNP without any change in tax rates, is called _____ _____.

16. The marginal tax rate on the largest corporations, those with taxable incomes exceeding $335,000, is ___ percent, while that on the wealthiest individuals is ___ percent.

17. Interest received on _____ bonds is generally not subject to federal income taxes. This feature makes them particularly attractive to investors in _____ tax brackets.

18. In order to qualify as a long-term capital gain or loss, an asset must be held for more than ___ months.

19. Gains or losses on assets held less than one year are referred to as _____ - _____ transactions.

20. Interest income received by a corporation is taxed as _____ income. However, only ___ percent of dividends received from another corporation is subject to taxation.

21. Another important distinction exists between interest and dividends paid by a corporation. Interest payments are ____ _____, while dividend payments are not.

22. Ordinary corporate operating losses can first be carried back ___ years and then forward ___ years.

23. A firm that refuses to pay dividends in order to help stockholders avoid personal income taxes may be subject to a penalty for _____ _____ of earnings.

24. A corporation that owns 80 percent or more of another corporation's stock may choose to file _____ tax returns.

25. The Tax Code permits a corporation (that meets certain restrictions) to be taxed at the owners' personal tax rates and avoid the impact of _____ taxation of dividends. This type of corporation is called an ____ corporation.

Conceptual

26. If management is sure that the economy is at the peak of a boom, and is about to enter a recession, a firm which needs to borrow money should probably use short-term rather than long-term debt.

    a. True b. False

©1992 The Dryden Press
All rights reserved.

27. Long-term interest rates reflect expectations about future inflation. Inflation has varied greatly from year to year over the last 10 years, and, as a result, long-term rates have fluctuated more than short-term rates.

   a. True   **b.** False

28. The fact that 70 percent of the dividends received by a corporation is excluded from taxable income has encouraged debt financing over equity financing.

   a. True   **b.** False

29. An individual with substantial personal wealth and income is considering the possibility of opening a new business. The business will have a relatively high degree of risk, and losses may be incurred for the first several years. Which legal form of business organization would probably be best?

   a. Proprietorship   **b.** Corporation   **c.** Partnership
   d. S corporation   **e.** Limited partnership

30. Assume interest rates on 30-year government and corporate bonds were as follows: T-bond = 7.72%; A = 9.64%; AAA = 8.72%; BBB = 10.18%. The differences in rates among these issues are caused primarily by:

   a. Tax effects.   **b.** Default risk differences.   **c.** Maturity risk differences.
   d. Inflation differences.   **e.** Both b and d.

31. Which of the following statements is most *correct*?

   a. The introduction of a new technology, such as computers, might be expected to improve labor productivity, making businesses more able and willing to pay a higher price for capital. This would put upward pressure on interest rates. However, the productivity improvements might give rise to lower inflationary expectations, which would put downward pressure on interest rates. Thus, the net effect of the new technology on interest rates might be uncertain.
   b. If future inflation were expected to remain constant at 6 percent for all future years, then for all bonds (government and corporate combined) we could measure the maturity risk premium as the difference between the yields on 30-year and 1-year bonds.
   c. If investors expect the inflation rate to *decrease* over time, e.g., the expected inflation rate in Year t exceeds the expected rate in Year t + 1 for all values of t, then we can be *certain* that the yield curve for U.S. Treasury securities will be downward sloping.
   d. Each of the above statements is correct.
   e. Statements a and c are both correct.

© 1992 The Dryden Press
All rights reserved.

SELF-TEST PROBLEMS

1. You have determined the following data for a given bond: Real risk-free rate (k^*) = 3%; inflation premium = 8%; default risk premium = 2%; liquidity premium = 2%; and maturity risk premium = 1%. What is the nominal risk-free rate, k_{RF}?

   a. 10%   b. 11%   c. 12%   d. 13%   e. 14%

2. Refer to the previous problem. What is the interest rate on long-term Treasury securities, or T-bonds, of the relevant maturity?

   a. 10%   b. 11%   c. 12%   d. 13%   e. 14%

3. Assume that a 3-year Treasury note has no maturity risk nor liquidity risk, and that the real risk-free rate of interest falls to 2 percent. A 3-year T-note carries a yield to maturity of 12 percent. If the expected inflation rate is 12 percent for the coming year and 10 percent the year after, what is the implied expected inflation rate for the third year?

   a. 8%   b. 9%   c. 10%   d. 11%   e. 12%

4. Wayne Corporation had income from operations of $385,000, it received interest payments of $15,000, it paid interest of $20,000, it received dividends from another corporation of $10,000, and it paid $40,000 in dividends to its common stockholders. What is Wayne's federal income tax?

   a. $122,760   b. $130,220   c. $141,700   d. $155,200   e. $163,500

5. A firm purchases $10 million of corporate bonds which paid a 16 percent interest rate, or $1.6 million in interest. If the firm's marginal tax rate is 34 percent, what is the after-tax interest yield?

   a. 7.36%   b. 8.64%   c. 10.56%   d. 13.89%   e. 14.72%

6. Refer to the previous problem. The firm also invests in the common stock of another company having a 16 percent before-tax dividend yield. What is the after-tax dividend yield?

   a. 7.36%   b. 8.64%   c. 10.56%   d. 13.89%   e. 14.37%

7. The Carter Company's taxable income and income tax payments are shown below for 1988 through 1991:

©1992 The Dryden Press
All rights reserved.

Year	Taxable Income	Tax Payment
1988	$10,000	$1,500
1989	5,000	750
1990	10,000	1,500
1991	5,000	750

Assume that Carter's tax rate for all 4 years was a flat 15 percent; that is, each dollar of taxable income was taxed at 15 percent. In 1992, Carter incurred a loss of $17,000. Using corporate loss carry-back, what is Carter's adjusted tax payment for 1991?

a. $850   b. $750   c. $610   d. $550   e. $450

8. A firm can undertake a new project which will generate a before-tax return of 20 percent or it can invest the same funds in the preferred stock of another company which yields 13 percent before taxes. If the only consideration is which alternative provides the highest relevant (after-tax) return, and the applicable tax rate is 34 percent, should the firm invest in the project or the preferred stock?

a. Preferred stock; its relevant return is 12 percent.
b. Project; its relevant return is 1.53 percentage points higher.
c. Preferred stock; its relevant return is 0.22 percentage points higher.
d. Project; its before-tax return is 20 percent.
e. Either alternative can be chosen; they have the same relevant return.

9. Assume that the real risk-free rate, k*, is 4 percent, and that inflation is expected to be 7 percent in Year 1, 4 percent in Year 2, and 3 percent thereafter. Assume also that all Treasury bonds are highly liquid and free of default risk. If 2-year and 5-year Treasury bonds both yield 11 percent, what is the difference in the maturity risk premiums (MRPs) on the two bonds; that is, what is $MRP_5 - MRP_2$?

a. 0.5%   b. 1.0%   c. 2.25%   d. 1.5%   e. 1.25%

10. Cooley Corporation has $20,000 which it plans to invest in marketable securities. It is choosing between MCI bonds which yield 10 percent, State of Colorado municipal bonds which yield 7 percent, and MCI preferred stock with a dividend yield of 8 percent. Cooley's corporate tax rate is 25 percent, and 70 percent of its dividends received are tax exempt. What is the after-tax rate of return on the highest yielding security?

a. 7.4%   b. 7.0%   c. 7.5%   d. 6.5%   e. 6.0%

©1992 The Dryden Press
All rights reserved.

ANSWERS TO SELF-TEST QUESTIONS

1. money; capital
2. primary; secondary
3. intermediary
4. investment banking
5. organized exchanges; over-the-counter (OTC)
6. default
7. U.S. Treasury
8. inflation
9. inflation; default; liquidity; maturity
10. term structure; yield
11. upward
12. segmentation; liquidity; expectations
13. short-term; long-term; equity
14. progressive
15. bracket creep
16. 34; 31
17. municipal; high
18. 12
19. short-term
20. ordinary; 30
21. tax deductible
22. 3; 15
23. improper accumulation
24. consolidated
25. double; S

26. a. The firm should borrow short-term until interest rates drop due to the recession, then go long-term. Predicting interest rates is extremely difficult, for managers can rarely be sure about what is going to happen to the economy.

27. b. Fluctuations in long-term rates are smaller because the long-term inflation premium is an average of inflation expectations over many years, and hence the IP on long-term bonds is quite stable relative to the IP on short-term bonds. Also, short-term rates fluctuate as a result of Federal Reserve policy (the Fed intervenes in the short-term rather than the long-term market).

28. b. Debt financing is encouraged by the fact that interest payments are tax deductible while dividend payments are not.

29. d. The S corporation limits the liability of the individual, but permits losses to be deducted against personal income.

30. b. $k = k^* + IP + DRP + LP + MRP$. Since each of these bonds has a 30-year maturity, the MRP and IP would all be equal. Thus, the differences in the interest rates among these issues are the default risk and liquidity premiums.

31. a. Statement b is false because $k = k^* + IP + DRP + LP + MRP$. $k^* + IP$ would be the same for the two bonds; however, the default risk premium and liquidity premium would not be the same for the two bonds. Thus, you could not simply subtract the two yields to determine the MRP. Statement c is false because the expectations theory is not the only theory proposed to explain the shape of the yield curve. The market segmentation theory states that the slope depends on supply/demand conditions and the liquidity preference theory states that under normal conditions a positive maturity risk premium exists. So, we cannot be certain that the yield curve would be downward sloping.

©1992 The Dryden Press
All rights reserved.

SOLUTIONS TO SELF-TEST PROBLEMS

1. b. $k_{RF} = k* + IP = 3\% + 8\% = 11\%$.

2. c. There is virtually no risk of default on a U.S. Treasury security, and they trade in active markets, which provide liquidity, so

$$k = k* + IP + DRP + LP + MRP$$
$$= 3\% + 8\% + 0\% + 0\% + 1\%$$
$$= 12\%.$$

3. a.
$$k = k* + IP + DRP + LP + MRP$$
$$12\% = 2\% + X + 0\% + 0\% + 0\%$$
$$X = 10\%.$$

Thus, the average expected inflation rate over the next 3 years is 10 percent. Given that the average expected inflation rate over the next three years is 10%, we can find the implied expected inflation rate for the third year by solving the equation that sets the two known plus the one unknown expected inflation rates equal to 10%:

$$\frac{12\% + 10\% + Y}{3} = 10\%$$
$$Y = 8\%.$$

4. b. The first step is to determine taxable income:

Income from operations	$385,000
Interest income (fully taxable)	15,000
Interest expense (fully deductible)	(20,000)
Dividend income (30% taxable)	3,000
Taxable income	$383,000

(Note that dividends are paid from after-tax income and do not affect taxable income.)

Based on the current corporate tax table, the tax calculation is as follows:

Tax = $113,900 + 0.34($383,000 - $335,000) = $113,900 + $16,320 = $130,220.

5. c. The after-tax yield (or dollar return) equals the before-tax yield (or dollar return) multiplied by one minus the effective tax rate, or   AT = BT(1 - Effective T). Therefore, AT = 16%(1 - 0.34) = 16%(0.66) = 10.56%.

©1992 The Dryden Press
All rights reserved.

6. e. Since the dividends are received by a corporation, only 30 percent are taxable, and the Effective T = Tax rate × 30%:

$$
\begin{aligned}
AT &= BT(1 - \text{Effective T}) \\
&= 16\%[1 - 0.34(0.30)] \\
&= 16\%(1 - 0.102) \\
&= 16\%(0.898) \\
&= 14.37\%.
\end{aligned}
$$

7. e.

Year	Taxable Income	Tax Payment	Adjusted Taxable Income	Adjusted Tax Payment
1988	$10,000	$1,500	$10,000	$1,500
1989	5,000	750	0	0
1990	10,000	1,500	0	0
1991	5,000	750	3,000	450

The carry-back can only go back 3 years. Thus, there was no adjustment made in 1988. After $5,000 of adjustment in 1989 and $10,000 in 1990, there was a $2,000 loss remaining to apply to 1991. The 1991 adjusted tax payment is $3,000(0.15) = $450. Thus, Carter received a total of $2,550 in tax refunds after the adjustment.

8. b. The project is fully taxable; thus its after-tax return is as follows:

$$
AT = 20\%(1 - 0.34) = 20\%(0.66) = 13.2\%.
$$

But only 30 percent of the preferred stock dividends are taxable; thus its after-tax yield is $AT = 13\%[(1 - 0.34(0.30)] = 13\%(1 - 0.102) = 13\%(0.898) = 11.67\%$. Therefore, the new project should be chosen since its after-tax return is 1.53 percentage points higher.

9. d. First, note that we will use the equation $k_t = 4\% + IP_t = MRP_t$. We have the data needed to find the IPs:

$$
IP_5 = (7\% + 4\% + 3\% + 3\% + 3\%)/5 = 20\%/5 = 4\%.
$$

$$
IP_2 = (7\% + 4\%)/2 = 5.5\%.
$$

Now we can substitute into the equation:

$$
k_2 = 4\% + 5.5\% + MRP = 11\%.
$$

$$
k_5 = 4\% + 4\% + MRP = 11\%.
$$

Now we can solve for the MRPs, and find the difference:

$$
MRP_5 = 11\% - 8\% = 3\%.
$$
$$
MRP_2 = 11\% - 9.5\% = 1.5\%.
$$

Difference = $3\% - 1.5\% = 1.5\%$.

©1992 The Dryden Press
All rights reserved.

10. c. AT yield on Colorado bond = 7%.

AT yield on MCI bond = 10% − Taxes = 10% − 10%(0.25) = 7.5%.

Check: Invest $20,000 at 10% = $2,000 interest.

Pay 25% tax, so AT income = $2,000(1 − T) = $2,000(0.75) = $1,500.

AT rate of return = $1,500/$20,000 = 7.5%.

AT yield on MCI preferred stock:
AT yield = 8% − Taxes = 8% − 0.3(8%)(0.25) = 8% − 0.6% = 7.4%.

Therefore, invest in MCI bonds.

©1992 The Dryden Press
All rights reserved.

CHAPTER 4
RISK AND RATES OF RETURN

OVERVIEW

Risk is an important concept in financial analysis, especially in terms of how it affects security prices and rates of return. Investment risk is associated with the probability of low or negative future returns. There are two types of risk pertinent to investors: *diversifiable* and *nondiversifiable risk*, the sum of which is the investment's *total risk*. Diversifiable risk is not important to rational, informed investors, because they will eliminate its effects by diversifying it away. The significant risk is nondiversifiable risk, which cannot be eliminated.

An attempt has been made to quantify market risk with a measure called beta. Beta is a measurement of how a particular firm's stock returns move relative to overall movements of stock market returns. The Capital Asset Pricing Model (CAPM), using the concept of beta and investors' aversion to risk, specifies the relationship between market risk and the required rate of return. This relationship can be visualized graphically with the Security Market Line (SML). The slope of the SML can change, or the line can shift upward or downward, in response to changes in risk or required rates of return.

OUTLINE

I. **Risk refers to the chance that some unfavorable event will occur. Investment risk is related to the probability of actually earning less than the expected return; thus, the greater the chance of low or negative returns, the riskier the investment.**

A. The *probability distribution* is the listing of all possible outcomes, or events, with a probability (chance of occurrence) assigned to each outcome. The sum of these probabilities must equal 1.0.

B. If you buy a bond, the higher the probability of failure in receiving the interest payments, the riskier the bonds, and the higher the risk, the higher your required rate of return on the bond.

C. The *expected rate of return* $(\hat{k})$ is the sum of the products of each possible outcome times its associated probability—it is a weighted average of the various possible outcomes, with the weights being their probabilities of occurrence:

$$\text{Expected rate of return} = \hat{k} = \sum_{i=1}^{n} P_i k_i.$$

D. Where the number of possible outcomes is virtually unlimited, *continuous probability distributions* are used in determining the expected rate of return.

©1992 The Dryden Press
All rights reserved.

1. The tighter, or more peaked, the probability distribution, the more likely it is that the actual outcome will be close to the expected value, and thus, the lower the risk assigned to a stock.
2. One measure for determining the tightness of the probability distribution is the standard deviation, σ:

$$\text{Standard deviation} = \sigma = \sqrt{\sum_{i=1}^{n} (k_i - \hat{k})^2 P_i}.$$

3. Thus, the standard deviation is a probability-weighted average deviation from the expected value, and it gives you an idea of how far above or below the expected value the actual value is likely to be.
4. Another useful measure of risk is the coefficient of variation (CV), which is the standard deviation divided by the expected return. It shows the risk per unit of return and provides a more meaningful basis for comparison when the expected returns on two alternatives are not the same:

$$\text{Coefficient of variation (CV)} = \frac{\sigma}{\hat{k}}.$$

E. Most investors are *risk averse*. This means that for two alternatives with the same expected rate of return, investors will choose the one with the lower risk. Therefore, in market equilibrium, riskier securities must have higher expected returns than less risky ones.

II. **A stock held as part of a portfolio is less risky than the same stock held in isolation. Most institutions and individual investors hold portfolios of securities rather than one stock. This fact has been incorporated into a generalized framework called the Capital Asset Pricing Model (CAPM).**

A. From the investor's standpoint, what is important is the return on his or her portfolio, and the portfolio's risk—not the fact that a particular stock goes up or down. Thus, the risk and return of an individual security should be analyzed in terms of how it affects the risk and return of the portfolio in which it is held.
1. The expected return on a portfolio, $\hat{k}_p$, is the weighted average expected return of the individual stocks in the portfolio, with the weights being the fraction of the total portfolio invested in each stock:

$$\hat{k}_p = \sum_{i=1}^{n} w_i \hat{k}_i.$$

2. The riskiness of a portfolio, σ_p, is generally *not* a weighted average of the standard deviations of the individual securities in the portfolio. The riskiness of a portfolio depends not only on the standard deviations of the individual stocks, but also on the *correlation between the stocks*.
a. The correlation coefficient, r, measures this tendency of two variables to move together.

©1992 The Dryden Press
All rights reserved.

b. Diversification does nothing to reduce risk if the portfolio consists of perfectly positively correlated stocks.

c. As a rule, the riskiness of a portfolio will be reduced as the number of stocks in the portfolio increases.

B. While very large portfolios end up with a substantial amount of risk, it is not as much risk as if all the money were invested in only one stock. Almost half of the riskiness inherent in an average individual stock can be eliminated if the stock is held in a reasonably well-diversified portfolio, which is one containing 40 or more stocks.

1. Company-specific (also known as diversifiable or unsystematic) risk is that part of the risk of a stock which can be eliminated. It is caused by events particular to the firm.

2. Market (also known as nondiversifiable or systematic) risk is that part of the risk which cannot be eliminated, and it stems from factors which systematically affect all firms, such as war, inflation, recessions, and high interest rates. Thus, market risk is the relevant risk, which reflects a security's contribution to the portfolio's risk.

III. **The tendency of a stock to move with the market is reflected in its beta coefficient, b, which is a measure of the stock's volatility relative to that of an average stock.**

A. An average-risk stock is defined as one that tends to move up and down in step with the general market. By definition it has a beta of 1.0.

B. A stock that is twice as volatile as the market will have a beta of 2.0, while a stock that is half as volatile as the market will have a beta coefficient of 0.5.

C. The beta coefficient of a portfolio of securities is the weighted average of the individual securities' betas:

$$b_p = \sum_{i=1}^{n} w_i b_i.$$

D. Since a stock's beta measures its contribution to the riskiness of a portfolio, beta is the appropriate measure of the stock's relevant risk.

IV. **The Capital Asset Pricing Model (CAPM) employs the concept of beta, which measures risk as the relationship between a particular stock's movements and the movements of the overall stock market. The CAPM uses a stock's beta, in conjunction with the average investor's degree of risk aversion, to calculate the return that investors require, k_s, on that particular stock.**

A. The Security Market Line (SML) shows the relationship between risk as measured by beta and the required rate of return for individual securities. The SML equation can be used to find the required rate of return on Stock i:

©1992 The Dryden Press
All rights reserved.

SML Equation: $k_i = k_{RF} + (k_M - k_{RF})b_i$.

Here k_{RF} is the rate of interest on risk-free securities, b_i is the ith stock's beta, and k_M is the return on the market or, alternatively, on an average stock.

1. The term, $k_M - k_{RF}$, is the market risk premium, RP_M. This is a measure of the additional return over the risk-free rate needed to compensate investors for assuming an average amount of risk.

2. In the CAPM the *market risk premium*, $k_M - k_{RF}$, is multiplied by the stock's beta to determine the additional premium over the risk-free rate that is required to compensate investors for the risk inherent in a particular stock.

3. This premium may be larger or smaller than the premium required on an average stock, depending on the riskiness of that stock in relation to the overall market as measured by the stock's beta.

4. The risk premium calculated by $(k_M - k_{RF})b_i$ is added to the risk-free rate, k_{RF} (the rate on Treasury securities), to determine the total rate of return required by investors on a particular stock, k_s.

B. The SML equation can be expressed in graph form. The slope of the SML reflects the degree of risk aversion in the economy.

C. The risk-free (also known as nominal or quoted) rate of interest consists of two elements: (1) a real inflation-free rate of return, k^*, and (2) an inflation premium, IP, equal to the anticipated rate of inflation.

1. The real rate on long-term Treasury bonds has historically ranged from 2 to 4 percent.

2. As the expected rate of inflation increases, a higher premium must be added to the real risk-free rate of return to compensate for the loss of purchasing power.

3. As risk aversion increases, so does the risk premium and, thus, the slope of the SML.

4. Many factors can affect a company's beta. When such changes occur, the required rate of return also changes.

V. A word of caution is in order regarding betas and the Capital Asset Pricing Model. The entire theory is based on ex ante, or expected, conditions, yet we have available only ex post, or past, data. Thus, the betas we calculate show how volatile a stock has been in the past, but conditions may change, and its future volatility, which is the item of real concern to investors, might be quite different from its past volatility.

VI. Because returns on foreign investments are not perfectly positively correlated with returns on U.S. assets, it has been argued that multinational corporations are less risky than companies which operate strictly within the boundaries of any one country.

VII. Appendix 4A presents a discussion on the calculation of beta coefficients. The discussion concentrates on graphic and least squares regression techniques.

©1992 The Dryden Press
All rights reserved.

SELF-TEST QUESTIONS

Definitional

1. Investment risk is associated with the _____ of low or negative returns; the greater the chance of loss, the riskier the investment.

2. A listing of all possible _____, with a probability assigned to each, is known as a probability _____.

3. Weighting each possible outcome of a distribution by its _____ of occurrence and summing the results give the expected _____ of the distribution.

4. One measure of the tightness of a probability distribution is the _____ _____.

5. Investors who prefer outcomes with a high degree of certainty to those that are less certain are described as being _____ _____.

6. Owning a portfolio of securities enables investors to benefit from _____.

7. Diversification of a portfolio can result in lower _____ for the same level of return.

8. Diversification of a portfolio is achieved by selecting securities that are not perfectly _____ correlated with each other.

9. That part of a stock's risk that can be reduced by diversification is known as _____ -_____ risk, while the portion that cannot be eliminated is called _____ risk.

10. The _____ coefficient measures a stock's relative volatility as compared with a stock market index.

11. A stock that is twice as volatile as the market would have a beta coefficient of ____, while a stock with a beta of 0.5 would be only _____ as volatile as the market.

12. The beta coefficient of a portfolio is the _____ _____ of the betas of the individual stocks.

13. The expected value of a probability distribution of future returns is known as the _____ rate of return. The minimum expected return that will induce investors to buy a particular security is the _____ rate of return.

14. The security used to measure the _____ - _____ rate is the return available on U.S. Treasury securities.

©1992 The Dryden Press
All rights reserved.

15. The difference between the required rate of return on a risky asset and the risk-free rate is referred to as a _____ _____.

16. The risk premium for a stock may be calculated by multiplying the market risk premium times the stock's _____ _____.

17. A stock's required rate of return is equal to the _____-_____ rate plus the stock's _____ _____.

18. The risk-free rate on a short-term Treasury security is made up of two parts: an inflation-free or _____ rate of return plus an _____ premium.

19. Changes in investors' risk aversion alter the _____ of the Security Market Line.

Conceptual

20. The Y-axis intercept of the Security Market Line (SML) indicates the required rate of return on an individual stock with a beta of 1.0.

    a. True   b. False

21. If a stock has a beta of zero, it will be riskless when held in isolation.

    a. True   b. False

22. Which is the best measure of risk for an asset held in a well-diversified portfolio?

    a. Variance   b. Standard deviation   c. Beta
    d. Semi-variance   e. Expected value

23. In a portfolio of three different stocks, which of the following could *not* be true?

    a. The riskiness of the portfolio is less than the riskiness of each stock held in isolation.
    b. The riskiness of the portfolio is greater than the riskiness of one or two of the stocks.
    c. The beta of the portfolio is less than the beta of each of the individual stocks.
    d. The beta of the portfolio is greater than the beta of one or two of the individual stocks.
    e. The beta of the portfolio is equal to the beta of one of the individual stocks.

©1992 The Dryden Press
All rights reserved.

24. If investors expected inflation to increase in the future, and they also became more risk averse, what could be said about the change in the Security Market Line (SML)?

    a. The SML would shift up and the slope would increase.
    b. The SML would shift up and the slope would decrease.
    c. The SML would shift down and the slope would increase.
    d. The SML would shift down and the slope would decrease.
    e. The SML would remain unchanged.

25. Which of the following statements is most *correct*?

    a. The SML relates required returns to firms' systematic (or market) risk. The slope and intercept of this line *cannot* be controlled by the financial manager.
    b. The slope of the SML is determined by the value of beta.
    c. If you plotted the returns of a given stock against those of the market, and if you found that the slope of the regression line was negative, then the CAPM would indicate that the required rate of return on the stock should be less than the risk-free rate for a well-diversified investor, assuming that the observed relationship is expected to continue on into the future.
    d. If investors become less risk averse, the slope of the Security Market Line will increase.
    e. Statements a and c are both true.

26. Which of the following statements is most *correct*?

    a. Normally, the Security Market Line has an upward slope. However, at one of those unusual times when the yield curve on bonds is downward sloping, the SML will also have a downward slope.
    b. The market risk premium, as it is used in the CAPM theory, is equal to the required rate of return on an average stock minus the required rate of return on an average company's bonds.
    c. If the marginal investor's aversion to risk decreases, then the slope of the yield curve would, other things held constant, tend to increase. If expectations for inflation also increased at the same time risk aversion was decreasing—say the expected inflation rate rose from 5 percent to 8 percent—the net effect could possibly result in a parallel upward shift in the SML.
    d. According to the text, it is theoretically possible to combine two stocks, each of which would be quite risky if held as your only asset, and to form a 2-stock portfolio that is riskless. However, the stocks would have to have a correlation coefficient of expected future returns of -1.0, and it is hard to find such stocks in the real world.
    e. Each of the above statements is false.

4-7

©1992 The Dryden Press
All rights reserved.

27. Which of the following statements is most *correct*?

    a. The expected future rate of return, $\hat{k}$, is always *above* the past realized rate of return, $\bar{k}$, except for highly risk-averse investors.

    b. The expected future rate of return, $\hat{k}$, is always *below* the past realized rate of return, $\bar{k}$, except for highly risk-averse investors.

    c. The expected future rate of return, $\hat{k}$, is always *below* the required rate of return, k, except for highly risk-averse investors.

    d. There is no logical reason to think that any relationship exists between the expected future rate of return, $\hat{k}$, on a security and the security's required rate of return, k.

    e. Each of the above statements is false.

SELF-TEST PROBLEMS

1. Stock A has the following probability distribution of expected returns:

Probability	Rate of Return
0.1	-15%
0.2	0
0.4	5
0.2	10
0.1	25

What is Stock A's expected rate of return and standard deviation?

    a. 8.0%; 9.5% **b.** 8.0%; 6.5% **c.** 5.0%; 3.5% **d.** 5.0%; 6.5% **e.** 5.0%; 9.5%

2. If k_{RF} = 5%, k_M = 11%, and b = 1.3 for Stock X, what is k_X, the required rate of return for Stock X?

    a. 18.7%   **b.** 16.7%   **c.** 14.8%   **d.** 12.8%   **e.** 11.9%

3. Refer to the previous problem. What would k_X be if investors expected the inflation rate to increase by 2 percentage points?

    a. 18.7%   **b.** 16.7%   **c.** 14.8%   **d.** 12.8%   **e.** 11.9%

4. Refer to Self-Test Problem 2. What would k_X be if an increase in investors' risk aversion caused the market risk premium to increase by 3 percentage points? k_{RF} remains at 5 percent.

    a. 18.7%   **b.** 16.7%   **c.** 14.8%   **d.** 12.8%   **e.** 11.9%

©1992 The Dryden Press
All rights reserved.

5. Refer to Self-Test Problem 2. What would k_X be if investors expected the inflation rate to increase by 2 percentage points *and* their risk aversion increased by 3 percentage points?

   a. 18.7%   **b.** 16.7%   **c.** 14.8%   **d.** 12.8%   **e.** 11.9%

6. The Apple Investment Fund has a total investment of $450 million in five stocks.

Stock	Investment (Millions)	Beta
1	$130	0.4
2	110	1.5
3	70	3.0
4	90	2.0
5	50	1.0

What is the fund's overall, or weighted average, beta?

   a. 1.14   **b.** 1.22   **c.** 1.35   **d.** 1.46   **e.** 1.53

7. Refer to the previous problem. If the risk-free rate is 12 percent, and the market risk premium is 6 percent, what is the required rate of return on the Apple Fund?

   a. 20.76%   **b.** 19.92%   **c.** 18.81%   **d.** 17.62%   **e.** 15.77%

8. You are managing a portfolio of 10 stocks which are held in equal dollar amounts. The current beta of the portfolio is 1.8, and the beta of Stock A is 2.0. If Stock A is sold, and the proceeds are used to purchase a replacement stock, what does the beta of the replacement stock have to be to lower the portfolio beta to 1.7?

   a. 1.4   **b.** 1.3   **c.** 1.2   **d.** 1.1   **e.** 1.0

9. Consider the following information for the Alachua Retirement Fund, with a total investment of $4 million.

Stock	Investment	Beta
A	$ 400,000	1.2
B	600,000	-0.4
C	1,000,000	1.5
D	2,000,000	0.8
	$4,000,000	

The market required rate of return is 12 percent, and the risk-free rate is 6 percent. What is its required rate of return?

   a. 9.98%   **b.** 10.45%   **c.** 11.01%   **d.** 11.50%   **e.** 12.56%

©1992 The Dryden Press
All rights reserved.

10. You are given the following distribution of returns:

Probability	Return
0.4	$30
0.5	25
0.1	-20

What is the coefficient of variation of the expected dollar returns?

a. 206.2500   **b.** 0.6383   **c.** 14.3614   **d.** 0.7500   **e.** 1.2500

11. If the risk-free rate is 8 percent, the expected return on the market is 13 percent, and the expected return on Security J is 15 percent, then what is the beta of Security J?

a. 1.40   **b.** 0.90   **c.** 1.20   **d.** 1.50   **e.** 0.75

Appendix 4A

4A-1. Given the information below, calculate the betas for Stocks A and B.

Year	Stock A	Stock B	Market
1	-5%	10%	-10%
2	10	20	10
3	25	30	30

(Hint: Think rise over run.)

a. 1.0; 0.5   **b.** 0.75; 0.5   **c.** 0.75; 1.0   **d.** 0.5; 0.5   **e.** 0.75; 0.25

ANSWERS TO SELF-TEST QUESTIONS

1. probability
2. outcomes; distribution
3. probability; return
4. standard deviation
5. risk averse
6. diversification
7. risk
8. positively
9. company-specific (or unsystematic); market (or systematic)

10. beta
11. 2.0; half
12. weighted average
13. expected; required
14. risk-free
15. risk premium
16. beta coefficient
17. risk-free; risk premium
18. real; inflation
19. slope

20. b. The Y-axis intercept of the SML is k_{RF}, which is the required rate of return of a security with a beta of zero.

©1992 The Dryden Press
All rights reserved.

21. b. A zero beta stock could be made riskless if it were combined with enough other zero beta stocks, but it would still have company-specific risk and be risky when held in isolation.

22. c. The beta coefficient, which is a measure of the extent to which the returns on a given stock move with the stock market.

23. c. The beta of the portfolio is a weighted average of the individual securities' betas, so it could not be less than the betas of all of the stocks.

24. a. The increase in inflation would cause the SML to shift up, and investors becoming more risk averse would cause the slope to increase.

25. e. Statement b is false because the slope of the SML is $k_M - k_{RF}$. Statement d is false because as investors become less risk averse the slope of the SML decreases. Statement a is correct because the financial manager has no control over k_M or k_{RF}. ($k_M - k_{RF}$ = slope and k_{RF} = intercept of the SML.) Statement c is correct because the slope of the regression line is beta and beta would be negative; thus, the required return would be less than the risk-free rate.

26. d. Statement a is false. The yield curve determines the value of k_{RF}; however, SML = $k_{RF} + (k_M - k_{RF})b$. The average return on the market will always be greater than the risk-free rate; thus, the SML will always be upward sloping. Statement b is false because RP_M is equal to $k_M - k_{RF}$. k_{RF} is equal to the risk-free rate, not the rate on an average company's bonds. Statement c is false. A decrease in an investor's aversion to risk would indicate a downward sloping yield curve. A decrease in risk aversion and an increase in inflation would cause the SML slope to decrease and to shift upward simultaneously.

27. e. All the statements are false. For equilibrium to exist the expected return must equal the required return.

SOLUTIONS TO SELF-TEST PROBLEMS

1. e. $\hat{k}_A = 0.1(-15\%) + 0.2(0\%) + 0.4(5\%) + 0.2(10\%) + 0.1(25\%) = 5.0\%$.

$$\text{Variance} = 0.1(-0.15 - 0.05)^2 + 0.2(0.0 - 0.05)^2 + 0.4(0.05 - 0.05)^2$$
$$+ 0.2(0.10 - 0.05)^2 + 0.1(0.25 - 0.05)^2$$

$$= 0.009.$$

Standard deviation = $\sqrt{0.009} = 0.0949 \approx 9.5\%$.

2. d. $k_X = k_{RF} + (k_M - k_{RF})b_X = 5\% + (11\% - 5\%)1.3 = 12.8\%$.

©1992 The Dryden Press
All rights reserved.

3. c. $k_X = k_{RF} + (k_M - k_{RF})b_X = 7\% + (13\% - 7\%)1.3 = 14.8\%$.

A change in the inflation premium does *not* change the market risk premium ($k_M - k_{RF}$) since both k_M and k_{RF} are affected.

4. b. $k_X = k_{RF} + (k_M - k_{RF})b_X = 5\% + (14\% - 5\%)1.3 = 16.7\%$.

5. a. $k_X = k_{RF} + (k_M - k_{RF})b_X = 7\% + (16\% - 7\%)1.3 = 18.7\%$.

6. d. $b_p = \sum_{i-1}^{5} w_i b_i$

$$= \frac{\$130}{\$450}(0.4) + \frac{\$110}{\$450}(1.5) + \frac{\$70}{\$450}(3.0) + \frac{\$90}{\$450}(2.0) + \frac{\$50}{\$450}(1.0) = 1.46.$$

7. a. $k_p = k_{RF} + (k_M - k_{RF})b_p = 12\% + (6\%)1.46 = 20.76\%$.

8. e. First find the beta of the remaining 9 stocks:

$1.8 = 0.9(b_R) + 0.1(b_A)$
$1.8 = 0.9(b_R) + 0.1(2.0)$
$1.8 = 0.9(b_R) + 0.2$
$1.6 = 0.9(b_R)$
$b_R = 1.78$.

Now find the beta of the new stock that produces $b_p = 1.7$.

$1.7 = 0.9(1.78) + 0.1(b_N)$
$1.7 = 1.6 + 0.1(b_N)$
$0.1 = 0.1(b_N)$
$b_N = 1.0$.

9. c. Determine the weight each stock represents in the portfolio:

Stock	Investment	w_i	Beta	$w_i \times$ Beta
A	$ 400,000	0.10	1.2	0.1200
B	600,000	0.15	-0.4	-0.0600
C	1,000,000	0.25	1.5	0.3750
D	2,000,000	0.50	0.8	0.4000
			$b_p =$	0.8350 Portfolio beta

Write out the SML equation, and substitute known values including the portfolio beta. Solve for the required portfolio return.

©1992 The Dryden Press
All rights reserved.

$$k_p = k_{RF} + (k_M - k_{RF})b_p = 0.06 + (0.12 - 0.06)0.8350$$

$$= 0.06 + 0.0501 = 0.1101 = 11.01\%.$$

10. b. Use the given probability distribution of returns to calculate the expected value, variance, standard deviation, and coefficient of variation.

P_i	k_i	$P_i k_i$	k_i	$\hat{k}$	$(k_i - \hat{k})$	$(k_i - \hat{k})^2$	$P(k_i - \hat{k})^2$
$0.4 \times$	30% =	12.0%	30% -	22.5% =	7.5%	56.25%	22.500%
$0.5 \times$	25 =	12.5	25 -	22.5 =	2.5	6.25	3.125
$0.1 \times$	-20 =	-2.0	-20 -	22.5 =	-42.5	1,806.25	180.625
	$\hat{k} =$	22.5%				$\sigma^2 =$ Variance =	206.250%

The standard deviation (σ) of $\hat{k}$ is $\sqrt{206.25\%}$ - 14.3614%.

Use the standard deviation and the expected return to calculate the coefficient of variation: 14.3614%/22.5% = 0.6383.

11. a. Use the SML equation, substitute in the known values, and solve for beta.

$$k_{RF} = 0.08; \ k_M = 0.13.$$

$$k_j = k_{RF} + (k_M - k_{RF})b_j$$

$$0.15 = 0.08 + (0.13 - 0.08)b_j$$

$$0.07 = (0.05)b$$

$$b_j = 1.4.$$

Appendix 4A

4A-1. b. Stock A: b_A - $\dfrac{\text{Rise}}{\text{Run}}$ - $\dfrac{10 - (-5)}{10 - (-10)}$ - $\dfrac{15}{20}$ - 0.75.

Stock B: b_B - $\dfrac{\text{Rise}}{\text{Run}}$ - $\dfrac{20 - 10}{10 - (-10)}$ - $\dfrac{10}{20}$ - 0.50.

4-13

© 1992 The Dryden Press
All rights reserved.

CHAPTER 5
TIME VALUE OF MONEY

OVERVIEW

A dollar in the hand today is worth more than a dollar to be received in the future because, if you had it now, you could invest that dollar and earn interest. Of all the techniques used in finance, none is more important than the concept of time value of money, or discounted cash flow (DCF) analysis. Future value and present value techniques can be applied to lump sums, ordinary annuities, annuities due, and irregular cash flow streams. Future and present values can be calculated using interest factor tables, a regular calculator, or a calculator with financial functions. When compounding occurs more frequently than once a year, the effective rate of interest is greater than the stated rate.

OUTLINE

I. **The time line is one of the most important tools in time value of money calculations. Time lines help to visualize what is happening in a particular problem. Cash flows are placed directly below the tick marks, and interest rates are shown directly above the time line; unknown cash flows are indicated by question marks. Thus, to find the future value of $100 after 5 years at 5 percent interest, the following time line can be set up:**

$$
\begin{array}{lccccccc}
\text{Time:} & 0 & & 1 & 2 & 3 & 4 & 5 \\
& & 5\% & & & & & \\
\text{Cash flows:} & -100 & & & & & & FV_5 = ?
\end{array}
$$

II. **Finding the future value (FV), or compounding, is the process of going from today's values (or present values) to future amounts (or future values). It can be calculated as**

$$FV_n = PV(1 + i)^n,$$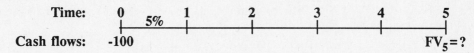

where PV = present value, or beginning amount; i = interest rate per year; and n = number of periods involved in the analysis. This equation can be solved in one of three ways: numerically, with interest tables, or with a financial calculator. For calculations, assume the following data presented in the time line above: present value = $100, interest rate = 5%, and number of years = 5.

A. **To solve numerically, use a regular calculator to find 1 + i = 1.05 raised to the fifth power, which equals 1.2763. Multiply this figure by PV = $100 to get the final answer of FV_5 = $127.63.**

©1992 The Dryden Press
All rights reserved.

B. To solve with interest tables, look at Table A-3 at the end of your textbook for future value interest factors. Look down the first column to Period 5, then look across that row to the 5% column for the number 1.2763. Multiplying by PV = $100 results in FV_5 = $127.63.

C. With a financial calculator, the future value can be found by using the time value of money input keys, where N = number of periods, I = interest rate per period, PV = present value, PMT = payment, and FV = future value. By entering PV = 100, I = 5, and N = 5, and then pressing the FV key, the answer 127.63 is displayed.
  1. Some financial calculators require that all cash flows be designated as either inflows or outflows, thus an outflow must be entered as a negative number (for example, PV = -100 instead of PV = 100).
  2. Some calculators require you to press a "Compute" key before pressing the FV key.

D. Note that small rounding differences will often occur among the various solution methods.

E. A graph of the compounding process shows how any sum grows over time at various rates of interest. The greater the rate of interest, the faster is the rate of growth.

III. Finding present values is called discounting, and it is simply the reverse of compounding. In general, the present value of a cash flow due n years in the future is the amount which, if it were on hand today, would grow to equal the future amount. By solving for PV in the future value equation, the present value, or discounting, equation can be developed and written in several forms:

$$PV = \frac{FV_n}{(1 + i)^n} = FV_n\left(\frac{1}{1 + i}\right)^n = FV(PVIF_{i,n}).$$

A. To solve for the present value of $127.63 discounted back 5 years at a 5% opportunity cost rate, one can utilize any of the three solution methods:
  1. Numerical solution: Divide $127.63 by 1.05 five times to get PV = $100.
  2. Tabular solution: Refer to Table A-1 in Appendix A of the text for the present value interest factors ($PVIF_{i,n}$). The value of $PVIF_{i,n}$ for i = 5% and n = 5 is 0.7835. Multiply this number by $127.63 to get PV = $100.
  3. Financial calculator solution: Enter N = 5, I = 5, and FV = 127.63, and then press the PV key to get PV = -100.

B. A graph of the discounting process shows how the present value of any sum to be received in the future diminishes as the years to receipt increases. At relatively high interest rates, funds due in the future are worth very little today, and even

© 1992 The Dryden Press
All rights reserved.

at a relatively low discount rate, the present value of a sum due in the very distant future is quite small.

IV. **There are four variables in the time value of money equations: PV, FV, i, and n. If three of the four variables are known, you can find the value of the fourth.**

   A. If we are given PV, FV, and n, we can determine i by substituting the known values into either the present value or future value equations, and then solving for i. Thus, if you can buy a security at a price of $78.35 which will pay you $100 after 5 years, what is the interest rate earned on the investment?
      1. Numerical solution: Use a trial and error process to reach the 5% value for i. This is a tedious and inefficient process.
      2. Tabular solution: Find the interest rate in Table A-3 of the text that corresponds to the future value interest factor of 1.2763 (calculated by dividing $100 by $78.35).
      3. Financial calculator solution: Enter N = 5, PV = -78.35, and FV = 100, then press the I key, and I = 5 is displayed.

   B. Likewise, if we are given PV, FV, and i, we can determine n by substituting the known values into either the present value or future value equations, and then solving for n. Thus, if you can buy a security with a 5 percent interest rate at a price of $78.35, how long will it take for your investment to return $100?
      1. Numerical solution: Use a trial and error process to reach the value of 5 for n. This is a tedious and inefficient process.
      2. Tabular solution: Find the value of n in Table A-3 of the text that corresponds to the future value interest factor of 1.2763 (found by dividing $100 by $78.35).
      3. Financial calculator solution: Enter PV = -78.35, FV = 100, and I = 5, then press the N key, and N = 5 is displayed.

V. **An annuity is a series of equal payments at fixed intervals for a specified number of periods. If the payments occur at the end of each period, as they typically do, the annuity is an ordinary (or deferred) annuity. If the payments occur at the beginning of each period, it is called an annuity due.**

   A. The future value of an annuity is the total amount one would have at the end of the annuity period if each payment were invested at a given interest rate and held to the end of the annuity period.
      1. Defining FVA_n as the compound sum of an ordinary annuity of n years, and PMT as the periodic payment, we can write

$$FVA_n = PMT \sum_{t=1}^{n} (1 + i)^{n-t} = PMT(FVIFA_{i,n}).$$

      2. $FVIFA_{i,n}$ is the future value interest factor for an ordinary annuity. FVIFAs may be found in Table A-4 of the text.

©1992 The Dryden Press
All rights reserved.

3. For example, the future value of a 3-year, 5 percent ordinary annuity of $100 per year would be $100(3.1525) = $315.25.
4. The same calculation can be made using the financial functions of a calculator. Enter N = 3, I = 5, and PMT = -100. Then press the FV key, and 315.25 is displayed.
5. For an annuity due, each payment is compounded for one additional period, so the future value of the entire annuity is equal to the future value of an ordinary annuity compounded for one additional period. Thus:

$$FVA_n \text{ (Annuity due)} = PMT(FVIFA_{i,n})(1 + i).$$

6. For example, the future value of a 3-year, 5 percent annuity due of $100 per year is $100(3.1525)(1.05) = $331.01.
7. Most financial calculators have a switch, or key, marked "DUE" or "BEG" that permits you to switch from end-of-period payments (an ordinary annuity) to beginning-of-period payments (an annuity due). Switch your calculator to beginning mode, and calculate as for an ordinary annuity. Do not forget to switch your calculator back to "END" mode when you are finished.

B. The present value of an annuity is the lump-sum payment today that would be equivalent to the annuity payments spread over the annuity period. It is the amount today that would permit withdrawals of an equal amount (PMT) at the end (or beginning for an annuity due) of each period for n periods.
1. Defining PVA_n as the present value of an ordinary annuity of n years and PMT as the periodic payment, we can write

$$PVA_n = PMT \sum_{t-1}^{n} \left(\frac{1}{1 + i} \right)^t = PMT(PVIFA_{i,n}).$$

2. $PVIFA_{i,n}$ is the present value interest factor for an ordinary annuity. PVIFAs may be found in Table A-2 at the back of the text.
3. For example, an annuity of $100 per year for 3 years at 5 percent would have a present value of $100(2.7232) = $272.32.
4. Using a financial calculator, enter N = 3, I = 5, and PMT = -100, and then press the PV key, for an answer of $272.32.
5. The present value for an annuity due is

$$PVA_n \text{ (Annuity due)} = PMT(PVIFA_{i,n})(1 + i).$$

6. For example, the present value of a 3-year, 5 percent annuity due of $100 is $100(2.7232)(1.05) = $285.94.
7. Using a financial calculator, switch to the beginning-of-period mode, and then enter N = 3, I = 5, and PMT = -100, and then press PV to get the answer, $285.94. Again, do not forget to switch your calculator back to "END" mode when you are finished.

5-4

©1992 The Dryden Press
All rights reserved.

VI. **An annuity that goes on indefinitely is called a perpetuity. The payments of a perpetuity constitute an infinite series.**

    A. The present value of a perpetuity is:

$$PV \ (Perpetuity) = Payment/Interest \ rate = PMT/i.$$

    B. For example, if the interest rate were 12 percent, a perpetuity of $1,000 a year would have a present value of $1,000/0.12 = $8,333.33.

VII. **Many financial decisions require the analysis of uneven, or nonconstant, cash flows rather than a stream of fixed payments such as an annuity.**

    A. The present value of an uneven stream of income is the sum of the PVs of the individual cash flow components. Similarly, the future value of an uneven stream of income is the sum of the FVs of the individual cash flow components.

        1. With a financial calculator, enter each cash flow (beginning with the $t=0$ cash flow) in the cash flow register, CF_j, enter the appropriate interest rate, and then press the NPV key to obtain the PV of the cash flow stream.

        2. Some calculators have a net future value (NFV) key which allows you to obtain the FV of the cash flow stream.

    B. If one knows the relevant cash flows, the effective interest rate can be calculated efficiently with a financial calculator. Enter each cash flow (beginning with the $t=0$ cash flow) in the cash flow register, CF_j, and then press the IRR key to obtain the interest rate of the cash flow stream.

VIII. **Semiannual, quarterly, and other compounding periods more frequent than on an annual basis are often used in financial transactions. Compounding on a non-annual basis requires an adjustment to both the compounding and discounting procedures discussed previously.**

    A. The *effective annual rate* is the rate that would have produced the final compound value under annual compounding. The effective annual percentage rate is given by the following formula:

$$Effective \ annual \ rate \ (EAR) = (1 + i_{Nom}/m)^m - 1.0,$$

where i_{Nom} is the nominal, or quoted, annual rate and m is the number of compounding periods per year. The EAR is useful in comparing securities with different compounding periods.

    B. For example, to find the effective annual rate if the nominal rate is 6 percent and semiannual compounding is used, we have:

$$Effective \ annual \ rate = (1 + 0.06/2)^2 - 1.0 = 6.09\%.$$

5-5

©1992 The Dryden Press
All rights reserved.

C. For annual compounding use the formula to find the future value of a lump sum:

$$FV_n = PV(1 + i)^n.$$

When compounding occurs more frequently than once a year, use this formula:

$$FV_n = PV(1 + i_{Nom}/m)^{mn}.$$

Here m is the number of times per year compounding occurs, and n is the number of years.

D. The amount to which $1,000 will grow after 5 years if quarterly compounding is applied to a nominal 8 percent interest rate is found as follows:

$$FV_n = \$1,000(1 + 0.08/4)^{(4)(5)} = \$1,000(1.02)^{20} = \$1,485.95.$$

1. Tabular solution: Divide the interest rate by 4, so i = 8%/4 = 2% and multiply the number of years by 4, so n = 5 × 4 = 20. Look down the first column of Table A-3 to Period 20 and then across to the 2% column to find $FVIF_{2\%,20}$ = 1.4859. FV = 1.4859 × $1,000 = $1,485.90.
2. Financial calculator solution: Enter N = 20, I = 2, PV = -1,000, and then press the FV key to find FV = $1,485.95.

E. The present value of a 5-year future investment equal to $1,485.95, with an 8 percent nominal interest rate, compounded quarterly, is found as follows:

$$\$1,485.95 = PV(1 + 0.08/4)^{(4)(5)}$$
$$PV = \frac{\$1,485.95}{(1.02)^{20}} = \$1,000.$$

1. Tabular solution: Use Table A-1, look down to Period 20 and across to the 2% column to find $PVIF_{2\%,20}$ = 0.6730. PV = $1,485.95 × 0.6730 = $1,000.04.
2. Financial calculator solution: Enter N = 20, I = 2, FV = 1,485.95, and then press the PV key to find PV = $1,000.00.

IX. **Fractional time periods are used when payments occur within periods, instead of at either the beginning or the end of periods. Solving these problems requires using the fraction of the time period for n, number of periods, and then solving either numerically or with a financial calculator.**

X. **An important application of compound interest involves amortized loans, which are paid off in equal installments over time.**

A. **The amount of each payment, PMT, is found as follows: PV of the annuity = PMT(PVIFA$_{i,n}$), so PMT = PV of the annuity/PVIFA$_{i,n}$.**

©1992 The Dryden Press
All rights reserved.

B. With a financial calculator, enter N (number of years), I (interest rate), and PV (amount borrowed), and then press the PMT key to find the periodic payment.

C. Each payment consists partly of interest and partly of the repayment of principal. This breakdown is often developed in a loan amortization schedule.
  1. The interest component is largest in the first period, and it declines over the life of the loan.
  2. The repayment of principal is smallest in the first period, and it increases thereafter.

XI. Appendix 5A discusses the formulas necessary for continuous compounding and discounting. The equation for continuous compounding is $FV_n = PV(e^{in})$ where e is the value 2.7183; the equation for continuous discounting is $PV = FV_n(e^{-in})$.

SELF-TEST QUESTIONS

Definitional

1. The beginning value of an account or investment in a project is known as its _____ _____.

2. Using a savings account as an example, the difference between the account's present value and its future value at the end of the period is due to _____ earned during the period.

3. The equation $FV_n = PV(1 + i)^n$ determines the future value of a sum at the end of n periods. The factor $(1 + i)^n$ is known as the _____ _____ _____ _____.

4. The process of finding present values is often referred to as _____ and is the reverse of the _____ process.

5. The $PVIF_{i,n}$ for a 5-year, 5 percent investment is 0.7835. This value is the _____ of the $FVIF_{i,n}$ for 5 years at 5 percent.

6. For a given number of time periods, the $PVIF_{i,n}$ will decline as the _____ _____ increases.

7. A series of payments of a constant amount for a specified number of periods is an _____. If the payments occur at the end of each period it is an _____ annuity, while if the payments occur at the beginning of each period it is an annuity ____.

8. The present value of an uneven stream of future payments is the ____ of the PVs of the individual payments.

©1992 The Dryden Press
All rights reserved.

9. Since different types of investments use different compounding periods, it is important to distinguish between the quoted, or _____, rate and the _____ annual interest rate.

10. To use the interest factor tables when compounding occurs more than once a year, divide the _____ _____ by the number of times compounding occurs and multiply the years by the number of _____ _____ per year.

Conceptual

11. You have determined the profitability of a planned project by finding the present value of all the cash flows from that project. Which of the following would cause the project to look less appealing, that is, have a lower present value?

    a. The discount rate decreases.
    b. The cash flows are extended over a longer period of time.
    c. The discount rate increases.
    d. Statements b and c are both correct.
    e. Statements a and b are both correct.

12. If a bank uses quarterly compounding for savings accounts, the nominal rate will be greater than the effective annual rate (EAR).

    a. True   b. False

13. If money has time value, the future value of some amount of money will always be more than the amount invested. The present value of some amount to be received in the future is always less than the amount to be received.

    a. True   b. False

14. At an inflation rate of 9 percent, the purchasing power of $1 would be cut in half in just over 8 years (some calculators round to 9 years). How long, to the nearest year, would it take for the purchasing power of $1 to be cut in half if the inflation rate were only 4 percent?

    a. 12 years   b. 15 years   c. 18 years   d. 20 years   e. 23 years

15. As the discount rate increases without limit, the present value of a future cash inflow

    a. Gets larger without limit.
    b. Stays unchanged.
    c. Approaches zero.
    d. Gets smaller without limit; that is, approaches minus infinity.
    e. Goes to e^{in}.

©1992 The Dryden Press
All rights reserved.

16. Which of the following statements is most correct?

    a. For all positive values of i and n, $FVIF_{i,n} \geq 1.0$ and $PVIFA_{i,n} \geq n$.

    b. You may use the PVIF tables to find the present value of an uneven series of payments. However, the PVIFA tables can never be of use, even if some of the payments constitute an annuity (for example, $100 each year for Years 3, 4, 5, and 6), because the entire series does not constitute an annuity.

    c. If a bank uses quarterly compounding for savings accounts, the nominal rate will be greater than the effective annual rate.

    d. The present value of a future sum decreases as either the nominal interest rate or the number of discounting periods per year increases.

    e. All of the above statements are false.

SELF-TEST PROBLEMS

(Note: In working these problems, you may get an answer which differs from ours by a few cents due to differences in rounding. This should not concern you; just pick the closest answer.)

1. Assume that you purchase a 6 year, 8 percent savings certificate for $1,000. If interest is compounded annually, what will be the value of the certificate when it matures?

    a. $630.17   **b.** $1,469.33   **c.** $1,677.10   **d.** $1,586.90   **e.** $1,766.33

2. A savings certificate similar to the one in the previous problem is available with the exception that interest is compounded semiannually. What is the difference between the ending value of the savings certificate compounded semiannually and the one compounded annually?

    a. The semiannual is worth $14.10 more than the annual.
    b. The semiannual is worth $14.10 less than the annual.
    c. The semiannual is worth $21.54 more than the annual.
    d. The semiannual is worth $21.54 less than the annual.
    e. The semiannual is worth the same as the annual.

3. A friend promises to pay you $600 two years from now if you loan him $500 today. What annual interest rate is your friend offering?

    a. 7.5%   **b.** 8.5%   **c.** 9.5%   **d.** 10.5%   **e.** 11.5%

4. You are offered an investment opportunity with the "guarantee" that your investment will double in 5 years. Assuming annual compounding, what annual rate of return would this investment provide?

    a. 40.00%   **b.** 100.00%   **c.** 14.87%   **d.** 20.00%   **e.** 18.74%

5-9

$$2x = x(FVIF_{8,5})$$
$$2 =$$

©1992 The Dryden Press
All rights reserved.

5. You decide to begin saving toward the purchase of a new car in 5 years. If you put $1,000 in a savings account paying 6 percent compounded annually at the end of each of the next 5 years, how much will you accumulate after 5 years?

a. $6,691.13   b. $5,637.10   c. $1,338.23   d. $5,975.33   e. $5,732.00

6. Refer to the previous problem. What would be the ending amount if the payments were made at the beginning of each year?

a. $6,691.13   b. $5,637.10   c. $1,338.23   d. $5,975.33   e. $5,732.00

7. Refer to Self-Test Problem 5. What would be the ending amount if $500 payments were made at the end of each 6-month period for 5 years and the account paid 6 percent compounded semiannually?

a. $6,691.13   b. $5,637.10   c. $1,338.23   d. $5,975.33   e. $5,732.00

8. Calculate the present value of $1,000 to be received at the end of 8 years. Assume an interest rate of 7 percent.

a. $582.00   b. $1,718.19   c. $531.82   d. $5,971.30   e. $649.37

9. How much would you be willing to pay today for an investment that would return $800 each year at the end of each of the next 6 years? Assume a discount rate of 5 percent.

a. $5,441.53   b. $4,800.00   c. $3,369.89   d. $4,060.56   e. $4,632.37

10. You have applied for a mortgage of $60,000 to finance the purchase of a new home. The bank will require you to make annual payments of $7,047.55 at the end of each of the next 20 years. Determine the interest rate in effect on this mortgage.

a. 8.0%   b. 9.8%   c. 10.0%   d. 51.0%   e. 11.2%

11. If you would like to accumulate $7,500 over the next 5 years, how much must you deposit each six months, starting six months from now, given a 6 percent interest rate and semiannual compounding?

a. $1,330.47   b. $879.23   c. $654.22   d. $569.00   e. $732.67

12. A company is offering bonds which pay $100 per year indefinitely. If you require a 12 percent return on these bonds—that is, the discount rate is 12 percent—what is the value of each bond?

a. $1,000.00   b. $962.00   c. $904.67   d. $866.67   e. $833.33

© 1992 The Dryden Press
All rights reserved.

13. What is the present value (t = 0) of the following cash flows if the discount rate is 12 percent?

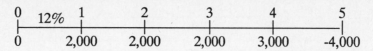

0	12%	1	2	3	4	5
0		2,000	2,000	2,000	3,000	-4,000

   a. $4,782.43   **b.** $4,440.50   **c.** $4,221.79   **d.** $4,041.23   **e.** $3,997.98

14. What is the effective annual percentage rate (EAR) of 12 percent compounded monthly?

   a. 12.00%   **b.** 12.55%   **c.** 12.68%   **d.** 12.75%   **e.** 13.00%

15. Self-Test Problem 10 refers to a 20-year mortgage of $60,000. This is an amortized loan. How much principal will be repaid in the second year?

   a. $1,152.30   **b.** $1,725.70   **c.** $5,895.25   **d.** $7,047.55   **e.** $1,047.55

16. You have $1,000 invested in an account which pays 16 percent compounded annually. A commission agent (called a "finder") can locate for you an equally safe deposit which will pay 16 percent, compounded quarterly, for 2 years. What is the maximum amount you should be willing to pay him now as a fee for locating the new account?

   a. $10.92   **b.** $13.78   **c.** $16.14   **d.** $16.81   **e.** $21.13

17. The present value (t = 0) of the following cash flow stream is $11,958.20 when discounted at 12 percent annually. What is the value of the missing t = 2 cash flow?

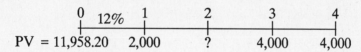

0	12%	1	2	3	4
PV = 11,958.20		2,000	?	4,000	4,000

   a. $4,000.00   **b.** $4,500.00   **c.** $5,000.00   **d.** $5,500.00   **e.** $6,000.00

18. Today is your birthday and you decide to start saving for your college education. You will begin college on your 18th birthday and will need $4,000 per year at the *end* of each of the following 4 years. You will make a deposit 1 year from today in an account paying 12 percent annually, and continue to make an identical deposit each year up to and including the year you begin college. If a deposit amount of $2,542.05 will allow you to reach your goal, what birthday are you celebrating today?

   a. 13   **b.** 14   **c.** 15   **d.** 16   **e.** 17

©1992 The Dryden Press
All rights reserved.

19. Assume that your aunt sold her house on December 31, and that she took a mortgage in the amount of $10,000 as part of the payment. The mortgage has a stated (or nominal) interest rate of 10 percent, but it calls for payments every 6 months, beginning on June 30, and the mortgage is to be amortized over 10 years. Now, one year later, your aunt must file a Form 1099 with the IRS and with the person who bought the house, informing them of the interest that was included in the two payments made during the year. (This interest will be income to your aunt and a deduction to the buyer of the house.) What is the total amount of interest that was paid during the first year?

    a. $1,604.86   **b.** $619.98   **c.** $984.88   **d.** $1,205.76   **e.** $750.02

20. Assume that you inherited some money. A friend of yours is working as an unpaid intern at a local brokerage firm, and her boss is selling some securities which call for four payments, $50 at the end of each of the next 3 years, plus a payment of $1,050 at the end of Year 4. Your friend says she can get you some of these securities at a cost of $900 each. Your money is now invested in a bank that pays an 8 percent nominal (quoted) interest rate, but with quarterly compounding. You regard the securities as being just as safe, and as liquid, as your bank deposit, so your required effective annual rate of return on the securities is the same as that on your bank deposit. You must calculate the value of the securities to decide whether they are a good investment. What is their present value to you?

    a. $957.75   **b.** $888.66   **c.** $923.44   **d.** $1,015.25   **e.** $893.26

21. Your company is planning to borrow $1,000,000 on a 5-year, 15 percent, annual payment, fully amortized term loan. What fraction of the payment made at the end of the second year will represent repayment of principal?

    a. 57.18%   **b.** 42.82%   **c.** 50.28%   **d.** 49.72%   **e.** 60.27%

Appendix 5A

5A-1. If you receive $30,000 today and can invest it at a 4 percent annual rate compounded continuously, then what will its future value be in 10 years?

    a. $31,224.32   **b.** $38,327   **c.** $40,765   **d.** $44,754.74   **e.** $42,121

5A-2. What is the present value of $125,000 due in 15 years, if the appropriate continuous discount rate is 6 percent?

    a. $44,754.74   **b.** $50,821.21   **c.** $38,327   **d.** $42,121   **e.** $40,765

©1992 The Dryden Press
All rights reserved.

ANSWERS TO SELF-TEST QUESTIONS

1. present value
2. interest
3. future value interest factor
4. discounting; compounding
5. reciprocal
6. interest rate
7. annuity; ordinary; due
8. sum
9. nominal; effective
10. nominal rate; compounding periods

11. d. The slower the cash flows come in and the higher the interest rate, the lower the present value.

12. b. The EAR is always greater than or equal to the nominal rate.

13. a. Both these statements are correct.

14. c.

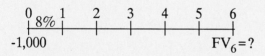

   With a financial calculator, input PV = -1.00, FV = 0.50, and I = 4. Solve for N = 17.67 ≈ 18 years.

15. c. As the discount rate increases, the present value of a future sum decreases and eventually approaches zero.

16. d. As a future sum is discounted over more and more periods, the present value will get smaller and smaller. Likewise, as the discount rate increases, the present value of a future sum decreases and eventually approaches zero.

SOLUTIONS TO SELF-TEST PROBLEMS

1. d.

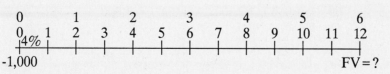

   $FV_n = PV(FVIF_{i,n}) = \$1,000(FVIF_{8\%,6}) = \$1,000(1.5869) = \$1,586.90.$

   With a financial calculator, input N = 6, I = 8, PV = -1,000, and solve for FV = $1,586.87.

2. a.

©1992 The Dryden Press
All rights reserved.

$FVIF_{i,n} = FVIF_{4\%,12} = 1.6010$.

Thus, $FV_n = \$1,000(1.6010) = \$1,601.00$. The difference, $\$1,601.00 - \$1,586.90 = \$14.10$, is the additional interest.

With a financial calculator, input $N = 12$, $I = 4$, $PV = -1,000$, and solve for $FV = \$1,601.03$. The difference, $\$1,601.03 - \$1,586.87 = \$14.16$.

3. c.

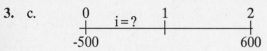

$$FV_2 = PV(FVIF_{i,2})$$
$$\$600 = \$500(FVIF_{i,2})$$
$$FVIF_{i,2} = 1.2000.$$

Looking across the Period 2 row in Table A-3, we see $FVIF_{9\%,2} = 1.1881$ and $FVIF_{10\%,2} = 1.2100$. Therefore, the annual interest rate is between 9% and 10%.

With a financial calculator, input $N = 2$, $PV = -500$, $FV = 600$, and solve for $I = 9.54\%$.

4. c.

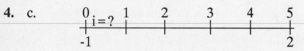

Assume any value for the present value and double it:

$$FV_5 = PV(FVIF_{i,5})$$
$$\$2 = \$1(FVIF_{i,5})$$
$$FVIF_{i,5} = 2.0000.$$

Looking across the Period 5 row in Table A-3, we see that 2.0000 occurs between 14% and 15%.

With a financial calculator, input $N = 5$, $PV = -1$, $FV = 2$, and solve for $I = 14.87\%$.

5. b.

```
0    6%    1         2         3         4         5
+----------+---------+---------+---------+---------+
         -1,000    -1,000    -1,000    -1,000    -1,000
                                                 FVA₅=?
```

$FVA_5 = PMT(FVIFA_{6\%,5}) = \$1,000(5.6371) = \$5,637.10$.

©1992 The Dryden Press
All rights reserved.

With a financial calculator, input N = 5, I = 6, PMT = -1,000, and solve for FV = $5,637.09.

6. d.

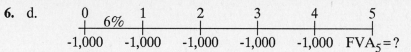

FVA_5(Annuity due) = PMT(FVIFA$_{6\%,5}$)(1 + i) = $1,000(5.6371)(1.06) = $5,975.33.

With a financial calculator, switch to "BEG" mode, then input N = 5, I = 6, PMT = -1,000, and solve for FV = $5,975.32. Be sure to switch back to "END" mode.

7. e.

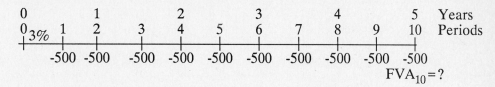

FVA_{10} = PMT(FVIFA$_{3\%,10}$) = $500(11.464) = $5,732.00.

With a financial calculator, input N = 10, I = 3, PMT = -500, and solve for FV = $5,731.94.

(Note: In order to use the annuity tables, the compounding period and payment period *must be the same*, in this case both are semiannual. If this is not the case, each cash flow must be treated individually.)

8. a.

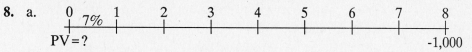

PV = FV_8(PVIF$_{7\%,8}$) = $1,000(0.5820) = $582.00.

With a financial calculator, input N = 8, I = 7, FV = -1,000, and solve for PV = $582.01.

(Note: Annual compounding is assumed if not otherwise specified.)

9. d.

PVA_6 = PMT(PVIFA$_{5\%,6}$) = $800(5.0757) = $4,060.56.

With a financial calculator, input N = 6, I = 5, PMT = -800, and solve for PV = $4,060.55.

©1992 The Dryden Press
All rights reserved.

10. c.

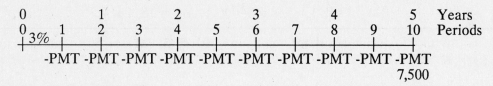

The amount of the mortgage ($60,000) is the present value of a 20-year ordinary annuity with payments of $7,047.55. Therefore,

$$PVA_{20} = PMT(PVIFA_{i,20})$$

$$\$60,000 = \$7,047.55(PVIFA_{i,20})$$

$$PVIFA_{i,20} = 8.5136$$

$$k = 10.00\% \text{ exactly.}$$

With a financial calculator, input N = 20, PV = -60,000, PMT = 7,047.55, and solve for I = 10.00%.

11. c.

	0		1		2		3		4		5	Years
0 3%	1	2	3	4	5	6	7	8	9	10	Periods

-PMT -PMT -PMT -PMT -PMT -PMT -PMT -PMT -PMT -PMT

7,500

$$FVA_{10} = PMT(FVIFA_{3\%,10})$$
$$\$7,500 = PMT(11.464)$$
$$PMT = \$654.22.$$

With a financial calculator, input N = 10, I = 3, FV = -7,500, and solve for PMT = $654.23.

12. e. PV = PMT/i = $100/0.12 = $833.33.

13. b.
$$PV = \$2,000(PVIFA_{12\%,3}) + \$3,000(PVIF_{12\%,4}) - \$4,000(PVIF_{12\%,5})$$

$$= \$2,000(2.4018) + \$3,000(0.6355) - \$4,000(0.5674)$$

$$= \$4,440.50.$$

With a financial calculator, using the cash flow register, CF_j, input 0; 2,000; 2,000; 2,000; 3,000; and -4,000. Enter I = 12 and solve for NPV = $4,440.51.

14. c. $$EAR = (1 + i_{Nom}/m)^m - 1.0$$

$$= (1 + 0.12/12)^{12} - 1.0$$

©1992 The Dryden Press
All rights reserved.

$$= (1.01)^{12} - 1.0$$

$$= 1.1268 - 1.0$$

$$= 0.1268 = 12.68\%.$$

15. a.

Year	Payment	Interest	Repayment on Principal	Remaining Principal Balance
1	$7,047.55	$6,000.00	$1,047.55	$58,952.45
2	7,047.55	5,895.25	1,152.30	57,800.15

16. d. Currently: $FV_n = \$1,000(FVIF_{16\%,2}) = \$1,000(1.3456) = \$1,345.60$.

With a financial calculator, input N = 2, I = 16, PV = -1,000, and solve for FV = $1,345.60.

New account: $FV_n = \$1,000(1 + i_{Nom}/m)^{mn} = \$1,000(1.3686) = \$1,368.60$.

With a financial calculator, input N = 8, I = 4, PV = -1,000, and solve for FV = $1,368.57.

Thus, the new account will be worth $1,368.60 − $1,345.60 = $23.00 more after 2 years. With a financial calculator, the new account will be worth $22.97 more after 2 years.

PV of difference = $23(PVIF_{4\%,8}) = \$23(0.7307) = \$16.81$. With a financial calculator, input N = 8, I = 4, FV = 22.97, and solve for PV = $16.78.

Therefore, the most you should be willing to pay the finder for locating the new account is $16.81.

17. e. $\$11,958.20 = \$2,000(PVIF_{12\%,1}) + X(PVIF_{12\%,2})$
$\qquad\qquad + \$4,000(PVIF_{12\%,3}) + \$4,000(PVIF_{12\%,4})$

$\$11,958.20 = \$2,000(0.8929) + X(0.7972) + \$4,000(0.7118) + \$4,000(0.6355)$
$\$11,958.20 = \$7,175.00 + 0.7972X$
$\quad\ 0.7972X = \$4,783.20$
$\qquad\quad\ X = \$6,000.00.$

With a financial calculator, input the cash flows in the cash flow register, using 0 as the value for the unknown cash flow, input I = 12, and then press the NPV key to solve for the present value of the unknown cash flow, $4,783.29. This value should be compounded by $(1.12)^2$, so that $4,783.29(1.2544) = $6,000.16.

18. b. First, how much must you accumulate on your 18th birthday?

5-17

©1992 The Dryden Press
All rights reserved.

$$PVA_n = \$4,000(PVIFA_{12\%,4}) = \$4,000(3.0373) = \$12,149.20.$$

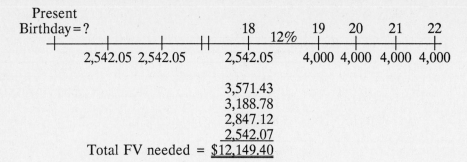

$$
\begin{array}{l}
3{,}571.43 \\
3{,}188.78 \\
2{,}847.12 \\
\underline{2{,}542.07}
\end{array}
$$

Total FV needed = $\underline{\$12,149.40}$

Using a financial calculator (with the calculator set for an ordinary annuity), enter $N = 4$, $I = 12$, $PMT = -4,000$, and solve for $PV = \$12,149.40$. This is the amount (or lump sum) that must be present in your bank account on your 18th birthday in order for you to be able to withdraw $4,000 at the end of each year for the next 4 years.

Now, how many payments must you make to accumulate $12,149.20?

$$FVA_n = \$12,149.20 = \$2,542.05(FVIFA_{12\%,n}).$$
$$FVIFA_{12\%,n} = 4.7793$$
$$n = 4.$$

Using a financial calculator, enter $I = 12$, $PMT = -2,542.05$, $FV = 12,149.40$, and solve for $N = 4$. Therefore, if you make payments at 18, 17, 16, and 15, you are now 14.

19. c. This can be done with a calculator by specifying an interest rate of 5 percent per period for 20 periods with 1 payment per period, or 10 percent interest, 20 periods, 2 payments per year. Either way, we get the payment each 6 months:

$I = 10\%/2 = 5\%.$
$N = 10 \times 2 = 20.$
$PV = \$10,000.$
$PMT = \$802.43.$

Set up an amortization table:

Period	Beginning Balance	Payment	Interest	Payment of Principal	Ending Balance
1	$10,000.00	$802.43	$500.00	$302.43	$9,697.57
2	9,697.57	802.43	484.88		
			$984.88		

©1992 The Dryden Press
All rights reserved.

You can really just work the problem with a financial calculator using the amortization function. Find the interest in each 6-month period, sum them, and you have the answer. Even simpler, with some calculators such as the HP 17B, just input 2 for periods and press INT to get the interest during the first year, $984.88.

20. e.

Discount rate: Effective annual rate on bank deposit:
EAR = $(1 + 0.08/4)^4 - 1 = 8.24\%$.

Input the cash flows in the cash flow register, input I = 8.24, and solve for PV = $893.26.

Alternatively, get PV = $893.26 by inputting N = 4, I = 8.24, PMT = 50, and FV = 1,000.

21. a. Input PV = -1,000,000, N = 5, and I = 15 to solve for PMT = $298,315.55.

Year	Beginning Balance	Payment	Interest	Payment of Principal	Ending Balance
1	$1,000,000.00	$298,315.55	$150,000.00	$148,315.55	$851,684.45
2	851,684.45	298,315.55	127,752.67	170,562.88	681,121.57

The fraction that is principal is $170,562.88/$298,315.55 = 57.18%.

Appendix 5A

5A-1. d. $FV_n = PV\ e^{in}$

$$FV_{10} = \$30,000\ e^{0.04(10)}$$

$$= \$30,000\ e^{0.4}$$

$$= \$44,754.74.$$

5A-2. b. PV = $FV_n\ e^{-in}$ = $125,000\ e^{-0.90}$ = $50,821.21.

©1992 The Dryden Press
All rights reserved.

CHAPTER 6
BOND AND STOCK VALUATION

OVERVIEW

This chapter uses the time value of money concept to determine the values of bonds and stocks. The value of any financial asset is the present value of the cash flows expected from that asset. Therefore, once the cash flows have been estimated, and a discount rate determined, the value of the financial asset can be calculated. A bond is valued as the present value of the stream of interest payments (an annuity) plus the present value of the par value which is received by the investor on the bond's maturity date. Depending on the relationship between the current interest rate and the bond's coupon rate, a bond can sell at its par value, at a discount, or at a premium. The total rate of return on a bond is comprised of two components: interest yield and capital gains yield.

The value of a share of preferred stock which is expected to pay a constant dividend forever is found as the dividend divided by the discount rate. A common stock is valued as the present value of the expected future dividend stream. The total rate of return on a stock is comprised of a dividend yield plus a capital gains yield. For both stocks and bonds, the total expected return must equal the average investor's required rate of return.

OUTLINE

I.   **Capital is raised in two primary forms—debt and equity. As the principal type of long-term debt, a bond is a long-term promissory note issued by a business or governmental unit.**

    A.   The *par value* is the stated face value of a bond, usually $1,000. This is the amount of money that the firm borrows and promises to repay at some future date.

    B.   The *maturity date* is the date on which the par value must be repaid. Most bonds have original maturities of from 10 to 40 years.

    C.   Most bonds have a *call provision*, whereby the issuer may pay off the bonds prior to maturity.

    D.   The *coupon interest payment* is the dollar amount that is paid yearly to a bondholder by the issuer for use of the $1,000 loan. This payment is a fixed amount, established at the time the bond is issued. The coupon interest rate is obtained by dividing the coupon payment by the par value of the bond.

    E.   A *new issue* is the term applied to a bond that has just been issued. At the time of issue, the coupon payment is generally set at a level that will force the market

©1992 The Dryden Press
All rights reserved.

price of the bond to equal its par value. Once the bond has been on the market for a while, it is classified as an outstanding bond, or a *seasoned issue*.

II.   Using these definitions, a basic bond valuation model can be constructed.

    A. A bond represents an annuity plus a lump sum, and its value is found as the present value of this payment stream:

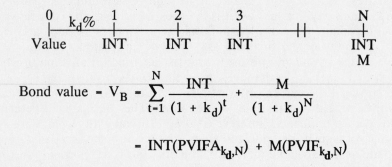

$$\text{Bond value} = V_B = \sum_{t=1}^{N} \frac{INT}{(1 + k_d)^t} + \frac{M}{(1 + k_d)^N}$$

$$= INT(PVIFA_{k_d,N}) + M(PVIF_{k_d,N})$$

    where INT = dollars of interest paid each year, M = par, or maturity, value, which is typically $1,000, k_d = rate of interest on the bond, and N = number of years until the bond matures.

    B. For example, consider a 15-year, $1,000 bond paying $150 annually, when the appropriate interest rate, k_d, is 15 percent. Utilizing the PVIFA and PVIF tables in the text, we find:

$$
\begin{aligned}
V_B &= \$150(5.8474) + \$1,000(0.1229) \\
&= \$877.11 + \$122.90 \\
&= \$1,000.01 \approx \$1,000.
\end{aligned}
$$

    Using a financial calculator, enter N = 15, PMT = 150, FV = 1,000, and k_d = I = 15, and then press the PV key for an answer of $1,000.

    C. Bond prices and interest rates are inversely related, that is, they tend to move in the opposite direction from one another.
        1. A bond will sell at par when its coupon interest rate is equal to the going rate of interest, k_d, as in the example above.
        2. When the going rate of interest is above the coupon rate, the bond will sell at a "discount" below its par value.
        3. If current interest rates are below the coupon rate, the bond will sell at a "premium" above its par value.
        4. The discount is equal to the present value of the amount of interest payment one sacrifices to buy a low-coupon old bond rather than a high-coupon new bond. The premium is equal to the present value of the additional interest payment one receives by buying a high-coupon old bond rather than a

©1992 The Dryden Press
All rights reserved.

low-coupon new bond. The exact amount can be obtained by using the formula:

$$\text{Discount or premium} = \left(\begin{array}{l} \text{Interest payment} \\ \text{on the old bond} \end{array} - \begin{array}{l} \text{Interest payment} \\ \text{on the new bond} \end{array} \right) (PVIFA_{k_d,N}).$$

D. The rate of interest earned on a bond if it is held until redeemed by the issuer is known as the *yield to maturity (YTM)*. The YTM for a bond that sells at par consists entirely of an interest yield, but if the bond sells at a price other than its par value, the YTM consists of the interest yield plus a positive or negative capital gains yield.

E. If current interest rates are well below an outstanding bond's coupon rate, then a *callable bond* is likely to be called, and investors should estimate the expected rate of return on the bond as the *yield to call (YTC)* rather than as the yield to maturity. To calculate the YTC, solve this equation for k_d:

$$\text{Price of bond} = \sum_{t=1}^{N} \frac{INT}{(1 + k_d)^t} + \frac{\text{Call price}}{(1 + k_d)^N}.$$

F. The bond valuation model must be adjusted when interest is paid semiannually:

$$V_B = \sum_{t=1}^{2N} \frac{INT/2}{(1 + k_d/2)^t} + \frac{M}{(1 + k_d/2)^{2N}}$$

$$= (INT/2)(PVIFA_{k_d/2,2N}) + M(PVIF_{k_d/2,2N}).$$

G. Interest rates fluctuate over time, and people or firms who invest in bonds are exposed to risk from changing interest rates, or *interest rate risk*. The longer the maturity of the bond, the greater the exposure to interest rate risk. However, the shorter the maturity of the bond, the greater the exposure to *reinvestment rate risk*.

III. Preferred stock is a hybrid—it is similar to bonds in some respects and to common stock in other respects.

A. Preferred dividends are similar to interest payments on bonds in that they are fixed in amount and generally must be paid before common stock dividends can be paid.

B. Most preferred stocks entitle their owners to regular fixed dividend payments. If the payments last forever, the issue is a perpetuity whose value, V_{ps}, is found as follows:

© 1992 The Dryden Press
All rights reserved.

$$V_{ps} = \frac{D_{ps}}{k_{ps}}.$$

Here D_{ps} is the dividend to be received in each year and k_{ps} is the required rate of return on the preferred stock.

IV. **Common stocks are also valued by finding the present value of the expected future cash flow stream.**

A. People typically buy common stock expecting to earn *dividends* plus a *capital gain* when they sell their shares at the end of some holding period. The capital gain may or may not be realized, but most people expect a gain or else they would not buy stocks.

B. The expected dividend yield on a stock during the coming year is equal to the expected dividend, D_1, divided by the current stock price, P_0. $(\hat{P}_1 - P_0)/P_0$ is the expected capital gains yield. The expected dividend yield plus the expected capital gains yield equals the expected total return.

C. The value of the stock today is calculated as the present value of an infinite stream of dividends. For any investor, cash flows consist of dividends plus the expected future sales price of the stock. This sales price, however, is dependent upon dividends expected by future investors:

$$\text{Value of stock} = \hat{P}_0 = \text{PV of expected dividends}$$

$$= \frac{D_1}{(1 + k_s)^1} + \frac{D_2}{(1 + k_s)^2} + \cdots + \frac{D_\infty}{(1 + k_s)^\infty}$$

$$= \sum_{t-1}^{\infty} \frac{D_t}{(1 + k_s)^t}.$$

Here k_s is the discount rate used to find the present value of the dividends.

D. Dividends are not expected to remain constant in the future, and dividends are harder to predict than bond interest payments. Thus, stock valuation is a more complex task than bond valuation.

E. If expected dividend growth is zero ($g = 0$), the value of the stock is found as follows: $\hat{P}_0 = D/k_s$. Since a zero growth stock is expected to pay a constant dividend, it can be thought of as a perpetuity. The expected rate of return is simply the dividend yield: $\hat{k}_s = D/P_0$.

F. For many companies, earnings and dividends are expected to grow at some normal, or constant, rate. Dividends in any future Year t may be forecasted as $D_t = D_0(1 + g)^t$, where D_0 is the last dividend paid and g is the expected rate of

© 1992 The Dryden Press
All rights reserved.

growth. For a company which last paid a $2.00 dividend and which has an expected 6 percent constant growth rate, the estimated dividend one year from now would be $D_1 = \$2.00(1.06) = \$2.12$; D_2 would be $\$2.00(1.06)^2 = \$2.25$, and the estimated dividend 4 years hence would be $D_t = D_0(1 + g)^t = \$2.00(1.06)^4 = \$2.525$. Using this method of estimating future dividends, the current price, P_0, is determined as follows:

$$\hat{P}_0 = \frac{D_0(1 + g)}{k_s - g} = \frac{D_1}{k_s - g}.$$

This equation for valuing a constant growth stock is often called the Gordon Model, after Myron J. Gordon, who developed it.

G. For all stocks, the total expected return is composed of an expected dividend yield plus an expected capital gains yield. For a constant growth stock the formula for the total expected return can be written as:

$$\hat{k}_s = \frac{D_1}{P_0} + g.$$

H. Firms typically go through periods of nonconstant growth, after which time their growth rate settles to a rate close to that of the economy as a whole. The value of such a firm is equal to the present value of its expected future dividends. To find the value of such a stock, we proceed in three steps:
   1. Find the present value of the dividends during the period of nonconstant growth.
   2. Find the price of the stock at the end of the nonconstant growth period, at which point it has become a constant growth stock, and discount this price back to the present.
   3. Add these two components to find the present value of the stock.

V. **The relationship between a stock's required and expected rates of return determines the equilibrium price level where buying and selling pressures will just offset each other.**

A. If the expected rate of return is less than the required rate, investors will desire to sell the stock; and there will be a tendency for the price to decline.

B. When the expected rate of return is greater than the required rate, investors will try to purchase shares of the stock; and this will drive the price upward.

C. Only at the equilibrium price, where the expected and required rates are equal, will the stock be stable.

D. Equilibrium will generally exist for a given stock because security prices adjust rapidly to new developments.

© 1992 The Dryden Press
All rights reserved.

E. Changes in the equilibrium price can be brought about (1) by a change in risk aversion, (2) by a change in the risk-free rate, (3) by a change in the stock's beta coefficient, or (4) by a change in the stock's expected rate of growth.

F. The *Efficient Markets Hypothesis (EMH)* hypothesizes that stocks are always in equilibrium and that it is impossible for an investor to consistently "beat the market."
   1. The *weak-form* of the EMH states that all information contained in past price movements is fully reflected in current market prices.
   2. The *semistrong-form* of the EMH states that current market prices reflect all *publicly available* information. If this is true, no abnormal returns can be gained by analyzing stocks.
   3. The *strong-form* of the EMH states that current market prices reflect all pertinent information, whether publicly available or privately held (inside information).

VI. **Anyone who has ever invested in the stock market knows that there can be, and generally are, large differences between expected and realized prices and returns.**

   A. Investors always expect positive returns from stock investments or else they would not buy them. However, in some years negative returns are actually earned.

   B. Even in bad years, some individual stocks do well; and the "name of the game" in security analysis is to pick the winners. Financial managers are trying to take those actions that will help put their companies in the winner's column.

SELF-TEST QUESTIONS

Definitional

1. A _____ is a long-term promissory note issued by a business firm or governmental unit.

2. The stated face value of a bond is referred to as its _____ value and is usually set at $_____.

3. The "coupon interest rate" on a bond is determined by dividing the _____ _____ by the ____ _____ of the bond.

4. The date at which the par value of a bond is repaid to each bondholder is known as the _____ _____.

5. A bond with annual coupon payments represents an annuity of INT dollars per year for N years, plus a lump sum of M dollars at the end of N years, and its value, V_B, is the _____ _____ of this payment stream.

©1992 The Dryden Press
All rights reserved.

6. At the time a bond is issued, the coupon interest rate is generally set at a level that will cause the _____ _____ and the ____ _____ of the bond to be approximately equal.

7. Market interest rates and bond prices move in _____ directions from one another.

8. The rate of interest earned by purchasing a bond and holding it until maturity is known as the bond's _____ ___ _____.

9. To adjust the bond valuation formula for semiannual coupon payments, the _____ _____ and _____ _____ must be divided by 2, and the number of _____ must be multiplied by 2.

10. Like other financial assets, the value of common stock is the _____ value of a future stream of income.

11. The income stream expected from a common stock consists of a _____ yield and a _____ _____ yield.

12. If the future growth rate of dividends is expected to be _____, the rate of return is simply the _____ yield.

13. Investors always expect a _____ return on stock investments, but in some years _____ returns may actually be earned.

Conceptual

14. Changes in economic conditions cause interest rates and bond prices to vary over time.

   a. True   b. False

15. If the appropriate rate of interest on a bond is greater than its coupon rate, the market value of that bond will be above par value.

   a. True   b. False

16. A 20-year, annual coupon bond with one year left to maturity has the same interest rate risk as a 10-year, annual coupon bond with one year left to maturity. Both bonds are of equal risk and have the same coupon rate. The prices of the two bonds are equal.

   a. True   b. False

© 1992 The Dryden Press
All rights reserved.

17. According to the valuation model developed in this chapter, the value that an investor assigns to a share of stock is independent of the length of time the investor plans to hold the stock.

    a. True   b. False

18. Which of the following assumptions would cause the constant growth stock valuation model to be invalid? The constant growth model is given below:

$$\hat{P}_0 = \frac{D_0(1 + g)}{k_s - g}.$$

    a. The growth rate is negative.
    b. The growth rate is zero.
    c. The growth rate is less than the required rate of return.
    d. The required rate of return is above 30 percent.
    e. None of the above assumptions would invalidate the model.

19. Which of the following statements is *false*? In all of the statements, assume that "other things are held constant."

    a. Price sensitivity—that is, the change in price due to a given change in the required rate of return—increases as a bond's maturity increases.
    b. For a given bond of any maturity, a given percentage point increase in the going interest rate (k_d) causes a *larger* dollar capital loss than the capital gain stemming from an identical decrease in the interest rate.
    c. For any given maturity, a given percentage point increase in the interest rate causes a *smaller* dollar capital loss than the capital gain stemming from an identical decrease in the interest rate.
    d. From a borrower's point of view, interest paid on bonds is tax-deductible.
    e. A 20-year zero-coupon bond has less reinvestment rate risk than a 20-year coupon bond.

20. Which of the following statements is most correct?

    a. Ignoring interest accrued between payment dates, if the required rate of return on a bond is less than its coupon interest rate, and k_d remains below the coupon rate until maturity, then the market value of that bond will be below its par value until the bond matures, at which time its market value will equal its par value.
    b. Assuming equal coupon rates, a 20-year original maturity bond with one year left to maturity has more interest rate risk than a 10-year original maturity bond with one year left to maturity.
    c. Regardless of the size of the coupon payment, the price of a bond moves in the same direction as interest rates; for example, if interest rates rise, bond prices also rise.

© 1992 The Dryden Press
All rights reserved.

d. For bonds, price sensitivity to a given change in interest rates generally increases as years remaining to maturity increases.

e. Because short-term interest rates are much more volatile than long-term rates, you would, in the real world, be subject to more interest rate risk if you purchased a 30-*day* bond than if you bought a 30-*year* bond.

21. Which of the following statements is most correct?

   a. If two firms have the same expected D_1 and the same expected growth rate, their stocks must sell at the same current price, or else the market will not be in equilibrium.

   b. Interest rate (or price) risk and reinvestment rate risk tend to move in the same direction; that is, if a bond provides a lot of protection against interest rate risk, then it probably also provides a lot of protection against reinvestment rate risk.

   c. The existence of a positive maturity risk premium is an indication that investors, in general, regard interest rate (or price) risk as being more important than reinvestment rate risk.

   d. The constant growth stock valuation model requires that k be greater than g, that g be constant for all future years, and that g be equal to or greater than zero.

   e. All of the above statements are false.

SELF-TEST PROBLEMS

1. Delta Corporation has a bond issue outstanding with an annual coupon rate of 7 percent and 4 years remaining until maturity. The par value of the bond is $1,000. Determine the current value of the bond if present market conditions justify a 14 percent required rate of return. The bond pays interest annually.

   a. $1,126.42   b. $1,000.00   c. $796.06   d. $791.00   e. $536.42

2. Refer to the previous problem. Suppose the bond had a semiannual coupon. Now what would be the current value?

   a. $1,126.42   b. $1,000.00   c. $796.06   d. $791.00   e. $536.42

3. Refer to Self-Test Problem 1. Assume an annual coupon, but 20 years remaining to maturity. What is the current value under these conditions?

   a. $1,126.42   b. $1,000.00   c. $796.06   d. $791.00   e. $536.42

4. Acme Products has a bond issue outstanding with 8 years remaining to maturity, a coupon rate of 10 percent with interest paid annually, and a par value of $1,000. If the current market price of the bond issue is $814.45, what is the yield to maturity, k_d?

   a. 12%   b. 13%   c. 14%   d. 15%   e. 16%

© 1992 The Dryden Press
All rights reserved.

5. Stability Inc. has maintained a dividend rate of $4 per share for many years. The same rate is expected to be paid in future years. If investors require a 12 percent rate of return on similar investments, determine the present value of the company's stock.

   a. $15.00   **b.** $30.00   **c.** $33.33   **d.** $35.00   **e.** $40.00

6. Your sister-in-law, a stockbroker at Invest Inc. is trying to sell you a stock with a current market price of $25. The stock's last dividend (D_0) was $2.00, and earnings and dividends are expected to increase at a constant growth rate of 10 percent. Your required return on this stock is 20 percent. From a strict valuation standpoint, you should:

   a. Buy the stock; it is fairly valued.
   b. Buy the stock; it is undervalued by $3.00.
   c. Buy the stock; it is undervalued by $2.00.
   d. Not buy the stock; it is overvalued by $2.00.
   e. Not buy the stock; it is overvalued by $3.00.

7. Lucas Laboratories' last dividend was $1.50. Its current equilibrium stock price is $15.75, and its expected growth rate is a constant 5 percent. If the stockholders' required rate of return is 15 percent, what is the expected dividend yield and expected capital gains yield for the coming year?

   a. 0%; 15%   **b.** 5%; 10%   **c.** 10%; 5%   **d.** 15%; 0%   **e.** 15%; 15%

8. The Canning Company has been hard hit by increased competition. Analysts predict that earnings (and dividends) will decline at a rate of 5 percent annually into the foreseeable future. If Canning's last dividend (D_0) was $2.00, and investors' required rate of return is 15 percent, what will be Canning's stock price *in 3 years*?

   a. $8.15   **b.** $9.50   **c.** $10.00   **d.** $10.42   **e.** $10.96

   (The following data relate to Self-Test Problems 9 through 11.)

   The Club Auto Parts Company has just recently been organized. It is expected to experience no growth for the next 2 years as it identifies its market and acquires its inventory. However, Club will grow at an annual rate of 5 percent in the third year, and, beginning with the fourth year, should attain a 10 percent growth rate which it will sustain thereafter. The first dividend (D_1) to be paid at the end of the first year is expected to be $0.50 per share. Investors require a 15 percent rate of return on Club's stock.

9. What is the current equilibrium stock price?

   a. $5.00   **b.** $8.75   **c.** $9.57   **d.** $12.43   **e.** $15.00

©1992 The Dryden Press
All rights reserved.

10. What will Club's stock price be at the end of the first year (P_1)?

    a. $5.00   **b.** $8.76   **c.** $9.56   **d.** $12.43   **e.** $15.00

11. What dividend yield and capital gains yield should an investor in Club expect for the first year?

    a. 0%; 15%   **b.** 3%; 12%   **c.** 6%; 9%   **d.** 10%; 5%   **e.** 12%; 3%

12. You have just been offered a bond for $863.73. The coupon rate is 8 percent, payable annually, and interest rates on new issues with the same degree of risk are 10 percent. You want to know how many more interest payments you will receive, but the party selling the bond cannot remember. If the par value is $1,000, how many interest payments remain?

    a. 10   **b.** 11   **c.** 12   **d.** 13   **e.** 14

13. Johnson Corporation's stock is currently selling at $45.83 per share. The last dividend paid (D_0) was $2.50. Johnson is a constant growth firm. If investors require a return of 16 percent on Johnson's stock, what do they think Johnson's growth rate will be?

    a. 6%   **b.** 7%   **c.** 8%   **d.** 9%   **e.** 10%

14. Assume that the average firm in your company's industry is expected to grow at a constant rate of 7 percent, and its dividend yield is 8 percent. Your company is about as risky as the average firm in the industry, but it has just successfully completed some R&D work which leads you to expect that its earnings and dividends will grow at a rate of 40 percent ($D_1 = D_0(1 + g) = D_0(1.40)$) this year and 20 percent the following year, after which growth should match the 7 percent industry average rate. The last dividend paid (D_0) was $1. What is the value per share of your firm's stock?

    a. $22.47   **b.** $24.15   **c.** $21.00   **d.** $19.48   **e.** $22.00

15. Assume that as investment manager of Florida Electric Company's pension plan (which is exempt from income taxes), you must choose between Exxon bonds and GM preferred stock. The bonds have a $1,000 par value; they mature in 20 years, they pay $35 each 6 months; they are callable at Exxon's option at a price of $1,150 after 5 years (ten 6-month periods); and they sell at a price of $815.98 per bond. The preferred stock is a perpetuity; it pays a dividend of $1.50 each quarter, and it sells for $75 per share. What is the most likely effective annual rate of return (EAR) on the *higher* yielding security?

    a. 9.20%   **b.** 8.24%   **c.** 9.00%   **d.** 8.00%   **e.** 8.50%

© 1992 The Dryden Press
All rights reserved.

ANSWERS TO SELF-TEST QUESTIONS

1. bond
2. par; 1,000
3. coupon payment; par value
4. maturity date
5. present value
6. market price; par value
7. opposite
8. yield to maturity
9. coupon payment; interest rate; years
10. present
11. dividend; capital gains
12. zero; dividend
13. positive; negative

14. a. For example, if inflation increases, the interest rate (or required return) will increase, resulting in a decline in bond price.

15. b. It will sell at a discount.

16. a. Both bonds are valued as 1-year bonds regardless of their original issue dates, and since they are of equal risk and have the same coupon rate, their prices must be equal.

17. a. The model considers all future dividends. This produces a current value which is appropriate for all investors independent of their expected holding period.

18. e. The model would be invalid, however, if the growth rate *exceeded* the required rate of return.

19. b. Statements a, d, and e are all true. To determine which of the remaining statements is false, it is best to use an example. Assume you have a 10-year, 10 percent annual coupon bond which sold at par. If interest rates increase to 13 percent, the value of the bond decreases to $837.21, while if interest rates decrease to 7 percent, the value of the bond increases to $1,210.71. Thus, the capital gain is greater than the capital loss and statement b is false.

20. d. Statement a is false because the bond would have a premium and thus sell above par value. Statement b is false because both bonds would have the same interest rate risk because they both have one year left to maturity. Statement c is false because the price of a bond moves in the opposite direction as interest rates. Statement e is false because the 30-year bond would have more interest rate risk than the 30-day bond. Statement d is correct. As years to maturity increases for a bond, the number of discount periods used in finding the current bond value also increases. Therefore, bonds with longer maturities will have more price sensitivity to a given change in interest rates.

21. c. Statement a is false. $\hat{P}_0 = D_1/(k_s - g)$. Thus, if the two stocks had different required rates of return, their prices would be different. Statement b is false because interest rate risk and reinvestment risk move in the opposite direction. Statement d is false because g can be less than zero. Statement c is correct. The

© 1992 The Dryden Press
All rights reserved.

maturity risk premium (MRP) compensates investors for interest rate risk. As a given security's maturity increases, the MRP also increases. If reinvestment rate risk was regarded as more important, then short-term securities would have a higher required yield than long-term securities. However, this is not true because of the existence of a positive MRP. Statement d is false because g may be negative in the constant growth stock valuation model, but it cannot be greater than k_s, the required return.

SOLUTIONS TO SELF-TEST PROBLEMS

1. c. $V_B = INT(PVIFA_{k_d,N}) + M(PVIF_{k_d,N})$

    $= \$70(PVIFA_{14\%,4}) + \$1,000(PVIF_{14\%,4})$

    $= \$70(2.9137) + \$1,000(0.5921) = \$796.06.$

    Calculator solution: Input $N = 4$, $I = 14$, $PMT = 70$, $FV = 1,000$, and solve for $PV = \$796.04$.

2. d. $V_B = (INT/2)(PVIFA_{k_d/2,2N}) + M(PVIF_{k_d/2,2N})$

    $= \$35(PVIFA_{7\%,8}) + \$1,000(PVIF_{7\%,8})$

    $= \$35(5.9713) + \$1,000(0.5820) = \$791.00.$

    Calculator solution: Input $N = 8$, $I = 7$, $PMT = 35$, $FV = 1,000$, and solve for $PV = \$791.00$.

3. e. $V_B = INT(PVIFA_{k_d,N}) + M(PVIF_{k_d,N})$

    $= \$70(PVIFA_{14\%,20}) + \$1,000(PVIF_{14\%,20})$

    $= \$70(6.6231) + \$1,000(0.0728) = \$536.42.$

    Calculator solution: Input $N = 20$, $I = 14$, $PMT = 70$, $FV = 1,000$, and solve for $PV = \$536.38$.

4. c. $V_B = INT(PVIFA_{k_d,N}) + M(PVIF_{k_d,N})$

    $\$814.45 = \$100(PVIFA_{k_d,8}) + \$1,000(PVIF_{k_d,8}).$

    Now use trial and error techniques. Try $I = k_d = 12\%$:

    $\$814.45 = \$100(4.9676) + \$1,000(0.4039) = \$900.66.$

© 1992 The Dryden Press
All rights reserved.

Since \$814.45 ≠ \$900.66, the yield to maturity is not 12 percent. The calculated value is too large. Therefore, increase the value of I to 14 percent to lower the calculated value: \$814.45 = \$100(4.6389) + \$1,000(0.3506) = \$814.49. This is close enough to conclude that k_d = yield to maturity = 14%.

Calculator solution: Input N = 8, PV = -814.45, PMT = 100, FV = 1,000, and solve for I = k_d = 14.00%.

5. c. This is a zero-growth stock, or perpetuity: $\hat{P}_0 = D/k_s = \$4.00/0.12 = \$33.33$.

6. e. $\hat{P}_0 = \dfrac{D_0(1 + g)}{k_s - g} = \dfrac{\$2.00(1.10)}{0.20 - 0.10} = \$22.00$.

Since the stock is currently selling for \$25.00, the stock is not in equilibrium and is overvalued by \$3.00.

7. c. $\text{Dividend yield} = \dfrac{D_1}{P_0} = \dfrac{D_0(1 + g)}{P_0} = \dfrac{\$1.50(1.05)}{\$15.75} = 0.10 = 10\%$.

$\text{Capital gains yield} = \dfrac{\hat{P}_1 - P_0}{P_0} = \dfrac{P_0(1 + g) - P_0}{P_0} = \dfrac{\$16.54 - \$15.75}{\$15.75} = g = 5\%$.

For a constant growth stock, the capital gains yield is equal to g.

8. a. $\hat{P}_0 = \dfrac{D_0(1 + g)}{k_s - g} = \dfrac{\$2.00(0.95)}{0.15 - (-0.05)} = \dfrac{\$1.90}{0.20} = \$9.50$.

$\hat{P}_3 = \hat{P}_0(1 + g)^3 = \$9.50(0.95)^3 = \$9.50(0.8574) = \$8.15$.

The Gordon model can also be used:

$\hat{P}_3 = \dfrac{D_4}{k_s - g} = \dfrac{D_0(1 + g)^4}{0.15 - (-0.05)} = \dfrac{\$2.00(0.95)^4}{0.20} = \dfrac{\$2.00(0.8145)}{0.20} = \$8.15$.

9. b. To calculate the current value of a nonconstant growth stock, follow these steps:

(1) Determine the expected stream of dividends during the nonconstant growth period. Also, calculate the expected dividend at the end of the first year of constant growth that will be used later to calculate stock price.

$D_1 = \$0.50.$
$D_2 = D_1(1 + g) = \$0.50(1 + 0.0) = \$0.50.$
$D_3 = D_2(1 + g) = \$0.50(1.05) = \$0.525.$
$D_4 = D_3(1 + g) = \$0.525(1.10) = \$0.5775.$

6-14

© 1992 The Dryden Press
All rights reserved.

(2)   Discount the expected dividends during the nonconstant growth period at the investor's required rate of return to find their present value.

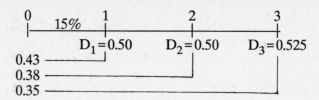

(3)   Calculate the expected stock price at the end of the final year of nonconstant growth. This occurs at the end of Year 3. Use the Gordon model for this calculation.

$$\hat{P}_3 = \frac{D_4}{k_s - g} = \frac{\$0.5775}{0.15 - 0.10} = \$11.55.$$

Then discount this stock price back 3 periods at the investor's required rate of return to find its present value.

$$PV = \$11.55(PVIF_{15\%,3}) = \$11.55(0.6575) = \$7.59.$$

(4)   Add the present value of the stock price expected at the end of Year 3 plus the dividends expected in Years 1, 2, and 3 to find the present value of the stock, P_0.

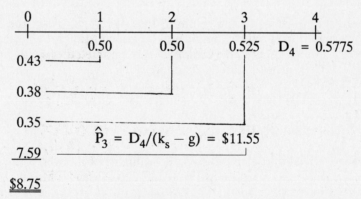

Alternatively, input 0, 0.5, 0.5, 12.075 (0.525 + 11.55) into the cash flow register, input I = 15, and then solve for NPV = $8.75.

10.   c.   To calculate the expected stock price at the end of Year 1, P_1, follow the same procedure you did to find the value of the nonconstant growth stock in Problem 9. However, discount values to Year 1 instead of Year 0. Also, remember that the dividend in Year 1, D_1, is not included in the valuation because it has already been

© 1992 The Dryden Press
All rights reserved.

paid and therefore adds nothing to the wealth of the investor buying the stock at the end of Year 1.

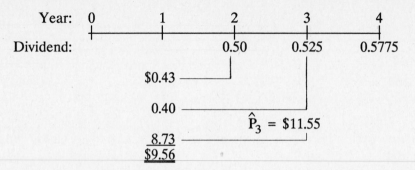

Alternatively, input 0, 0.5, 12.075 (0.525 + 11.55) into the cash flow register, input I = 15, and then solve for NPV = $9.57.

11. c. $\dfrac{\text{Dividend}}{\text{yield}} = \dfrac{D_1}{P_0} = \dfrac{\$0.50}{\$8.75} = 5.71\% \approx 6\%.$

$\dfrac{\text{Capital}}{\text{gains yield}} = \dfrac{\hat{P}_1 - P_0}{P_0} = \dfrac{\$9.56 - \$8.75}{\$8.75} = 0.093 \approx 9\%.$

The total yield = dividend yield + capital gains yield = 6% + 9% = 15%. The total yield must equal the required rate of return. Also, the capital gains yield is not equal to the growth rate during the nonconstant growth phase of a nonconstant growth stock. Finally, the dividend and capital gains yields are not constant until the constant growth state is reached.

12. c. $V_B = \text{INT}(\text{PVIFA}_{k_d,N}) + M(\text{PVIF}_{k_d,N})$

$\$863.73 = \$80(\text{PVIFA}_{10\%,N}) + \$1,000(\text{PVIF}_{10\%,N})$

Now use trial and error to find the value of N for which the equality holds. For N = 12, $863.73 = $80(6.8137) + $1,000(0.3186) = $863.70. Or using a financial calculator, input I = 10, PV = -863.73, PMT = 80, FV = 1,000, and solve for N = 12.

© 1992 The Dryden Press
All rights reserved.

13. e.

$$P_0 = \frac{D_0(1 + g)}{k_s - g}$$

$$\$45.83 = \frac{\$2.50(1 + g)}{0.16 - g}$$

$$\$7.33 - \$45.83g = \$2.50 + \$2.50g$$
$$\$48.33g = \$4.83$$
$$g = 0.0999 \approx 10\%.$$

14. d. $D_0 = \$1.00$; $k_s = 8\% + 7\% = 15\%$; $g_1 = 40\%$; $g_2 = 20\%$; $g_n = 7\%$.

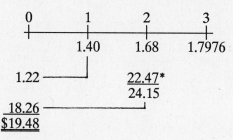

$$*\hat{P}_2 = \frac{\$1.7976}{0.15 - 0.07} = \$22.47.$$

15. a. Bonds: Price = \$815.98, Maturity = 20 years, PMT = \$35/6 mos., and callable at \$1,150 after 10 periods (5 years).

Will the bond's YTM or YTC be applicable? The bond is selling at a discount, so k_d > coupon interest rate. Therefore, the bond is not likely to be called, so calculate the YTM.

Input N = 40, PV = -815.98, PMT = 35, FV = 1,000, and solve for I = $k_d/2$ = 4.5%. EAR = $(1.045)^2 - 1 = 9.2\%$.

Preferred: D = \$1.50/quarter and P_0 = \$75.

k_{ps} = \$1.50/\$75 = 2% = periodic rate.

EAR = $(1.02)^4 - 1 = 8.24\%$.

© 1992 The Dryden Press
All rights reserved.

CHAPTER 7
THE COST OF CAPITAL

OVERVIEW

The firm's marginal cost of capital (MCC) schedule is developed in the following manner: First, the cost of capital must be estimated for each component of the firm's capital structure. These components are normally debt, preferred stock, and common equity. The next task is to combine the component costs to form a weighted average cost of capital. The weights are based on the firm's target capital structure. Capital typically has an increasing cost if the firm expands beyond certain limits. The point at which the cost of capital increases is called a break point, and the MCC schedule is often drawn as a step-function which increases due to increases in one or more of the capital components.

The investment opportunity schedule (IOS) is a plot of the firm's potential projects arrayed in descending order of their rates of return. The intersection of the MCC and the IOS schedules defines the firm's optimal capital budget as well as the relevant marginal cost of capital used to evaluate all new projects with the same risk as the firm's other assets.

OUTLINE

I. **Determining the firm's cost of capital, or the proper discount rate for use in calculating the present value of the cash inflows for the firm's projects, is an important element of the capital budgeting process.**

   A. *Capital components* are items on the right-hand side of the balance sheet such as debt, preferred stock, common stock, and retained earnings.

   B. Each element of capital has a *component cost* which can be identified as follows:
   1. k_d = interest rate on the firm's new debt, before tax.
   2. $k_d(1 - T)$ = after-tax cost of debt where T is the marginal tax rate.
   3. k_p = component cost of preferred stock.
   4. k_s = component cost of retained earnings; it is equal to the required rate of return on common stock.
   5. k_e = cost of external capital obtained by issuing additional common stock; it must be distinguished from equity raised through retained earnings due to the flotation costs when new stock is issued.
   6. WACC = the weighted average cost of capital.

II. **The cost of each capital component can be determined as follows:**

   A. The after-tax cost of debt, $k_d(1 - T)$, is defined as the interest rate on debt, k_d, less the tax savings that result because interest is tax deductible.

©1992 The Dryden Press
All rights reserved.

1. For example, if a firm has a tax rate of 40 percent and can borrow at a rate of 10 percent, then its after-tax cost of debt is $k_d = 10\%(1 - 0.40) = 10\%(0.60) = 6.0\%$.
2. The tax deductibility of interest payments has the effect of causing the federal government to pay part of the interest charges.
3. k_d is the interest rate on new debt, not that on already outstanding debt.

B. The component cost of preferred stock, k_p, is the preferred dividend, D_p, divided by the net issuing price, P_n, or the price the firm receives after deducting flotation costs: $k_p = D_p/P_n$. No tax adjustments are made when calculating k_p because preferred dividends, unlike interest expense on debt, are not deductible, and hence there are no tax savings.

C. The cost of retained earnings, k_s, is the rate of return stockholders require on equity capital the firm obtains from earnings. There are three approaches used to determine k_s.
1. The *Capital Asset Pricing Model (CAPM)* works as follows:
   a. Estimate the risk-free rate, k_{RF}, usually based on U.S. Treasury securities.
   b. Estimate the stock's beta coefficient as an index of risk.
   c. Estimate the expected rate of return on the market, or on an "average" stock, k_M.
   d. Substitute the preceding values into the CAPM equation, $k_s = k_{RF} + (k_M - k_{RF})b$, to estimate the required rate of return on the stock in question.
   e. Thus, if $k_{RF} = 8\%$, $k_M = 13\%$, and the beta is 0.7, then $k_s = 8\% + (13\% - 8\%)0.7 = 11.5\%$.
2. The *bond-yield-plus-risk-premium approach* estimates k_s by adding a risk premium of three to five percentage points to the firm's own bond yield. Thus, k_s = Bond yield + Risk premium.
   a. If the firm uses a risk premium of 4 percentage points, and its bond rate is 9 percent, then $k_s = 9\% + 4\% = 13\%$.
   b. Because the risk premium is a judgmental estimate, this method is not likely to produce a precise cost of equity; however, it does get us "into the right ballpark."
3. The required rate of return, k_s, may also be estimated by the *discounted cash flow (DCF) approach*. This approach combines the expected dividend yield, D_1/P_0, with the expected future growth rate, g, of earnings and dividends, or

$$k_s - \hat{k}_s - \frac{D_1}{P_0} + \text{Expected g.}$$

   a. The DCF approach assumes that stocks are normally in equilibrium and that growth is expected to be at a constant rate. If growth is not constant, then a nonconstant growth model must be used.
   b. The expected growth rate may be based on projections of past growth rates, if they have been relatively stable, or on expected future growth rates as estimated in some other manner.

©1992 The Dryden Press
All rights reserved.

c. If the firm's next expected dividend is $1.24, its expected growth rate is 8 percent per year, and its stock is selling for $23 per share, then

$$k_s = \hat{k}_s = \frac{\$1.24}{\$23} + 8.0\% = 13.4\%.$$

4. If the firm cannot earn about 13.4 percent on reinvested equity capital, then it should pay its earnings to stockholders and let them invest directly in other assets that do provide this return. Thus, k_s is an *opportunity cost*.
5. It is recommended that all three approaches be used in estimating the required rate of return on common stock. When the methods produce widely different results, judgment must be used in selecting the best estimate.

D. The cost of new common equity, or external equity capital, k_e, is higher than the cost of retained earnings, k_s, because of *flotation costs* involved in selling new common stock.
   1. To allow for flotation costs, F, we must adjust the DCF formula for the required rate of return as follows:

$$k_e = \frac{D_1}{P_0(1 - F)} + g.$$

   2. If the firm has a flotation cost of 10 percent, its cost of new outside equity is computed as follows:

$$k_e = \frac{\$1.24}{\$23(1 - 0.10)} + 8.0\% = 14.0\%.$$

   3. If the firm can earn 14 percent on investments financed by new common stock, then earnings, dividends, and the growth rate will be maintained, and the price per share will not fall. If it earns more than 14 percent, the price will rise; while if it earns less, the price will fall.

III. **The target proportions of debt, preferred stock, and common equity, along with the component costs of capital, are used to calculate the firm's weighted average cost of capital (WACC).**

A. The calculation of the weighted average cost of capital is shown below for a firm which finances 30 percent with debt, 10 percent with preferred stock, and 60 percent with common equity and which has the following after-tax component costs:

7-3

©1992 The Dryden Press
All rights reserved.

Component	Weight	×	After-tax Cost	=	Weighted Cost
Debt	0.3	×	8.4%	=	2.52%
Preferred	0.1	×	12.6	=	1.26
Common	0.6	×	16.0	=	9.60
				WACC =	13.38%

B. In more general terms, and in equation format,

$$\text{WACC} = w_d k_d (1 - T) + w_p k_p + w_s (k_s \text{ or } k_e).$$

C. The capital structure that minimizes a firm's weighted average cost of capital also maximizes its stock price.

IV. **The marginal cost of capital (MCC) is defined as the cost of the last dollar of new capital that the firm raises, and the marginal cost rises as more and more capital is raised during a given period.**

A. Firms raise capital in accordance with their target capital structures.

B. As companies raise larger and larger sums during a given time period, the component costs begin to rise. This causes an increase in the weighted average cost of each additional dollar of new capital.

C. Suppose that a firm needs $500,000 in new capital. Its capital structure is 60 percent common equity, 30 percent debt and 10 percent preferred stock, and its marginal tax rate is 40 percent. The before-tax cost of debt is 14 percent and the cost of preferred stock is 12.6 percent. The firm will need to raise 0.6($500,000) = $300,000 in common equity. It expects retained earnings for the year to be $100,000; therefore, it needs to sell $300,000 - $100,000 = $200,000 of new common stock. The cost of retained earnings is 16.0 percent, but the cost of new equity is 16.8 percent. The average cost of capital, using new equity, is:

$$
\begin{aligned}
\text{WACC} &= w_d k_d (1 - T) + w_p k_p + w_s k_e \\
&= 0.3(14\%)(0.60) + 0.1(12.6\%) + 0.6(16.8\%) \\
&= 13.86\%.
\end{aligned}
$$

D. The point at which the marginal cost of capital increases is called a *break point*. The retained earnings break point is calculated as Retained earnings/Equity fraction. For the firm discussed above, this break point is $100,000/0.6 = $166,667. That is, when $166,667 of new capital is raised, the firm will have used 0.6($166,667) = $100,000 of retained earnings. After that, more costly new common equity must be used. Other break points for the other capital components can be calculated in a similar manner.

V. **The marginal cost of capital (MCC) schedule shows the relationship between the cost of each dollar raised, WACC, and the total amount of capital raised during the year.**

7-4

©1992 The Dryden Press
All rights reserved.

The MCC schedule can be used to help determine the discount rate to be used in the capital budgeting process.

A. The optimal capital structure is the one that produces the lowest MCC schedule.

B. In general, a break will occur in the MCC schedule any time the cost of one of the components rises.

   1. The break point is determined by the following equation:

$$\text{Break point} = \frac{\text{Total amount of lower-cost capital of a given type}}{\text{Fraction of this type of capital in the capital structure}}.$$

   2. If there are no break points, there will be one MCC. If there are n break points, there will be n + 1 different MCCs.

C. For ease in calculating the MCC schedule, first identify the points where breaks occur, then determine the cost of capital for each component in the intervals between the breaks, and, finally, calculate the weighted averages of these costs for each interval.

VI. **The investment opportunity schedule (IOS) shows the rate of return that is expected on each potential investment opportunity.**

A. The investment opportunity schedule (IOS) is a plot of the firm's potential projects in descending order of each project's rate of return.

B. The WACC at the point where the IOS intersects the MCC curve is defined as the "corporate cost of capital," which reflects the marginal cost of capital to the corporation.

SELF-TEST QUESTIONS

Definitional

1. The firm should calculate its cost of capital as a _____ _____ of the after-tax costs of the various types of funds it uses.

2. Capital components are items on the right-hand side of the balance sheet such as the following: (1) _____, (2) _____ _____, (3) _____ _____, and (4) _____ _____.

3. The cost of equity capital is defined as the _____ _____ _____ stockholders require on the firm's common stock.

©1992 The Dryden Press
All rights reserved.

4. There are _____ approaches that can be used to determine the cost of retained earnings.

5. Assigning a cost to retained earnings is based on the _____ _____ principle.

6. The cost of external equity capital is higher than the cost of retained earnings due to _____ _____.

7. Using the Capital Asset Pricing Model (CAPM), the required rate of return on common stock is found as a function of the _____ - _____ _____, the firm's _____ _____, and the required rate of return on an average _____.

8. The cost of common equity may also be found by adding a _____ _____ to the interest rate on the firm's own _____ _____.

9. The required rate of return may also be estimated as the _____ _____ on the common stock plus the expected future _____ _____ of the dividends.

10. The proportions of _____, _____ _____, and _____ _____ in the target capital structure should be used to calculate the _____ _____ cost of capital.

11. The _____ cost of capital is the cost of raising another dollar of new capital.

12. The MCC schedule can be used to help determine the _____ _____ to be used in the capital budgeting process.

13. The _____ _____ _____ graphs a firm's capital projects in descending order of each project's _____ _____ _____.

Conceptual

14. If a firm obtains all of its common equity from retained earnings, its MCC schedule would always be flat; that is, there would be no break points.

    a. True   b. False

15. If there are n break points in the MCC schedule, there will be n + 1 different MCCs.

    a. True   b. False

16. Funds acquired by the firm through preferred stock have a cost to the firm equal to the preferred dividend divided by the price investors paid for one share.

    a. True   b. False

©1992 The Dryden Press
All rights reserved.

17. Which of the following statements could be true concerning the costs of debt and equity?

   a. The cost of debt for Firm A is greater than the cost of equity for Firm A.
   b. The cost of debt for Firm A is greater than the cost of equity for Firm B.
   c. The cost of retained earnings for Firm A is less than its cost of external equity.
   d. The cost of retained earnings for Firm A is less than its cost of debt.
   e. Statements b and c could both be true.

18. Which of the following statements is most correct?

   a. If Congress raised the corporate tax rate, this would lower the effective cost of debt but probably would also reduce the amount of retained earnings available to corporations, so the effect on the marginal cost of capital is uncertain.
   b. For corporate investors, 70 percent of the dividends received on both common and preferred stocks is exempt from taxes. However, neither preferred nor common dividends may be deducted by the issuing company. Therefore, the dividend exclusion has no effect on a company's cost of capital, so its WACC would probably not change at all if the dividend exclusion rule were rescinded by Congress.
   c. Normally, the MCC schedule is drawn with an upward slope, reflecting the fact that as more capital is raised, the cost of capital increases. However, if the firm uses a lot of short-term debt, then its MCC schedule could, according to the text, have a U shape.
   d. Each of the above statements is true.
   e. Each of the above statements is false.

19. Which of the following statements is most correct?

   a. Three procedures for determining the cost of retained earnings were discussed in the text: the CAPM, the DCF, and the WACC.
   b. One reason why new common stock has a higher cost than retained earnings is because, to raise capital by selling stock, the firm must attract new investors who are less sanguine (that is, less optimistic) about the firm's prospects. This requires that the price of the stock be reduced, and this price reduction is built into the flotation cost. Therefore, the steeper the demand curve for the stock, the greater the differential between the cost of new equity and the cost of retained earnings.
   c. Logically, one can think of a high dividend payout stock as being similar to a shorter-term bond, and of a low payout stock as being similar to a longer-term bond, because cash flows come in faster if the payout is higher. Because of this factor, the differential between the cost of retained earnings and the cost of new outside equity should normally be *greater* for a low payout stock, other things held constant.
   d. When calculating the WACC for a firm which will obtain equity both from retained earnings and by selling new stock, the cost of equity used in the WACC formula should normally be a weighted average of k_s and k_e, that is, the equity component will be $w_e(k_s + k_e)$.
   e. Each of the above statements is false.

©1992 The Dryden Press
All rights reserved.

20. Which of the following statements is most correct?

   a. If a firm which has income and pays dividends estimates its MCC schedule on out to a very large amount of new capital, there will always be at least one break in the MCC, due to running out of retained earnings. However, once the IOS is considered, then, for capital budgeting purposes, the MCC may turn out to be constant over the range of funds the company will actually raise, that is, there will be only one relevant WACC.
   b. If there is more than one break in the MCC, we can be absolutely sure that the firm's investment bankers have told it that if it wants to sell more than some given amount of new stock, the flotation costs on new stock issues will rise.
   c. As the situation was explained in the text, the firm's WACC should be calculated using constant weights for debt, preferred, and common equity so long as all equity comes from retained earnings, but if new common stock must be sold, then the weight used for equity must be increased.
   d. The MCC-IOS concept is used by firms as they make plans for some future period. Further, we know that the WACC will eventually increase if the firm uses larger and larger amounts of capital during a given year, which means that the MCC can rise. If this situation occurs, then the NPVs of high IRR projects, which will be financed with the earlier, low-cost capital, should be determined with a lower WACC than that used for later projects.
   e. All of the above statements are false.

SELF-TEST PROBLEMS

1. Roland Corporation's next expected dividend (D_1) is $2.50. The firm has maintained a constant payout ratio of 50 percent during the past 7 years. Seven years ago its EPS was $1.50. The firm's beta coefficient is 1.2. The required return on an average stock in the market is 13 percent, and the risk-free rate is 7 percent. Roland's A-rated bonds are yielding 10 percent, and its current stock price is $30. Which of the following values is the most reasonable estimate of Roland's cost of retained earnings, k_s?

   a. 10%   b. 12%   c. 14%   d. 20%   e. 26%

2. The director of capital budgeting for See-Saw Inc., manufacturers of playground equipment, is considering a plan to expand production facilities in order to meet an increase in demand. He estimates that this expansion will produce a rate of return of 11 percent. The firm's target capital structure calls for a debt/equity ratio of 0.8. See-Saw currently has a bond issue outstanding which will mature in 25 years and has a 7 percent annual coupon rate. The bonds are currently selling for $804. The firm has maintained a constant growth rate of 6 percent. See-Saw's next expected dividend is $2 and its current stock price is $40. Its tax rate is 40 percent. Should it undertake the expansion? (Assume that there is no preferred stock outstanding and that any new debt will have a 25 year maturity.)

©1992 The Dryden Press
All rights reserved.

a. No; the expected return is 2.5 percentage points lower than the cost of capital.
b. No; the expected return is 1.0 percentage points lower than the cost of capital.
c. Yes; the expected return is 0.5 percentage points higher than the cost of capital.
d. Yes; the expected return is 1.0 percentage points higher than the cost of capital.
e. Yes; the expected return is 2.5 percentage points higher than the cost of capital.

3. Midterm Corporation's present capital structure, which is also its target capital structure, calls for 50 percent debt and 50 percent common equity. The firm has only one potential project, an expansion program with a 10.2 percent rate of return and a cost of $20 million but which is completely divisible; that is, Midterm can invest any amount up to $20 million. Midterm expects to retain $3 million of earnings next year. It can raise up to $5 million in new debt at a before-tax cost of 8 percent, and all debt after the first $5 million will have a cost of 10 percent. The cost of retained earnings is 12 percent; Midterm can sell any amount of new common stock desired at a constant cost of new equity of 15 percent. The firm's marginal tax rate is 40 percent. What is Midterm's optimal capital budget?

a. $0 million   b. $5 million   c. $6 million   d. $10 million   e. $20 million

4. The management of Florida Phosphate Industries (FPI) is planning next year's capital budget. FPI projects net income of $10,500, and its payout ratio is 40 percent. The company's earnings and dividends are growing at a constant rate of 5 percent. The last dividend, D_0, was $0.90; and the current equilibrium stock price is $8.59. FPI can raise up to $10,000 of debt at a 12 percent before-tax cost, the next $10,000 will cost 14 percent, and all debt after $20,000 will cost 16 percent. If FPI issues new common stock, a 10 percent flotation cost will be incurred on the first $16,000 issued, while flotation costs will be 20 percent on all new stock issued after the first $16,000. FPI is at its optimal capital structure, which is 40 percent debt and 60 percent equity, and the firm's marginal tax rate is 40 percent. FPI has the following independent, indivisible, and equally risky investment opportunities:

Project	Cost	Rate of Return
A	$15,000	17%
B	15,000	16
C	12,000	15
D	20,000	14

What is FPI's optimal capital budget?

a. $62,000   b. $42,000   c. $30,000   d. $15,000   e. $0

5. Gator Products Company (GPC) is at its optimal capital structure of 70 percent common equity and 30 percent debt. GPC's MCC and IOS schedules for next year intersect at a 14 percent marginal cost of capital. At the intersection, the IOS schedule is vertical and the MCC schedule is horizontal. GPC has a marginal tax rate of 40 percent. Next year's dividend is expected to be $2.00 per share, and GPC has a

©1992 The Dryden Press
All rights reserved.

constant growth in earnings and dividends of 6 percent. The after-tax cost of equity used in the MCC at the intersection is based on new equity with a flotation cost of 10 percent, while the before-tax cost of debt is 12 percent. What is GPC's current equilibrium stock price?

a. $12.73   **b.** $17.23   **c.** $20.37   **d.** $23.70   **e.** $37.20

(The following data apply to Self-Test Problems 6 and 7.)

Sun Products Company (SPC) uses only debt and equity. It can borrow unlimited amounts at an interest rate of 12 percent so long as it finances at its target capital structure, which calls for 45 percent debt and 55 percent common equity. Its last dividend was $2.40, its expected constant growth rate is 5 percent, its stock sells for $30 per share, and new stock would net the company $24 per share after flotation costs. SPC's tax rate is 40 percent, and it expects to have $120 million of retained earnings this year. Two projects are available: Project A has a cost of $240 million and a rate of return of 13 percent, while Project B has a cost of $150 million and a rate of return of 10 percent. All of the company's potential projects are equally risky.

6. What is SPC's cost of equity from newly issued stock?

     a. 15.50%   **b.** 13.40%   **c.** 7.20%   **d.** 12.50%   **e.** 16.00%

7. What is SPC's marginal cost of capital? In other words, what WACC cost rate should it use to evaluate capital budgeting projects (these two projects plus any others that might arise during the year, provided the cost of capital schedule remains as it is currently)?

     a. 12.05%   **b.** 13.40%   **c.** 11.77%   **d.** 12.50%   **e.** 10.61%

ANSWERS TO SELF-TEST QUESTIONS

1. weighted average
2. debt; preferred stock; common stock; retained earnings
3. rate of return
4. three
5. opportunity cost
6. flotation costs
7. risk-free rate (k_{RF}); beta coefficient (b); stock (k_M)

8. risk premium; bond yield
9. dividend yield; growth rate
10. debt; preferred stock; common equity; weighted average
11. marginal
12. discount rate
13. Investment Opportunity Schedule (IOS); rate of return

14. b. The component cost of debt and/or preferred equity might increase, thus causing break points in the MCC schedule.

15. a. This statement is correct.

16. b. Flotation costs must be subtracted from the investor's cost to get the net issuance price, which is then used to calculate the cost of preferred stock.

17. e. If Firm A has more business risk than Firm B, Firm A's cost of debt could be greater than Firm B's cost of equity. Also, the cost of retained earnings is less than the cost of external equity because of flotation costs.

18. a. Statement a is correct. If Congress were to raise the tax rate, this would lower the cost of debt; however, a bigger chunk of the firm's earnings would go to Uncle Sam. The effect on the MCC would depend on which had the greater effect on the MCC. Statement b is false. Preferred stock generally has a lower cost than debt due to the dividend exclusion; however, if the dividend exclusion were omitted, preferred stock would have an increased cost. Statement c is false because short-term debt is not considered in the MCC schedule. The MCC schedule is usually drawn as a step function; however, at some point numerous break points would occur and the MCC would rise almost continuously beyond some level of new financing.

19. b. Statement a is false. The three methods for determining the cost of equity are the DCF, the CAPM, and the Bond-yield-plus-risk-premium. Statement b is correct. Statement c is false. The differential for the cost of retained earnings and the cost of new stock is discussed in statement b. Statement d is false. The MCC will contain a break where retained earnings are used up and new common stock is used, and there would be 2 different MCC's calculated—one using k_s and one using k_e.

20. a. Statement a is true. Statement b is false; breaks in the MCC can occur due to increased costs at different levels of debt and/or preferred stock financing. Statement c is false; the weights used in calculating the WACC depend on the optimal capital structure used and do not change because retained earnings are used up and new equity must be used. Statement d is false because the intersection of the MCC and IOS curve determines the WACC that should be used in evaluating all average-risk projects. The method for adjusting the WACC for low- and high-risk projects will be discussed in Chapter 10.

SOLUTIONS TO SELF-TEST PROBLEMS

1. c. Use all three methods to estimate k_s.

   CAPM: $k_s = k_{RF} + (k_M - k_{RF})b = 7\% + (13\% - 7\%)1.2 = 14.2\%$.

   Risk Premium: k_s = Bond yield + Risk premium = $10\% + 4\% = 14\%$.

   DCF: $k_s = D_1/P_0 + g = \$2.50/\$30 + g$, where g can be estimated as follows:

© 1992 The Dryden Press
All rights reserved.

$0.75 = \$2.50(PVIF_{k,7})$

$PVIF_{k,7} = \$0.75/\$2.50 = 0.3000.$

Thus k, which is the compound growth rate, g, is about 19%, or, using a calculator, 18.8%. Therefore, $k_s = 0.083 + 0.188 = 27.1\%$.

Roland Corporation has apparently been experiencing supernormal growth during the past 7 years, and it is not reasonable to assume that this growth will continue. The first two methods yield a k_s of about 14 percent, which appears reasonable.

2. e. Cost of equity $= k_s = \$2/\$40 + 0.06 = 0.11 = 11\%$.

Cost of debt $= k_d =$ Yield to maturity on outstanding bonds based on current market price.

$$V_B = INT(PVIFA_{k_d,25}) + M(PVIF_{k_d,25}),$$

$$\$804 = \$70(PVIFA_{k_d,25}) + \$1,000(PVIF_{k_d,25}).$$

Solving by trial and error gives $k_d = 9\%$. Alternatively, with a financial calculator: Input N = 25, PV = -804, PMT = 70, FV = 1,000, and solve for I = k_d = 9%.

In determining the capital structure weights, note that debt/equity = 0.8 or, for example, 4/5. Therefore, debt/assets is

$$\frac{D}{A} = \frac{Debt}{Debt + Equity} = \frac{4}{4+5} = \frac{4}{9},$$

and equity/assets = 5/9. Hence, the weighted average cost of capital is calculated as follows:

$$
\begin{aligned}
WACC &= k_d(1-T)(D/A) + k_s(1-D/A) \\
&= 0.09(1-0.4)(4/9) + 0.11(5/9) \\
&= 0.024 + 0.061 \\
&= 0.085 = 8.5\%.
\end{aligned}
$$

The cost of capital is 8.5 percent, while the expansion project's rate of return is 11.0 percent. Since the expected return is 2.5 percentage points higher than the cost, the expansion should be undertaken.

3. d. First, look only at debt (in millions of dollars):

```
        8%     D₁  10%
 |-------------|----------------
$0            $5
```

7-12

©1992 The Dryden Press
All rights reserved.

Now, look only at equity (in millions of dollars):

$$\underset{\$0}{\vdash}\quad 12\% \quad \overset{E_1}{\underset{\$3}{\vdash}}\quad 15\%$$

Now combine debt and equity and look at total capital (in millions of dollars):

$$\underset{\$0}{\vdash}\quad A \quad \overset{E_1}{\underset{\$6}{\vdash}}\quad B \quad \overset{D_1}{\underset{\$10}{\vdash}}\quad C$$

The break points are calculated as follows:

$E_1 = \$3,000,000/0.5 = \$6,000,000.$
$D_1 = \$5,000,000/0.5 = \$10,000,000.$

Now, determine the weighted average cost of capital for intervals A, B, and C:

$$WACC = w_d(k_d)(1 - T) + w_s(k_s \text{ or } k_e).$$

A = 0.5(8%)(0.6) + 0.5(12%) = 8.4%.
B = 0.5(8%)(0.6) + 0.5(15%) = 9.9%.
C = 0.5(10%)(0.6) + 0.5(15%) = 10.5%.

Finally, graph the IOS and MCC schedules.

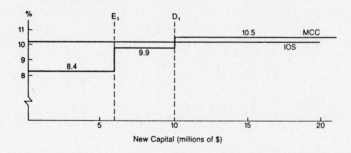

Thus, the optimal capital budget is $10 million.

4. b. First look only at debt:

$$\underset{\$0}{\vdash}\quad 12\% \quad \overset{D_1}{\underset{\$10,000}{\vdash}}\quad 14\% \quad \overset{D_2}{\underset{\$20,000}{\vdash}}\quad 16\%$$

©1992 The Dryden Press
All rights reserved.

Now, look only at equity:

$$
\begin{array}{cccccc}
& 16\% & E_1 & 17.22\% & E_2 & 18.75\% \\
\hline
\$0 & & \$6{,}300 & & \$22{,}300 &
\end{array}
$$

Retained earnings are forecast to be $\$10{,}500(0.6) = \$6{,}300$. The cost of retained earnings is as follows:

$$
k_s = \frac{D_0(1 + g)}{P_0} + g = \frac{\$0.90(1.05)}{\$8.59} + 0.05 = 0.16 = 16.0\%.
$$

The cost of new equity is as follows:

$$
k_{e1} = \frac{D_0(1 + g)}{P_0(1 - F)} + g = \frac{\$0.90(1.05)}{\$8.59(1 - 0.10)} + 0.05 = 0.1722 = 17.22\%.
$$

$$
k_{e2} = \frac{\$0.90(1.05)}{\$8.59(1 - 0.20)} + 0.05 = 0.1875 = 18.75\%.
$$

Now, combine debt and equity and look at total capital:

$$
\begin{array}{ccccccccccc}
& A & E_1 & B & D_1 & C & E_2 & D & D_2 & E \\
\hline
\$0 & & \$10{,}500 & & \$25{,}000 & & \$37{,}167 & & \$50{,}000 &
\end{array}
$$

The break points are calculated as follows:

$E_1 = \$6{,}300/0.60 = \$10{,}500.$
$D_1 = \$10{,}000/0.40 = \$25{,}000.$
$E_2 = \$22{,}300/0.60 = \$37{,}167.$
$D_2 = \$20{,}000/0.40 = \$50{,}000.$

Now, determine the weighted average cost of capital for intervals A through E:

$$
\text{WACC} = w_d(k_d)(1 - T) + w_s(k_s \text{ or } k_e)
$$

$A = 0.4(12\%)(0.6) + 0.6(16.00\%) = 12.48\%.$
$B = 0.4(12\%)(0.6) + 0.6(17.22\%) = 13.21\%.$
$C = 0.4(14\%)(0.6) + 0.6(17.22\%) = 13.69\%.$
$D = 0.4(14\%)(0.6) + 0.6(18.75\%) = 14.61\%.$
$E = 0.4(16\%)(0.6) + 0.6(18.75\%) = 15.09\%.$

© 1992 The Dryden Press
All rights reserved.

Finally, graph the MCC and IOS schedules:

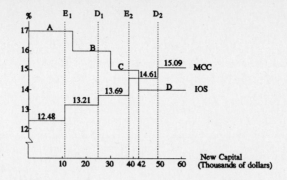

Therefore, the optimal capital budget is $42,000. Projects A, B, and C are accepted.

5. c. At the intersection of the IOS and MCC schedules, WACC = 14%. Therefore,

$$WACC = 14\% = w_d(k_d)(1 - T) + w_s(k_e)$$
$$14\% = 0.3(12\%)(0.6) + 0.7(k_e)$$
$$k_e = 16.91\%.$$

Now, at equilibrium:

$$\hat{k}_e = k_e = \frac{D_1}{P_0(1 - F)} + g$$

$$0.1691 = \frac{\$2.00}{P_0(1 - 0.10)} + 0.06$$

$$0.1091 = \frac{\$2.222}{P_0}$$

$$P_0 = \$20.37.$$

6. a. $k_e = [\$2.40(1.05)]/\$24 + 5\% = 0.1050 + 0.05 = 0.1550 = 15.50\%.$

7. c. $k_d = 12\%; k_d(1 - T) = 12\%(0.6) = 7.2\%.$
$k_s = [\$2.40(1.05)]/\$30 + 5\% = 13.40\%.$
$k_e = 15.50\%.$

RE = $120 million; BP_{RE} = $120/0.55 = $218.18 million.
D/A = 45%; E/A = 55%.

0 - $218.18 million: $WACC_1$ = 0.45(7.2%) + 0.55(13.40%) = 10.61%.
> $218.18 million: $WACC_2$ = 0.45(7.2%) + 0.55(15.50%) = 11.77%.

© 1992 The Dryden Press
All rights reserved.

CHAPTER 8
THE BASICS OF CAPITAL BUDGETING

OVERVIEW

Capital budgeting is similar in principle to security valuation in that future cash flows are estimated, risks are appraised and reflected in a cost of capital discount rate, and all cash flows are evaluated on a present value basis. Four methods can be used to determine which projects should be included in a firm's capital budget: (1) payback, (2) net present value (NPV), (3) internal rate of return (IRR), and (4) modified IRR (MIRR). The payback method has deficiencies, and thus should not be used as the sole criterion for making capital budgeting decisions. The NPV, IRR, and MIRR methods all lead to the same accept/reject decisions on independent projects. However, the methods may conflict when ranking mutually exclusive projects which differ in scale or timing. Under these circumstances, the NPV method should be used to make the final decision.

OUTLINE

I. **Capital budgeting is the process of analyzing fixed asset investment proposals.**

    A. A number of factors combine to make capital budgeting decisions perhaps the most important ones financial managers must make. Since the results of such decisions continue for many years, capital budgeting decisions have long-term consequences. Timing is also important since capital assets must be ready to come on line at the time they are needed.

    B. The same concepts developed for security analysis are involved in capital budgeting; however, whereas a set of stocks and bonds exists in the securities market from which investors select, capital budgeting projects are created by the firm.

    C. Analyzing capital expenditure proposals has a cost, so firms classify projects into different categories to help differentiate the level of analysis required:
        1. Replacement: maintenance of business
        2. Replacement: cost reduction
        3. Expansion of existing products or markets
        4. Expansion into new products or markets
        5. Safety and/or environmental projects
        6. Other miscellaneous projects

    D. Normally, a more detailed analysis is required for expansion and new product decisions than for simple replacement and maintenance decisions. Also, projects requiring larger investments will be analyzed more carefully than smaller projects.

©1992 The Dryden Press
All rights reserved.

E. The capital budgeting process involves the same procedures that are used in security valuation.

    1. The cost of the project must be determined.

    2. Cash flows from the project are estimated.

    3. The riskiness of these projected cash flows is determined.

    4. Given the riskiness of the projected cash flows, the appropriate cost of capital is determined at which cash flows are to be discounted.

    5. Cash flows are discounted to their present value to obtain an estimate of the asset's value to the firm.

    6. The present value of the benefits is compared with the required outlay, or cost. If the asset's value exceeds its cost, the project should be accepted; otherwise, it should be rejected.

II. **Four primary methods are currently used to rank projects and to decide whether or not they should be accepted for inclusion in the capital budget: (1) payback, (2) net present value (NPV), (3) internal rate of return (IRR), and (4) modified internal rate of return (MIRR). The MIRR is discussed in a later section.**

    A. The *payback period* is defined as the expected number of years required to recover the original investment in the project. Payback is a type of "breakeven" calculation in the sense that if cash flows come in at the expected rate until the payback year, then the project will break even.

        1. Although the payback method has some serious faults as a project ranking criterion, it does provide information on how long funds will be tied up in a project.

        2. A variant of the regular payback, the *discounted* payback period discounts the expected cash flows by the project's cost of capital, thus taking into account the effects of capital costs.

    B. The *net present value (NPV)* method of evaluating investment proposals is a discounted cash flow (DCF) technique that accounts for the time value of all cash flows from a project.

        1. To implement the NPV, proceed as follows: (a) Find the present value of each cash flow, discounted at the project's cost of capital, (b) sum these discounted cash flows to obtain the project's NPV, and (c) accept the project if the NPV is positive.

        2. The NPV is defined as follows:

$$\text{NPV} = \sum_{t=0}^{n} \frac{CF_t}{(1 + k)^t}.$$

        Here, CF_t is the expected net cash flow in Period t and k is the project's cost of capital. Cash outflows are treated as negative cash flows.

        3. If the NPV is positive, the project should be accepted; if negative, it should be rejected. If two projects are mutually exclusive (that is, only one can be

©1992 The Dryden Press
All rights reserved.

accepted), the one with the higher NPV should be chosen assuming that the NPV is positive. If both projects have negative NPVs, neither should be chosen.

4. Finding the NPV with a financial calculator is efficient and easy. Simply enter the different cash flows into the "cash flow register" along with the value of k = i, and then press the NPV key for the solution.

C. The *internal rate of return (IRR)* is defined as the discount rate which equates the present value of a project's expected cash inflows to the present value of its expected costs.

1. The equation for calculating the IRR is shown below:

$$\sum_{t=0}^{n} \frac{CF_t}{(1 + IRR)^t} = 0.$$

This equation has one unknown, IRR, and we can solve for the value of IRR that will make the equation equal to zero. The solution value of IRR is defined as the internal rate of return.

2. The IRR formula is simply the NPV formula solved for the particular discount rate that causes the NPV to equal zero.

3. The IRR can be found by trial and error, but most financial calculators and computers with financial analysis software can easily calculate IRRs and NPVs.

4. To find the IRR with a financial calculator, simply enter the different cash flows into the cash flow register, making sure to input the t=0 cash flow, and then press the IRR key for the solution.

D. The same basic equation is used for both the NPV and the IRR methods, but in the NPV method the discount rate, k, is specified and the NPV is found, whereas in the IRR method the NPV is specified to equal zero, and the value of IRR that forces this equality is determined.

E. A *net present value profile* is a graph which relates a project's NPV to the discount rate used to calculate its NPV.

1. The NPV profile crosses the Y-axis at the *undiscounted* NPV, while it crosses the X-axis at the IRR.

2. If two projects are *independent*, then the NPV and IRR criteria always lead to the same accept/reject decision.

3. If two *mutually exclusive* projects have NPV profiles which intersect in the upper righthand quadrant, then there may be a conflict in rankings between NPV and IRR methods. Two basic conditions can lead to conflicts between NPV and IRR:

   a. Project size (or scale) differences exist; that is, the cost of one project is larger than that of the other.

8-3

©1992 The Dryden Press
All rights reserved.

b. Timing differences exist such that cash flows from one project come in the early years and most of the cash flows from the other project come in the later years.

4. The critical issue in resolving conflicts between mutually exclusive projects is to determine how useful it is to generate cash flows earlier rather than later. Thus, the value of early cash flows depends on the rate at which we can reinvest these cash flows.

   a. The NPV method implicitly assumes that project cash flows are reinvested at the project's cost of capital.

   b. The IRR method implicitly assumes that project cash flows are reinvested at the project's IRR.

   c. The opportunity cost of a project's cash flows is the project's cost of capital. If these cash flows were not available to the firm, and if the firm needed capital to invest in new projects, then the funds would be obtained from the firm's capital suppliers; and the cost would be the overall cost of capital. Thus, the assumption of reinvestment at the cost of capital is the correct assumption, and NPV is the preferred method.

5. In summary, when projects are independent, the NPV and IRR methods both make exactly the same accept/reject decision. However, when evaluating mutually exclusive projects, especially those that differ in scale and/or timing, the NPV method should be used.

III. **Multiple IRRs can result when the IRR criterion is used with a project that has nonnormal cash flows. Nonnormal projects call for a large cash outflow either sometime during or at the end of its life. In such cases, the NPV criterion can be easily applied, and this method leads to conceptually correct capital budgeting decisions.**

IV. **Business executives often prefer to work with percentage rates of return, such as IRR, rather than dollar amounts of NPV when analyzing investments. To overcome some of the IRR's limitations a modified IRR, or MIRR, has been devised.**

A. The MIRR is defined as the discount rate which forces PV costs = PV terminal value, where terminal value (TV) is the future value of the inflows compounded at the project's cost of capital. Thus,

$$\sum_{t=0}^{n} \frac{COF_t}{(1+k)^t} = \frac{\sum_{t=0}^{n} CIF_t(1+k)^{n-t}}{(1+MIRR)^n}$$

$$PV \text{ costs} = \frac{TV}{(1+MIRR)^n}.$$

©1992 The Dryden Press
All rights reserved.

B. MIRR assumes that cash flows are reinvested at the cost of capital rather than the project's own IRR, making it a better indicator of a project's true profitability.

C. NPV and MIRR will lead to the same project selection decision if the two projects are of equal size. However, conflicts can still occur when projects differ in scale and, in this case, NPV should be used.

D. MIRR also avoids the problem of multiple IRRs, which can arise when a project is nonnormal or has negative cash flows after the project has gone into operation. NPV can be easily applied to such situations; however, MIRR can also overcome the multiple IRR problem because there is only one MIRR for any set of cash flows.

V. **In making the accept/reject decision, each of the four capital budgeting decision methods provides decision makers with a somewhat different piece of relevant information.**

A. Payback and discounted payback provide an indication of both the risk and the liquidity of a project.

B. NPV is important because it gives a direct measure of the dollar benefit (on a present value basis) of the project to the firm's shareholders, so it is regarded as the best single measure of profitability.

C. IRR also measures profitability, but expressed as a percentage rate of return, which many decision makers seem to prefer. Further, IRR contains information regarding a project's "safety margin" which is not inherent in NPV.

D. The modified IRR has all the virtues of the IRR, but it also incorporates the correct reinvestment rate assumption, and it avoids problems the IRR can have when applied to nonnormal projects.

VI. **An important aspect of the capital budgeting process is the post-audit, which involves comparing actual results with those predicted by the project's sponsors and explaining why any differences occurred. The results of the post-audit help to improve forecasts and to increase efficiency of the firm's operations.**

SELF-TEST QUESTIONS

Definitional

1. A firm's _____ _____ outlines its planned expenditures on fixed assets.

2. The most difficult step in the analysis of capital expenditure proposals involves estimating future _____ _____.

©1992 The Dryden Press
All rights reserved.

3. The number of years necessary to return the original investment in a project is known as the _____ _____.

4. The primary advantage of payback analysis is its _____.

5. One important weakness of payback analysis is the fact that _____ _____ beyond the payback period are _____.

6. The net present value (NPV) method of evaluating investment proposals is a _____ cash flow (DCF) technique.

7. A capital investment proposal should be accepted if its NPV is _____.

8. If two projects are _____ _____, the one with the _____ positive NPV should be selected.

9. In the IRR approach, a discount rate is sought which makes the NPV equal to _____.

10. A net present value profile shows the relationship between a project's _____ and the _____ _____ used to calculate the NPV.

11. If an independent project's _____ is greater than the project's cost of capital, it should be accepted.

12. If two mutually exclusive projects are being evaluated, and one project has a higher NPV while the other project has a higher IRR, the project with the higher _____ should be preferred.

13. The NPV method implicitly assumes reinvestment at the project's _____ _____ _____, while the IRR method implicitly assumes reinvestment at the _____ _____ _____ _____.

14. The MIRR method assumes reinvestment at the _____ _____ _____, making it a better indicator of a project's profitability than IRR.

15. The process of comparing a project's actual results with its projected results is known as a _____-_____.

16. The objective of the post-audit is to improve both _____ and _____.

17. The internal rate of return (IRR) is the _____ rate that equates the present value of the _____ _____ with the present value of the _____ _____.

©1992 The Dryden Press
All rights reserved.

18. The MIRR is defined as the discount rate which forces the present value of costs to equal the present value of the _____ _____.

Conceptual

19. The NPV of a project with cash flows that accrue relatively slowly is *more sensitive* to changes in the discount rate than is the NPV of a project with cash flows that come in more rapidly.

    a. True   b. False

20. The NPV method is preferred over the IRR method because the NPV method's reinvestment rate assumption is better.

    a. True   b. False

21. When you find the yield to maturity on a bond, you are finding the bond's net present value (NPV).

    a. True   b. False

22. Other things held constant, a decrease in the cost of capital (discount rate) will cause an *increase* in a project's IRR.

    a. True   b. False

23. The IRR method can be used in place of the NPV method for all independent projects.

    a. True   b. False

24. The NPV and MIRR methods lead to the same decision for mutually exclusive projects regardless of the projects' relative sizes.

    a. True   b. False

25. Nonnormal projects sometimes have multiple MIRRs.

    a. True   b. False

26. Projects A and B each have an initial cost of $5,000, followed by a series of positive cash inflows. Project A has total, undiscounted cash inflows of $12,000, while B has total undiscounted inflows of $10,000. Further, at a discount rate of 10 percent, the two projects have identical NPVs. Which project's NPV will be *more sensitive* to changes in the discount rate? (Hint: Projects with steeper NPV profiles are more sensitive to discount rate changes.)

©1992 The Dryden Press
All rights reserved.

a. Project A.
b. Project B.
c. Both projects are equally sensitive to changes in the discount rate since their NPVs are equal at all costs of capital.
d. Neither project is sensitive to changes in the discount rate, since both have NPV profiles which are horizontal.
e. The solution cannot be determined unless the timing of the cash flows is known.

27. Which of the following statements is most correct?

a. The IRR of a project whose cash flows accrue relatively rapidly is more sensitive to changes in the discount rate than is the IRR of a project whose cash flows come in more slowly.
b. There are many conditions under which a project can have more than one IRR. One such condition is where an otherwise normal project has a negative cash flow at the end of its life.
c. The phenomenon called "multiple internal rates of return" arises when two or more mutually exclusive projects which have different lives are being compared.
d. The modified IRR (MIRR) method has wide appeal to professors but most business executives prefer the NPV method to either the regular or modified IRR.
e. Each of the above statements is false.

SELF-TEST PROBLEMS

1. Your firm is considering a fast-food concession at the 1992 World's Fair. The cash flow pattern is somewhat unusual since you must build the stands, operate them for 2 years, and then tear the stands down and restore the sites to their original condition. You estimate the net cash flows to be as follows:

Time	Expected Net Cash Flow
0	($800,000)
1	700,000
2	700,000
3	(400,000)

What is the approximate IRR of this venture?

a. 5%   b. 15%   c. 25%   d. 35%   e. 45%

(The following data apply to Self-Test Problems 2 through 4.)

Toya Motors needs a new machine for production of its 1992 models. The financial vice president has appointed you to do the capital budgeting analysis. You have

©1992 The Dryden Press
All rights reserved.

identified two different machines that are capable of performing the job. You have completed the cash flow analysis, and the expected net cash flows are as follows:

	Expected Net Cash Flow	
Year	Machine B	Machine O
0	($5,000)	($5,000)
1	2,085	0
2	2,085	0
3	2,085	0
4	2,085	9,677

2. What is the payback period for Machine B?

   a. 1.0 years **b.** 2.0 years **c.** 2.4 years **d.** 2.6 years **e.** 3.0 years

3. The cost of capital is uncertain at this time, so you construct NPV profiles to assist in the final decision. The profiles for Machines B and O cross at what cost of capital?

   a. 6% **b.** 10% **c.** 18% **d.** 24%
   e. They do not cross in the upper righthand quadrant.

4. If the cost of capital for both projects is 14 percent at the time the decision is made, which project would you choose?

   a. Project B; it has the higher positive NPV.
   b. Project 0; it has the higher positive NPV.
   c. Neither; both have negative NPVs.
   d. Either; both have the same NPV.
   e. Project B; it has the higher IRR.

(The following data apply to Self-Test Problems 5 through 10.)

The director of capital budgeting for Giant Inc. has identified two mutually exclusive projects, L and S, with the following expected net cash flows:

	Expected Net Cash Flow	
Year	Project L	Project S
0	($100)	($100)
1	10	70
2	60	50
3	80	20

Both projects have a cost of capital of 10 percent.

©1992 The Dryden Press
All rights reserved.

5. What is the payback period for Project S?

   a. 1.6 years **b.** 1.8 years **c.** 2.1 years **d.** 2.5 years **e.** 2.8 years

6. What is Project L's NPV?

   a. $50.00 **b.** $34.25 **c.** $22.64 **d.** $18.79 **e.** $10.06

7. What is Project L's IRR?

   a. 18.1% **b.** 19.7% **c.** 21.4% **d.** 23.6% **e.** 24.2%

8. What is Project L's MIRR?

   a. 15.3% **b.** 16.5% **c.** 16.9% **d.** 17.1% **e.** 17.4%

9. What is Project S's MIRR?

   a. 15.3% **b.** 16.5% **c.** 16.9% **d.** 17.1% **e.** 17.4%

10. Plot the NPV profiles for the two projects. Where is the crossover point?

   a. 6.9% **b.** 7.8% **c.** 8.7% **d.** 9.6% **e.** 9.9%

11. Your company is considering two mutually exclusive projects, X and Y, whose costs and cash flows are shown below:

Year	Project X	Project Y
0	($2,000)	($2,000)
1	200	2,000
2	600	200
3	800	100
4	1,400	100

   The projects are equally risky, and their cost of capital is 10 percent. You must make a recommendation, and you must base it on the modified IRR. What is the MIRR of the better project?

   a. 11.50% **b.** 12.00% **c.** 11.70% **d.** 12.50% **e.** 13.10%

12. A company is analyzing two mutually exclusive projects, S and L, whose cash flows are shown below:

©1992 The Dryden Press
All rights reserved.

Year	Project S	Project L
0	($2,000)	($2,000)
1	1,800	0
2	500	500
3	20	800
4	20	1,600

The company's cost of capital is 9 percent, and it can get an unlimited amount of capital at that cost. What is the regular IRR (not MIRR) of the better project? (Hint: Note that the better project may or may not be the one with the higher IRR.)

a. 11.45%   **b.** 11.74%   **c.** 13.02%   **d.** 13.49%   **e.** 12.67%

ANSWERS TO SELF-TEST QUESTIONS

1. capital budget
2. cash flows
3. payback period
4. simplicity
5. cash flows; ignored
6. discounted
7. positive
8. mutually exclusive; higher
9. zero
10. NPV; discount rate
11. IRR
12. NPV
13. cost of capital; internal rate of return
14. cost of capital
15. post-audit
16. forecasts; operations
17. discount; cash inflows; cash outflows (or initial cost)
18. terminal value

19. a. The more the cash flows are spread over time, the greater is the effect of a change in discount rate. This is because the compounding process has a greater effect as the number of years increases.

20. a. Project cash flows are substitutes for outside capital. Thus, the opportunity cost of these cash flows is the firm's cost of capital, adjusted for risk. The NPV method uses this cost as the reinvestment rate, while the IRR method assumes reinvestment at the IRR.

21. b. The yield to maturity on a bond is the bond's IRR.

22. b. The computation of IRR is independent of the project's cost of capital.

23. a. Both the NPV and IRR methods lead to the same accept/reject decisions for independent projects. Thus, the IRR method can be used as a proxy for the NPV method when choosing independent projects.

24. b. NPV and MIRR may not lead to the same decision when the projects differ in scale.

©1992 The Dryden Press
All rights reserved.

25. b. Multiple IRRs occur in nonnormal projects, but there is only one MIRR for each project.

26. a. If we were to begin graphing the NPV profiles for each of these projects, we would know 2 of the points for each project. The Y-intercepts for Projects A and B would be $12,000 and $10,000, respectively, and the crossover rate would be 10 percent. Thus, from this information we can conclude that Project A's NPV profile would have the steeper slope and would be more sensitive to changes in the discount rate.

27. b. Statement a is false because the IRR is independent of the discount rate. Statement b is true; the situation identified is that of a nonnormal project, which has multiple IRRs. Statement c is false; multiple IRRs occur with nonnormal projects not with mutually exclusive projects with different lives. Statement d is false; business executives tend to prefer the IRR because it gives a measure of the project's safety margin.

SOLUTIONS TO SELF-TEST PROBLEMS

1. c. Unless you have a calculator that performs IRR calculations, the IRR must be obtained by trial and error or graphically. (The calculator solution is 25.48 percent.) Note that this project actually has multiple IRRs, with a second IRR at about -53 percent.

2. c. After Year 1, there is $5,000 - $2,085 = $2,915 remaining to pay back. After Year 2, only $2,915 - $2,085 = $830 is remaining. In Year 3, another $2,085 is collected. Assuming that the Year 3 cash flow occurs evenly over time, then payback occurs $830/$2,085 = 0.4 of the way through Year 3. Thus, the payback period is 2.4 years.

3. b. To solve graphically, construct the NPV profiles:

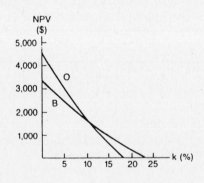

© 1992 The Dryden Press
All rights reserved.

The Y-intercept is the NPV when k = 0%. For B, 4($2,085) - $5,000 = $3,340. For O, $9,677 - $5,000 = $4,677. The X-intercept is the discount rate when NPV = $0, or the IRR. For B, $5,000 = $2,085(PVIFA$_{IRR,4}$); IRR ~ 24%. For O, $5,000 = $9,677(PVIF$_{IRR,4}$); IRR ~ 18%. The graph is an approximation since we are only using two points to plot lines that are curvilinear. However, it shows that there is a crossover point, and that it occurs somewhere in the vicinity of k = 10%. (Note that other data points for the NPV profiles could be obtained by calculating the NPVs for the two projects at different discount rates.)

Alternatively,

Year	B	O	Project Δ (B - O)
0	($5,000)	($5,000)	$ 0
1	2,085	0	2,085
2	2,085	0	2,085
3	2,085	0	2,085
4	2,085	9,677	(7,592)

The IRR of Project Δ, 10.00 percent, is the crossover point.

4. a. Refer to the NPV profiles. When k = 14%, we are to the right of the crossover point and Project B has the higher NPV. You can verify this fact by calculating the NPVs. When k = 14%, NPV$_B$ = $1,075 and NPV$_O$ = $730. Note that Project B also has the higher IRR. However, the NPV method should be used when evaluating mutually exclusive projects. Note that had the project cost of capital been 8 percent, then Project O would be chosen on the basis of the higher NPV.

5. a. After the first year, there is only $30 remaining to be repaid, and $50 is received in Year 2. Assuming an even cash flow throughout the year, the payback period is 1 + $30/$50 = 1.6 years.

6. d. NPV$_L$ = -$100 + $10/1.10 + $60/(1.10)^2 + $80/(1.10)^3 = -$100 + $9.09 + $49.59 + $60.11 = $18.79. Financial calculator solution: Input the cash flows into the cash flow register, I = k = 10, and solve for NPV = $18.78.

7. a. Input the cash flows into the cash flow register and solve for IRR = 18.1%.

8. b. $$\sum_{t=0}^{n} \frac{COF_t}{(1 + k)^t} = \frac{\sum_{t=0}^{n} CIF_t(1 + k)^{n-t}}{(1 + MIRR)^n}.$$

8-13

©1992 The Dryden Press
All rights reserved.

$$PV \text{ costs} = \frac{TV}{(1 + MIRR)^n}$$

$$\$100 = \frac{\$10(1.10)^2 + \$60(1.10)^1 + \$80(1.10)^0}{(1 + MIRR)^3}$$

$$= \frac{\$12.10 + \$66.00 + \$80.00}{(1 + MIRR)^3}$$

$$= \frac{\$158.10}{(1 + MIRR)^3}$$

$$MIRR_L = 16.50\%.$$

Alternatively, input N = 3, PV = -100, FV = 158.10, and solve for I = MIRR = 16.50%.

9. c. $$\$100 = \frac{\$70(1.10)^2 + \$50(1.10)^1 + \$20(1.10)^0}{(1 + MIRR)^3}$$

$$= \frac{\$84.70 + \$55.00 + \$20.00}{(1 + MIRR)^3}$$

$$= \frac{\$159.70}{(1 + MIRR)^3}$$

$$MIRR_S = 16.89\% \approx 16.9\%.$$

Alternatively, input N = 3, PV = -100, FV = 159.70, and solve for I = MIRR = 16.89%.

10. c. The NPV profiles plot as follows:

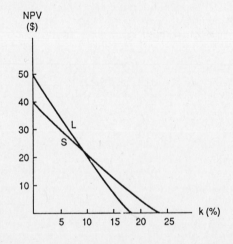

©1992 The Dryden Press
All rights reserved.

k	NPV_L	NPV_S
0%	$50	$40
5	33	29
10	19	20
15	7	12
20	(4)	5
25	(13)	(2)

By looking at the graph, the approximate crossover point is 8.7 percent.

Now to find the precise crossover point, determine the cash flows for Project Δ, which is the difference between the two projects' cash flows:

Year	L	S	Project Δ (L - S)
0	($100)	($100)	$ 0
1	10	70	(60)
2	60	50	10
3	80	20	60

The crossover point is the IRR of Project Δ, or 8.7 percent.

11. e. Project X:

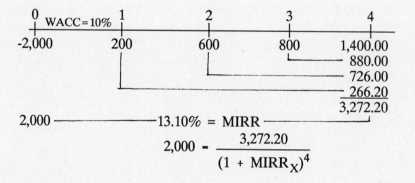

$$2,000 = \frac{3,272.20}{(1 + MIRR_X)^4}$$

Project Y:

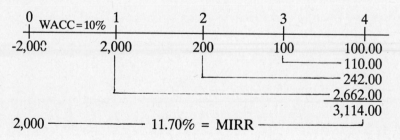

©1992 The Dryden Press
All rights reserved.

$$2{,}000 = \frac{3{,}114.00}{(1 + MIRR_Y)^4}$$

Project X has the higher MIRR; $MIRR_X = 13.10\%$.

Alternate step: You could calculate NPVs, see that X has the higher NPV, and just calculate $MIRR_X$. $NPV_X = \$234.96$ and $NPV_Y = \$126.90$.

12. b. Put the cash flows into the cash flow register, and then calculate NPV at 9% and IRR:

Project S: $NPV_S = \$101.83$; $IRR_S = 13.49\%$.

Project L: $NPV_L = \$172.07$; $IRR_L = 11.74\%$.

Because $NPV_L > NPV_S$, it is the better project. $IRR_L = 11.74\%$.

Alternatively, the PVIF table could be used to calculate the NPV; however, calculating the IRR by trial and error would be tedious.

©1992 The Dryden Press
All rights reserved.

CHAPTER 9
CASH FLOW ESTIMATION AND
OTHER TOPICS IN CAPITAL BUDGETING

OVERVIEW

One of the most critical steps in capital budgeting analysis is *cash flow estimation*. The key to correct cash flow estimation is to consider only *incremental cash flows*. However, the process is complicated by such factors as sunk costs, opportunity costs, externalities, net working capital changes, and salvage values. Cash flow estimation for replacement projects is similar to that for expansion projects, except that there are more flows to consider when analyzing replacement projects. Adjustments to the analysis must be made for projects with unequal lives as well as for the effects of inflation.

OUTLINE

I. **The most important, and also the most difficult, step in the analysis of a capital project is estimating its cash flows. Two key concepts in the process are important to recognize: (1) capital decisions must be based on cash flows, not accounting income, and (2) only incremental cash flows are relevant to the accept/reject decision.**

   A. In capital budgeting analysis, *annual cash flows, not accounting profits,* are used. While accounting profits are important for some purposes, determining the net cash flow (net income plus depreciation) is the most relevant for capital budgeting purposes.

   B. In evaluating a capital project, we are concerned only with those cash flows that result directly from the project. These *incremental cash flows* represent the changes in the firm's total cash flows that occur as a direct result of accepting or rejecting the project. Four special problems in determining incremental cash flows follow:
   1. A *sunk cost* is an outlay that has already occurred or has been committed and hence is not affected by the accept/reject decision. Sunk costs are not incremental, and hence should not be included in the analysis.
   2. *Opportunity costs*, which are cash flows that can be generated from assets the firm already owns provided they are not used for the project in question, must be included in the analysis.
   3. *Externalities* are the effects of a project on other parts of the firm, and their effects need to be considered in the incremental cash flows.
   4. *Shipping and installation costs* must be taken into account since it is part of the full cost of the equipment and is included in the depreciable basis when depreciation charges are calculated.

©1992 The Dryden Press
All rights reserved.

II. **Two types of capital budgeting decisions are (1) expansion project analysis and (2) replacement project analysis.**

    A.   An expansion project is one that calls for the firm to invest in new facilities to increase sales. Steps in the capital budgeting analysis for the project include:

        1.   Summarize the investment outlays required for the project. Changes in net working capital should be included as an outflow here; however, they should be considered as an inflow at the end of the project.

        2.   Estimate the cash flows that will occur once production begins, including effects of depreciation and salvage values.

        3.   Summarize the data by combining all the net cash flows on a time line and evaluate the project by payback period, IRR, MIRR, and NPV (at the appropriate cost of capital). If the project has a positive NPV, the project should be accepted.

        4.   The cost of capital may need to be increased if the project is deemed riskier than the firm's average project.

    B.   Replacement decision analysis is different from that for expansion projects because the cash flows from the old asset must be considered.

        1.   The following additional cash flows must be considered at time 0:

            a. The cash received from the sale of the old equipment is an inflow.

            b. However, the sale of the old machine will usually have tax effects. If the old equipment is sold below book value, there will be a tax savings; if the equipment is sold at a profit, taxes must be paid. The tax effect is equal to the loss or gain on the sale times the firm's marginal tax rate.

        2.   The cash flow from operations calculation must also be modified.

            a. First, look at the effects of the new equipment on revenues and costs. An incremental increase in revenues would produce a cash inflow, while an incremental increase in costs would produce a cash outflow, just as before. After combining the revenue and cost effects into a single incremental cash inflow, multiply by $(1 - T)$ to obtain the after-tax cash inflow.

            b. The depreciation expense on the old equipment must be subtracted from the depreciation expense on the new equipment to get the net change in depreciation. This amount is then multiplied by the tax rate to find the tax savings or loss from the change in depreciation.

            c. Any salvage value on the old machine, including tax effects, must be included as a cash outflow at the end of the project's life. Accepting the new project causes the firm to forgo the old machine's salvage value. Thus, it must be included as an opportunity cost. Of course, any salvage value on the new machine must also be included in the analysis.

III. **If two mutually exclusive projects have significantly different lives, the analysis must include an adjustment. Two procedures have been developed to deal with this problem: (1) the replacement chain method and (2) the equivalent annual annuity method.**

©1992 The Dryden Press
All rights reserved.

A. The replacement chain method extends one, or both, projects until an equal life is achieved.

   1. Suppose two mutually exclusive projects are being considered: Project A with a 2-year life, and Project B with a 3-year life. The projects' lives would be extended to a 6-year common life.

   2. Project A would have an extended NPV equal to NPV_A plus NPV_A discounted for 2 years at the project's cost of capital, plus NPV_A discounted for 4 years at the project's cost of capital. Project B would have an extended NPV equal to NPV_B plus NPV_B discounted for 3 years at the project's cost of capital.

   3. The project with the highest adjusted NPV would be chosen.

   4. This method assumes that the project can be repeated and that there is no change in cash flows.

B. Another way to deal with unequal lives is the equivalent annual annuity (EAA) method.

   1. First, find each project's NPV over its original life. Then find the constant annuity cash flow that has the same present value.

      a. This can be done by dividing the original NPV of each project by the PVIFA for the project's original life and cost of capital to find the equivalent annual annuity.

      b. With a financial calculator, enter N, I, and PV to solve for PMT.

   2. Assuming infinite replacement, the EAAs will continue on out to infinity; that is, they are perpetuities. Find the infinite horizon NPV of each project by dividing each EAA by the cost of capital.

   3. The project with the higher infinite horizon NPV would be chosen.

C. As a general rule, the unequal life issue does not arise for independent projects. Also, common life techniques can only be applied when the shorter-life project is actually expected to be replicated.

IV. Inflationary effects need to be recognized in capital budgeting decisions.

A. Inflationary expectations are built into interest rates and money costs (through the inflation premium). It is reflected in the WACC, which is used to find NPVs, and in the hurdle rate, if the IRR (or MIRR) method is used. The higher the inflation rate, the higher the k (or WACC), and the smaller will be the NPV.

B. If expected inflation is not built into the forecasted cash flows, then the calculated NPV will be incorrect; that is, it will be downwardly biased. Adjusting forecasted cash flows for inflation will produce an unbiased NPV.

V. Appendix 9A reviews depreciation concepts covered in accounting courses. The MACRS classes and asset lives are given, as well as the recovery allowance percentages for 3-year, 5-year, 7-year, and 10-year class personal property.

9-3

© 1992 The Dryden Press
All rights reserved.

SELF-TEST QUESTIONS

Definitional

1. An increase in net working capital would show up as a cash _____ at time 0 and then again as a cash _____ at the _____ of the project's life.

2. A _____ is a cash outlay which has already occurred or has been committed.

3. In general, a project's operating cash flow in any year is equal to the project's _____ _____ plus its _____ expense.

4. In replacement analysis, two cash flows that occur at t=0 that are not present in expansion projects are the price received from the sale of the _____ equipment and the _____ effects of the sale.

5. In replacement analysis, the depreciation tax savings or loss is based on the _____ in depreciation expense between the old and new asset.

6. An _____ cash flow represents the change in the firm's total cash flow that occurs as a direct result of project acceptance.

7. If two projects are _____, the fact that they have unequal lives will not affect the analysis.

8. If two mutually exclusive projects have unequal lives, either the _____ _____ or the _____ _____ _____ method may be used for the analysis.

9. If the cash flows are real, but the cost of capital is nominal, there will be a _____ bias to the calculated NPV.

10. Riskier projects should be evaluated with a higher _____ ____ _____ than average-risk projects.

Conceptual

11. In general, the value of land currently owned by a firm is irrelevant to a capital budgeting decision because the cost of that property is a sunk cost.

    a. True   b. False

12. McDonald's is planning to open a new store across from the student union. Annual revenues are expected to be $5 million. However, opening the new location will cause annual revenues to drop by $3 million at McDonald's existing stadium location. The relevant sales revenues for the capital budgeting analysis are $2 million per year.

©1992 The Dryden Press
All rights reserved.

a. True   **b.** False

13. In a replacement decision, the salvage value of the old asset need not be considered since the current market value of the asset is included in the analysis.

a. True   **b.** False

14. The equivalent annual annuity (EAA) for a project is determined by dividing the project's original NPV by

   a. The PVIF for the project's original life and cost of capital.
   b. The cost of the project.
   c. The cost of capital.
   d. The PVIFA for the project's original life and cost of capital.
   e. The number of years of the project's life.

15. Two corporations are formed. They are identical in all respects except for their methods of depreciation. Firm A uses MACRS depreciation, while Firm B uses the straight line method. Both plan to depreciate their assets for tax purposes over a 5-year life (6 calendar years), which is equal to the useful life, and both pay a 34 percent tax rate. (Note: The half-year convention will apply, so the firm using the straight line method will take 10 percent depreciation in Year 1 and 10 percent in Year 6.) Which of the following statements is *false*?

   a. Firm A will generate higher cash flows from operations in the first year than B.
   b. Firm A will pay more Federal corporate income taxes in the first year than B.
   c. If there is no change in tax rates over the 6-year period, and if we disregard the time value of money, the total amount of funds generated from operations by these projects for each corporation will be the same over the 6 years.
   d. Firm B will pay the same amount of federal corporate income taxes, over the 6-year period, as A.
   e. Firm A could, if it chose to, use straight line depreciation for stockholder reporting even if it used MACRS for tax purposes.

SELF-TEST PROBLEMS

1. The capital budgeting director of National Products Inc. is evaluating a new project that would decrease operating costs by $30,000 per year without affecting revenues. The project's cost is $50,000. The project will be depreciated using the MACRS method over its 3-year class life. It will have a *zero salvage value* after 3 years. The marginal tax rate of National Products is 34 percent, and the project's cost of capital is 12 percent. What is the project's NPV?

   a. $7,068   **b.** $8,324   **c.** $10,214   **d.** $11,326   **e.** $12,387

9-5

©1992 The Dryden Press
All rights reserved.

2. Your firm has a marginal tax rate of 40 percent and a cost of capital of 14 percent. You are performing a capital budgeting analysis on a new project that will cost $500,000. The project is expected to have a useful life of 10 years, although its MACRS class life is only 5 years. The project is expected to increase the firm's net income by $61,257 per year and to have a salvage value of $35,000 at the end of 10 years. What is the project's NPV?

   a. $95,356   b. $108,359   c. $135,256   d. $162,185   e. $177,902

3. The Board of Directors of National Brewing Inc. is considering the acquisition of a new still. The still is priced at $600,000 but would require $60,000 in transportation costs and $40,000 for installation. The still has a useful life of 10 years but will be depreciated over its 5-year MACRS life. It is expected to have a salvage value of $10,000 at the end of 10 years. The still would increase revenues by $120,000 per year and increase yearly operating costs by $20,000 per year. Additionally, the still would require a $30,000 increase in net working capital. The firm's marginal tax rate is 40 percent, and the project's cost of capital is 10 percent. What is the NPV of the still?

   a. $18,430   b. -$12,352   c. -$65,204   d. -$130,961   e. -$203,450

(The following data apply to Self-Test Problems 4 through 6.)

As the capital budgeting director of Union Mills Inc. you are analyzing the replacement of an automated loom system. The old system was purchased 5 years ago for $200,000; it falls into the MACRS 5-year class; and it has 5 years of remaining life and a $50,000 salvage value five years from now. The current market value of the old system is $100,000. The new system has a price of $300,000, plus an additional $50,000 in installation costs. The new system falls into the MACRS 5-year class, has a 5-year economic life, and a $100,000 salvage value. The new system will require a $40,000 increase in the spare parts inventory. The primary advantage of the new system is that it will decrease operating costs by $40,000 per year. Union Mills has a 12 percent cost of capital and a marginal tax rate of 34 percent.

4. What is the net cash investment at Year 0?

   a. $350,000   b. $319,920   c. $295,000   d. $40,000   e. $23,200

5. What is the annual net operating cash inflow in Year 1?

   a. $46,120   b. $43,950   c. $39,825   d. $33,350   e. $50,200

6. What is the net cash flow in the final year (Year 5)?

   a. $31,360   b. $43,060   c. $119,630   d. $121,930   e. $117,200

©1992 The Dryden Press
All rights reserved.

Buckeye Foundries builds railroad cars and then leases them to railroads and shippers. The company has some old boxcars which it plans to convert into specialized carriers. Its analysts foresee demand in two areas—cars to carry coal and cars to carry livestock. Each type of car will cost $50,000 per car to convert. Because of the greater weight they will carry, the coal cars will last only 10 years but will provide an after-tax cash flow of $9,500 per year. The livestock cars will last for 15 years, and their annual after-tax cash flow is estimated at $8,140. Buckeye's cost of capital is 10 percent. At the end of each car's original life, it can be rebuilt into "like new" condition at a cost expected to equal the original conversion cost. Also, since Buckeye has only a limited number of cars to convert, regard the two types of cars as being mutually exclusive.

7. Using the replacement chain method of evaluation, find the adjusted NPV for each alternative.

   a. $8,373; $11,913   **b.** $8,373; $14,765   **c.** $8,373; $16,212
   d. $12,846; $11,913   **e.** $12,846; $14,765

8. Which alternative should be taken according to the equivalent annual annuity method?

   a. Livestock cars, since they have an infinite horizon NPV of $11,913
   b. Livestock cars, since they have an infinite horizon NPV of $8,373.
   c. Livestock cars, since their infinite horizon NPV is $2,030 greater than the infinite horizon NPV of coal cars.
   d. Coal cars, since their infinite horizon NPV is $13,630.
   e. Coal cars, since their EAA is $1,363.

9. Central City Electric is considering two alternative ways to meet demand: It can build a coal-fired plant (Project C) at a cost of $1,000 million. This plant would have a 20-year life and would provide net cash flows of $120 million per year over its life. Alternatively, the company can build a gas-fired plant (Project G) that would cost $400 million and would produce net cash flows of $68 million per year for 10 years, after which the plant would have to be replaced. The power will be needed for exactly 20 years; the cost of capital for either plant is 10 percent; and inflation and productivity gains are expected to offset one another so as to leave expected costs and cash flows constant over time. What is the NPV of the better project, that is, how much (in millions) will the better project add to Central City's total value?

   a. $17.83   **b.** $21.63   **c.** $20.03   **d.** $24.70   **e.** $19.57

©1992 The Dryden Press
All rights reserved.

ANSWERS TO SELF-TEST QUESTIONS

1. outflow; inflow; end
2. sunk cost
3. net income; depreciation
4. old; tax
5. difference
6. incremental
7. independent
8. replacement chain; equivalent annual annuity
9. downward
10. cost of capital

11. b. The net market value of land currently owned is an opportunity cost of the project. If the project is not undertaken, the land could be sold to realize its current market value less any taxes and expenses. Thus, project acceptance means forgoing this cash inflow.

12. a. Incremental revenues, which are relevant in a capital budgeting decision, must consider the effects on other parts of the firm.

13. b. In an incremental analysis, the cash flows assuming replacement are compared with the cash flows assuming the old asset is retained. If the old asset is retained, it will produce a salvage value cash flow which must be included, with tax effects, in the replacement analysis.

14. d. The EAA is the annual constant cash flow which, over the project's original life, produces the project's original NPV. Thus, the divisor is the PVIFA.

15. b. Statement a is true; MACRS is an accelerated depreciation method, so Firm A will have a higher depreciation expense than Firm B. We are also given that both firms are identical except for depreciation methods used. Net cash flow is equal to net income plus depreciation. In Year 1, Firm A's depreciation expense is twice as great as Firm B's; however, Firm A's lower net income is more than compensated for by the addition of depreciation (which is twice as high as Firm B's). Thus, in Year 1, Firm A's net cash flow is greater than Firm B's. Statement b is false; because Firm A's depreciation expense is larger, it's earnings before taxes will be lower, and thus it will pay less income taxes than Firm B. Statements c, d, and e are all true.

SOLUTIONS TO SELF-TEST PROBLEMS

1. d. The only cash outflow is the $50,000 cost of the project. Cash inflows consist of the reduction in operating costs, equal to $30,000(0.66) = $19,800 on an after-tax basis, and depreciation. The value of the depreciation cash flows generated by the project is the amount of tax savings. After-tax depreciation cash flows are found by multiplying the depreciable basis, $50,000, by the recovery percentages in each year, and then multiplying this product by the tax rate. The allowances in each year are 0.33,

©1992 The Dryden Press
All rights reserved.

0.45, and 0.15 percent, respectively, and the depreciation tax savings in each year are as follows:

$Dep_1 = \$50,000(0.33)(0.34) = \$5,610.$
$Dep_2 = \$50,000(0.45)(0.34) = \$7,650.$
$Dep_3 = \$50,000(0.15)(0.34) = \$2,550.$

The project's cash flows are placed on a time line as follows:

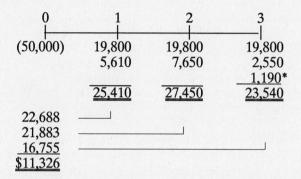

*Salvage value tax savings. National has taken $16,500 + $22,500 + $7,500 = $46,500 in total depreciation, and hence the book value at the end of the Year 3 is $50,000 - $46,500 = $3,500. Since the salvage value is $0, National can reduce its taxable income by $3,500, producing a 0.34($3,500) = $1,190 tax savings.

Alternatively, input the cash flows into the cash flow register, input I = 12, and then solve for NPV = $11,326.

2. e. In this case, the *net income* of the project is $61,257. Net cash flow = Net income + Depreciation = $61,257 + Depreciation. The depreciation allowed in each year is calculated as follows:

$Dep_1 = \$500,000(0.20) = \$100,000.$
$Dep_2 = \$500,000(0.32) = \$160,000.$
$Dep_3 = \$500,000(0.19) = \$95,000.$
$Dep_4 = \$500,000(0.12) = \$60,000.$
$Dep_5 = \$500,000(0.11) = \$55,000.$
$Dep_6 = \$500,000(0.06) = \$30,000.$
$Dep_{7\text{-}10} = \$0.$

In the final year (Year 10), the firm receives $35,000 from the sale of the machine. However, the book value of the machine is $0. Thus, the firm would have to pay 0.4($35,000) = $14,000 in taxes; and the net salvage value is $35,000 - $14,000 = $21,000. The time line is as follows:

©1992 The Dryden Press
All rights reserved.

0	1	2	3	4	5	6	7	8	9	10
(500,000)	61,257	61,257	61,257	61,257	61,257	61,257	61,257	61,257	61,257	61,257
	100,000	160,000	95,000	60,000	55,000	30,000				21,000
(500,000)	161,257	221,257	156,257	121,257	116,257	91,257	61,257	61,257	61,257	82,257

The project's NPV can be found by discounting each of the cash flows at the firm's 14 percent cost of capital. The project's NPV, found by using a financial calculator, is $177,902.

3. d. The initial net investment is $730,000:

Price	($600,000)
Transportation	(60,000)
Installation	(40,000)
Change in net working capital	(30,000)
Initial net investment	($730,000)

The annual net cash flows are equal to the net after-tax increase in revenues, 0.6($120,000 - $20,000) = $60,000, plus the depreciation tax savings. In Year 10, the firm will recover its investment in net working capital and gain the net salvage value. The depreciable basis is $700,000, thus, the annual depreciation tax savings is calculated as follows:

Dep_1 = $700,000(0.20)(0.4) = $56,000.
Dep_2 = $700,000(0.32)(0.4) = $89,600.
Dep_3 = $700,000(0.19)(0.4) = $53,200.
Dep_4 = $700,000(0.12)(0.4) = $33,600.
Dep_5 = $700,000(0.11)(0.4) = $30,800.
Dep_6 = $700,000(0.06)(0.4) = $16,800.
Dep_{7-10} = $0.

The net salvage value is $10,000(0.6) = $6,000. Therefore, the time line is as follows:

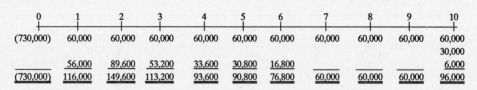

0	1	2	3	4	5	6	7	8	9	10
(730,000)	60,000	60,000	60,000	60,000	60,000	60,000	60,000	60,000	60,000	60,000
										30,000
	56,000	89,600	53,200	33,600	30,800	16,800				6,000
(730,000)	116,000	149,600	113,200	93,600	90,800	76,800	60,000	60,000	60,000	96,000

The project's NPV using a 10 percent cost of capital is -$130,961.

9-10

©1992 The Dryden Press
All rights reserved.

4. b.

Price of new machine	($300,000)
Installation	(50,000)
Sale of old machine	+100,000
Tax on sale*	(29,920)
Increase in net working capital	(40,000)
	($319,920)

*The old machine has been depreciated down to $12,000, since it falls into the MACRS 5-year class and it has been in operation for 5 years. Now, the old machine has a market value of $100,000. The $88,000 (purchase price minus book value) is treated as ordinary income and is taxed at 34 percent. Thus, Union Mills must pay a tax of 0.34($88,000) = $29,920 on the sale of the old asset.

5. a. The after-tax revenue/cost component is 0.66($40,000) = $26,400. As for the tax savings due to depreciation, the depreciable basis for the new machine is $350,000. Further, the MACRS depreciation allowance for Year 1 of a 5-year class asset is 20 percent. Thus, the depreciation expense on the new machine is 0.20($350,000) = $70,000. The old machine has not been fully depreciated, so its depreciation expense in Year 1 is $12,000, and the change in depreciation due to the replacement decision is an increase of $58,000. The tax savings is 0.34($58,000) = $19,720. Therefore, the Year 1 net cash flow from operations is $26,400 + $19,720 = $46,120.

6. c. In the final year, Year 5, the net cash flow is composed of 0.66($40,000) = $26,400 in after-tax cost decrease and 0.34(0.11)($350,000) = $13,090 in depreciation tax savings, for a total of $39,490, plus the applicable nonoperating cash flows. Thus, we have the following:

From operations	$ 39,490
Salvage value of new machine	100,000
Tax on new machine salvage value	(26,860)
Salvage value of old machine	(50,000)
Tax on old machine salvage value	17,000
Change in working capital	40,000
Net cash flow	$119,630

Note that the salvage value of the old machine is a cash outflow. This is an opportunity cost, since buying the new machine deprives Union Mills of the salvage value of the old machine. Additionally, salvage tax effects must be considered. Also note that the change in working capital considered at t = 0, an outflow, is exactly offset by an inflow at the end of the project. This is because it is assumed that the project will terminate and the increase in working capital is no longer required.

7. e. First, find each car's original NPV as follows:

©1992 The Dryden Press
All rights reserved.

$\text{NPV}_C = \$9,500(\text{PVIFA}_{10\%,10}) - \$50,000 = \$8,373.$

$\text{NPV}_L = \$8,140(\text{PVIFA}_{10\%,15}) - \$50,000 = \$11,913.$

Now look at the projects at a common life of 30 years:

Adjusted $\text{NPV}_C = \$8,373 + \$8,373(\text{PVIF}_{10\%,10}) + \$8,373(\text{PVIF}_{10\%,20}) = \$12,846.$

Adjusted $\text{NPV}_L = \$11,913 + \$11,913(\text{PVIF}_{10\%,15}) = \$14,765.$

Alternatively, once you've found the original NPV of each car, then the replication of the cars can be shown on the time line.

Coal:

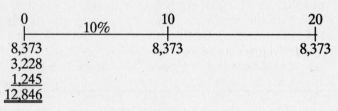

Livestock:

```
        0                    15                    30
        |         10%         |                     |
      11,913               11,913
       2,852
      14,765
```

8. c. The original NPVs were calculated above. Now:

$\text{EAA}_C = \$8,373/\text{PVIFA}_{10\%,10} = \$8,373/6.1446 = \$1,363.$ Alternatively, input N = 10, I = 10, PV = -8,373, and solve for PMT = $1,363.

$\text{EAA}_L = \$11,913/\text{PVIFA}_{10\%,15} = \$11,913/7.6061 = \$1,566.$ Alternatively, input N = 15, I = 10, PV = -11,913, and solve for PMT = $1,566.

Thus, the infinite horizon NPVs are as follows:

Infinite horizon $\text{NPV}_C = \$1,363/0.10 = \$13,630.$

Infinite horizon $\text{NPV}_L = \$1,566/0.10 = \$15,660.$

The difference is $15,660 - $13,630 = $2,030.

©1992 The Dryden Press
All rights reserved.

9. d. Project C:

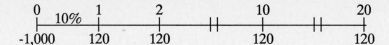

With a financial calculator, input the cash flows into the cash flow register, input I = 10, and then solve for NPV = $21.63 million.

Project G:

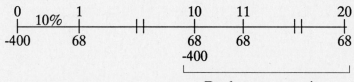

Replacement project

With a financial calculator input the cash flows for the first replication of the project into the cash flow register, input I = 10, and then solve for NPV = $17.83 million. However, this NPV must be adjusted for a 20-year common life. The NPV for the next replication can be calculated by inputting N = 10, I = 10, FV = 17.83, and then solving for NPV = $6.87. Thus, the extended NPV for Project G = $17.83 + $6.87 = $24.70 million:

$$\text{Extended NPV}_G = \$17.83 + (\text{PVIF}_{10\%,10})\$17.83$$

$$= \$17.83 + \$6.87 = \$24.70 \text{ million.}$$

©1992 The Dryden Press
All rights reserved.

CHAPTER 10
RISK ANALYSIS AND
THE OPTIMAL CAPITAL BUDGET

OVERVIEW

The analysis of project risk focuses on three issues: (1) the effect of a project on the firm's beta coefficient (market risk), (2) the project's effect on the probability of bankruptcy (corporate risk), and (3) the risk of the project independent of both the firm's other projects and investors' diversification (stand-alone risk). Market risk directly affects the value of the firm's stock. Corporate risk affects the financial strength of the firm, and this, in turn, influences its ability to use debt, and to maintain smooth operations over time. Stand-alone risk is measured by the variability of a project's expected returns. Techniques for measuring stand-alone risk include sensitivity analysis, scenario analysis, and Monte Carlo simulation.

Up to this point, the focus has been on how the cost of capital is used in project evaluations. However, capital budgeting and the cost of capital are interrelated. The optimal capital budget is determined by looking at both the cost of capital and the capital budget simultaneously.

OUTLINE

I.   **Three separate and distinct types of risk can be identified in capital budgeting: (1) stand-alone risk, (2) corporate (within-firm) risk, and (3) market (beta) risk.**

    A. Stand-alone risk is the risk an asset would have if it were a firm's only asset. It is measured by the variability of the asset's expected returns.

    B. Corporate risk is that risk which does not consider the effects of stockholders' diversification. It is measured by a project's effect on the firm's earnings variability.

    C. Market risk is that part of a project's risk that cannot be eliminated by diversification. It is measured by the project's beta coefficient.

II. **Stand-alone risk is by far the easiest to measure and may be done so in a number of ways. Because all three types of risk are usually highly correlated, stand-alone risk is generally a good proxy for hard-to-measure corporate and market risk. Three techniques for assessing a project's stand-alone risk are: (1) sensitivity analysis, (2) scenario analysis, and (3) Monte Carlo simulation.**

    A. *Sensitivity analysis* is a technique which indicates exactly how much a project's NPV will change in response to a given change in an input variable, other things held constant.

©1992 The Dryden Press
All rights reserved.

1. The analysis begins with expected values for unit sales, sales price, fixed costs, and variable costs to give an expected, or *base case*, NPV. A series of "what if" questions may then be asked to find the change in NPV, given a change in one of the input variables.
2. Each variable is changed by several specific percentage points above and below the expected value, holding other things constant. The resulting set of NPVs is plotted against the variable that was changed.
3. The steeper the slope, the more sensitive NPV is to changes in each of the inputs.
4. When comparing two projects, the one with the steeper sensitivity lines would be regarded as riskier, because for that project a relatively small error in estimating the input variable would produce a large error in the project's expected NPV.

B. *Scenario analysis* provides a more complete analysis, because in addition to the sensitivity of NPV to changes in key variables, it considers the range of likely values of these variables.
1. Worst case and best case scenarios are estimated and the input values from these scenarios are used to find the worst case NPV and the best case NPV.
2. Probabilities can be assigned to the best, worst, and base case NPVs to obtain the expected NPV.
3. The project's coefficient of variation can be compared to the coefficient of variation of the firm's "average" project to determine the relative stand-alone riskiness of the project.

C. *Monte Carlo simulation*, which ties together sensitivities and input variable probability distributions, requires a computer along with an efficient financial planning software package.
1. The computer repeatedly selects a random value for each uncertain variable based on its specified probability distribution, along with values for fixed factors. The end result is a continuous NPV probability distribution.
2. A simulation is more comprehensive than scenario analysis because it considers an infinite number of possible outcomes.

III. **Market (beta) risk measures risk from the standpoint of an equity investor holding a highly diversified portfolio.**

A. *Beta analysis* can be used to determine the appropriate project cost of capital.
1. The required rate of return on equity, k_s, is equal to the risk-free rate of return, k_{RF}, plus a risk premium equal to the market risk premium, $k_M - k_{RF}$, times the firm's beta coefficient, b:

$$k_s = k_{RF} + (k_M - k_{RF})b.$$

2. For example, if a firm has a beta of 1.1, $k_M = 12\%$, and $k_{RF} = 8\%$, then its required rate of return would be $k_s = 8\% + (12\% - 8\%)1.1 = 12.4\%$. Stock-

©1992 The Dryden Press
All rights reserved.

holders would be willing to let the firm invest their money if the firm could earn 12.4 percent on their equity capital.

3. Average-risk projects for this firm should be evaluated using a 12.4 percent cost of capital as the discount rate in the NPV method or as the hurdle rate in the IRR and MIRR methods.

B. The acceptance of a particular capital budgeting project may cause a firm's overall beta to rise or fall, causing a change in the required rate of return.

1. The impact of any one project on a firm's beta will depend upon the size of the project relative to its existing "portfolio" of projects.

2. The beta of a portfolio of assets is equal to the weighted average of the betas of the individual assets.

3. Holding other factors constant, an increase in a firm's beta coefficient will clearly result in a higher required return, k_s, and hence a decrease in price. To maintain a given price, there must be an *increase* in the expected rate of growth, dividends, or both. These factors, in turn, will result in an increase in the expected return. Therefore, an increase in the firm's beta coefficient will cause the stock price to decline unless the increased beta is offset by a higher expected rate of return.

4. A project with a high degree of corporate risk will not necessarily affect the firm's market risk to any great extent.

C. If the beta coefficient for each project can be determined, then individual projects' costs of equity capital can be found as follows:

$$k_{s(Project)} = k_{RF} + (k_M - k_{RF})b_{Project}.$$

High beta, or high-risk, projects will have a relatively high cost of equity capital, while low beta projects will have a correspondingly low cost of capital.

IV. **The estimation of project betas is even more difficult than that for stocks. However, two approaches have been developed for this purpose: the pure play method and the accounting beta method.**

A. In the *pure play method*, the company tries to find several single-product companies in the same line of business as the project being evaluated, and it then applies these betas to determine the cost of capital for its own product.

B. In the *accounting beta method*, a project's (or perhaps a division's) return on assets (ROA) is regressed against the average ROA of a large sample of firms, say the S&P 400. The resulting accounting beta is then used as a proxy for the market beta.

V. **Most firms use risk-adjusted discount rates to incorporate differential project risk in the capital budgeting process.**

©1992 The Dryden Press
All rights reserved.

A. A firm's cost of capital may be estimated with a fair degree of accuracy.

B. Increasing the discount rate for high-risk projects and lowering it for low-risk projects is a somewhat arbitrary and judgmental process, but it does force managers to at least consider a project's riskiness.

C. Diversified companies with divisions of varying risk may use a two-step process to determine a project's risk-adjusted discount rate.
   1. First, divisional costs of capital are established for each of the major operating divisions.
   2. Then, within the division, projects classified as high-risk would have an increased discount rate while low-risk projects would have a lowered discount rate.

VI. **Both the firm's investment opportunity schedule (IOS) and its marginal cost of capital (MCC) schedule are important elements in determining the optimal capital budget. The IOS is a plot of the firm's potential projects in descending order of IRR. The MCC is a plot of the firm's weighted average cost of capital.**

A. The optimal capital budget, along with the firm's marginal cost of capital, is found by combining the IOS and MCC schedules. The intersection of the IOS and MCC schedules defines the firm's marginal cost of capital.
   1. All projects that have "average" risk should be evaluated at this cost of capital. Note that for independent projects, the IRR method can be used as a proxy for the NPV method since both lead to the same accept/reject decision. Thus, all projects of average risk with IRRs exceeding the firm's marginal cost of capital should be accepted.
   2. However, for mutually exclusive projects, the NPV method should be used, and the appropriate discount rate for average-risk projects is the firm's marginal cost of capital.

B. The procedures set forth above are conceptually correct; however, most companies actually use a more judgmental, less quantitative process for establishing its final capital budget.
   1. A reasonably good estimate of the MCC is obtained from the treasurer, and the director of capital budgeting can get a "good fix" on the IOS schedule.
   2. The IOS and MCC schedules are combined to get a reasonably good approximation of the corporation's marginal cost of capital.
   3. The corporate MCC is scaled up or down to reflect each division's target capital structure and riskiness.
   4. Each project within each division is classified into one of three risk groups: high, low, or average risk.
   5. Each project's NPV is then determined, using its risk-adjusted project cost of capital. The optimal capital budget consists of all independent projects with positive risk-adjusted NPVs plus those mutually exclusive projects with the highest positive risk-adjusted NPVs.

© 1992 The Dryden Press
All rights reserved.

VII. Appendix 10A discusses capital rationing, which occurs when firms set an absolute limit on the size of their capital budgets such that the size of the budget is less than the level of investment called for by the NPV or IRR criterion.

SELF-TEST QUESTIONS

Definitional

1. The _____ *greater* _____ the risk associated with an investment, the greater the _____ _____ *required* _____ *return* _____ needed to compensate investors.

2. Three types of separate risk have been identified in capital budgeting decisions: market risk, _____ *stand* -, *alone* _____ risk, and _____ *corporate* _____ risk.

3. The required rate of return on a company's stock is equal to the _____ *stand* - *alone* rate plus a _____ for risk.

4. The risk premium on a stock is equal to the stock's _____ *b* _____ times the market risk premium.

5. An increase in the overall beta coefficient will cause the firm's stock price to _____ unless this increase is offset by a _____ expected rate of return.

6. Measuring corporate risk involves determining the uncertainty of a project's _____ _____.

7. Cash flow estimates are really _____ _____ taken from _____ distributions.

8. A commonly used method of risk analysis is based on constructing optimistic, pessimistic, and expected value estimates for the key variables. This method is called _____ _____.

9. In project analysis, changing one key variable at a time and determining the effect on its NPV is known as _____ *sensitivity* _____ *analysis* _____.

10. One purpose of sensitivity analysis is to determine which of the _____ *variables* _____ have the greatest influence on the project's NPV.

11. A project with a high degree of corporate risk will not necessarily affect the firm's _____ to any great extent.

12. Unless the cash flows are negative, riskier projects should be evaluated with a higher _____ *cost* *of* *capital* _____ than average-risk projects.

13. The _____ *Investment* *Opportunity* *Schedule* _____ is a plot of the firm's proposed projects, ranked in descending order of IRR, versus the dollars of new capital required.

10-5

©1992 The Dryden Press
All rights reserved.

14. The marginal cost of capital schedule is a plot of the firm's _____ _____ _____ _____ _____ versus the dollars of new capital raised.

15. The firm's _____ _____ _____ _____ is defined by the intersection of the MCC and IOS schedules.

16. All projects of _____ risk should be evaluated at the firm's marginal cost of capital.

17. In general, projects can be evaluated using the IRR method; however, _____ _____ projects must be evaluated by the NPV method.

18. _____ _____ occurs when firms set an absolute limit on the dollar amount of investment capital.

Conceptual

19. Even if the beta of a project being considered has a value of zero, acceptance of the project will affect the market risk of the firm.

    a. True   b. False

20. When independent projects of different risk are to be considered in capital budgeting, any project will be acceptable to the firm if the project's IRR is greater than the firm's weighted average cost of capital.

    a. True   b. False

21. If a cash *outflow* is judged to be riskier than average, then the firm's marginal cost of capital must be adjusted *downward* to reflect this differential.

    a. True   b. False

22. In capital budgeting decisions, corporate risk will be of least interest to:

    a. Employees.   b. Stockholders with few shares.
    c. Institutional investors.   d. Creditors.
    e. The local community.

23. Which of the following steps are commonly used in practice to establish a firm's optimal capital budget?

    a. Rough estimates of the MCC and IOS schedules are used to obtain the firm's MCC.
    b. The corporate MCC is scaled up or down to reflect each division's capital structure and risk characteristics.
    c. Each division's MCC is scaled up or down to reflect differential project risk.

©1992 The Dryden Press
All rights reserved.

d. Each project's NPV is then determined using its appropriate risk-adjusted cost of capital.

e. All the above steps are used.

24. The Pennsylvania Company is evaluating two mutually exclusive pollution control processes. Since the company's revenue stream will not be affected by the choice of control process, the projects are being evaluated by finding the PV of each set of costs. The firm's cost of capital is 10 percent, and it adds or subtracts 2 percentage points to adjust for project risk differences. Process A is judged to be a high-risk project—it might end up costing much more to operate than is expected. Process A's risk-adjusted cost of capital is

   a. 8 percent; this might seem illogical at first, but it correctly adjusts for risk where outflows, rather than inflows, are being discounted.

   b. 10 percent; the firm's cost of capital should not be adjusted when evaluating outflow only projects.

   c. 12 percent; since A is more risky, its cash flows should be discounted at a higher rate, because this correctly penalizes the project for its high risk.

   d. somewhere between 8 and 12 percent, with the answer depending on the riskiness of the relevant inflows.

   e. indeterminate, or, more accurately, irrelevant, because for such projects we would simply select the process that meets the requirements with the lowest required investment.

.7(1.3) + .3

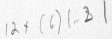

12 + (6)1-3 1

SELF-TEST PROBLEMS

1. Initially, United Products has a beta of 1.30. The risk-free rate is 12 percent, and the required rate of return on the market is 18 percent. The firm now sells 10 percent of its assets, having a beta of 1.30, and uses the proceeds to purchase a new product line with a beta of 1.00. What is the new overall required rate of return for United Products?

   a. 15.11%   **b.** 16.24%   **c.** 17.48%   **d.** 18.00%   **e.** 19.62%

2. Consolidated Inc. uses a weighted average cost of capital of 12 percent to evaluate average-risk projects and adds/subtracts two percentage points to evaluate projects of greater/lesser risk. Currently, two mutually exclusive projects are under consideration. Both have a net cost of $200,000 and last 4 years. Project A, which is riskier than average, will produce yearly after-tax net cash flows of $71,000. Project B, which has less-than-average risk, will produce an after-tax net cash flow of $146,000 in Years 3 and 4 only. What should Consolidated do?

   a. Accept Project B with an NPV of $9,412.

   b. Accept both projects since both NPVs are greater than zero.

   c. Accept Project A with an NPV of $6,874.

©1992 The Dryden Press
All rights reserved.

d. Accept neither project since both NPVs are less than zero.

e. Accept Project A with an NPV of $15,652.

3. Union Industries, an all equity-financed firm, is considering the purchase of a plant that produces plastic products. The plant is expected to generate a rate of return of 17 percent, and the plant's estimated beta is 2.00. The risk-free rate is 12 percent, and the market risk premium is 6 percent. Union should make the investment.

a. True   **b.** False

4. Diversified Products (DP) is considering the formation of a new division which will double the assets of the firm. DP is an all-equity firm which has a current required rate of return of 20 percent. The risk-free rate is 10 percent, and the market risk premium is 5 percent. If DP wants to reduce its required rate of return to 18 percent, what is the maximum beta the new division could have?

a. 1.00   **b.** 1.10   **c.** 1.20   **d.** 1.25   **e.** 1.30

5. Midwest Motors is choosing between two automobile washing/waxing machines on the basis of cost. The expected net costs of the two machines are as follows:

Year	Machine A	Machine B
0	($20,000)	($10,000)
1	(5,000)	(8,000)
2	(5,000)	(8,000)
3	(5,000)	(8,000)
4	(5,000)	(8,000)

The firm's cost of capital is 10 percent. Machine B is judged to be a riskier-than-average project, while Machine A is considered less risky than average. The firm's policy is to add or subtract 2 percentage points to adjust for risk. The firm should choose Machine B.

a. True   **b.** False

6. Consolidated Industries' overall cost of capital (WACC) is 10 percent. Division HR is riskier than average, Division AR has average risk, and Division LR is less risky than average. Consolidated adjusts for risk by adding or subtracting 2 percentage points. What is the risk-adjusted project cost of capital for a low-risk project in the HR division?

a. 6%   **b.** 8%   **c.** 10%   **d.** 12%   **e.** 14%

©1992 The Dryden Press
All rights reserved.

The Braxton Corporation has the following investment opportunities in the coming planning period:

Project	Net Investment	IRR
F	$300,000	18%
G	100,000	15
H	200,000	13
H*	200,000	12
I	100,000	10

Projects H and H* are mutually exclusive. The firm's MCC schedule is 10 percent up to $500,000 of new capital, and 11 percent thereafter.

7. What is the firm's marginal cost of capital?

   a. 10%   **b.** 11%   **c.** 12%   **d.** 13%   **e.** 15%

8. Assume that all projects have average risk. What is the dollar total of the firm's optimal capital budget?

   a. $300,000   **b.** $400,000   **c.** $500,000   **d.** $600,000   **e.** $700,000

9. Now assume that Project F is riskier than average and that Project I is less risky than average. The remaining projects have average risk. Braxton's policy is to adjust the marginal cost of capital up or down by 2 percentage points to account for risk. What is the effect of differential risk on Braxton's optimal capital budget?

   a. The capital budget is not changed.
   b. Project F is now unacceptable.
   c. The capital budget is now $700,000.
   d. Project I becomes acceptable.
   e. Both c and d are correct.

10. Florida Phosphate Company (FPC) can control ground water pollution using either "Project Average" or "Project Risky." Both will do the job, but the actual costs involved with Project Risky could be much higher than the expected cost levels. The cash outflows associated with Project Average are about as uncertain as the cash flows associated with the firm's average project. FPC's cost of capital for average-risk projects is *normally* set at 12 percent, and the company adds 3 percent for high-risk projects but subtracts 3 percent for low-risk projects. The two projects in question meet the criteria for high and average risk, but the financial manager is concerned about applying the normal rule to such cost-only projects. You must decide which project to recommend, and you should recommend the one with the lower PV of costs. What is the PV of costs of the better project?

©1992 The Dryden Press
All rights reserved.

Year	Project Risky	Project Average
0	($1,000)	($400)
1	(210)	(400)
2	(210)	(400)
3	(210)	(400)
4	(210)	(400)

a. -$1,680.34   **b.** -$1,599.55   **c.** -$1,614.94   **d.** -$1,541.99   **e.** -$1,637.84

ANSWERS TO SELF-TEST QUESTIONS

1. greater; rate of return
2. stand-alone; corporate (within-firm)
3. risk-free; premium
4. beta
5. fall; higher
6. cash flows
7. expected values; probability
8. scenario analysis
9. sensitivity analysis
10. variables
11. beta
12. cost of capital (or discount rate)
13. investment opportunity schedule
14. weighted average cost of capital
15. marginal cost of capital
16. average
17. mutually exclusive
18. Capital rationing

19. a. The addition of an asset with a beta of zero would normally lower the beta of the firm, thus lowering the firm's market risk. (The starting beta of most firms is greater than zero.)

20. b. The only time this statement holds is when all independent projects being evaluated have the same risk as the firm's current average project. Otherwise, the cost of capital must be adjusted for project risk.

21. a. The present value of a cash *outflow* (cash cost) must be *increased* to penalize it for above-average risk, and the present value will be increased only if the discount rate is *decreased*.

22. c. Institutional investors are well diversified and, therefore, more concerned with beta risk.

23. e. In fact, responses (a) through (d) are the steps normally followed, in the correct sequence.

24. a. When cash outflows are judged to be riskier than average, a project's marginal cost of capital must be adjusted downward to reflect this fact.

©1992 The Dryden Press
All rights reserved.

SOLUTIONS TO SELF-TEST PROBLEMS

1. e. New b = 0.9(1.30) + 0.1(1.00) = 1.27.

New k_s = 12% + (18% − 12%)1.27 = 19.62%.

2. a. Look at the time lines:

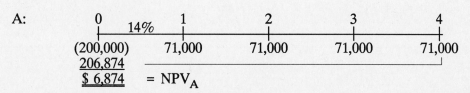

A:

0	14%	1	2	3	4
(200,000)		71,000	71,000	71,000	71,000

206,874
$6,874 = NPV$_A$

Alternatively, input the cash flows in the cash flow register, I = 14, and then solve for NPV$_A$ = $6,873.57.

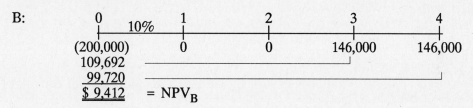

B:

0	10%	1	2	3	4
(200,000)		0	0	146,000	146,000

109,692
99,720
$9,412 = NPV$_B$

Alternatively, input the cash flows in the cash flow register, I = 10, and then solve for NPV$_B$ = $9,411.93.

Note that both discount rates are adjusted for risk. Since the projects are mutually exclusive, the project with the higher NPV is chosen.

3. b. The project's required rate of return on equity and overall cost of capital is 24 percent: $k_{s(Project)}$ = 12% + (6%)2 = 24%. Since the expected return is only 17 percent, the plant should not be purchased.

4. c. First, find the current beta of the firm: k_s = 10% + (5%)b = 20%, so b = 2.00.

Now find the beta required to lower the required rate of return to 18 percent: k_s = 10% + (5%)b = 18%, so b = 1.60.

Finally, if the firm doubles its size with the formation of the new division, 50 percent of the expanded firm's assets will be old assets, while 50 percent will be assets from the new division. Thus, 0.5(2.00) + 0.5(b$_{Div.}$) = 1.60; b$_{Div.}$ = 1.20.

5. b. These are cash outflows, so the risk adjustment process is reversed. Thus, the project cost of capital for Machine A is 12 percent, while the project cost of capital for B is 8 percent. PV$_{Project A}$ = -$35,187, and PV$_{Project B}$ = -$36,497.

©1992 The Dryden Press
All rights reserved.

We see that with the correct risk adjustment, the PV of costs for Machine A is less than the PV of costs for Machine B, and hence Machine A should be selected.

6. c. $k_{HR} = 10\% + 2\% = 12\%$; $k_{Project} = 12\% - 2\% = 10\%$.

7. b. First, plot the MCC and IOS schedules:

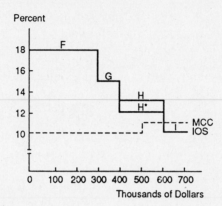

The intersection of the schedules defines the firm's marginal cost of capital. Thus, Braxton's MCC is 11 percent.

8. d. Since all projects have average risk, they are all evaluated at a project cost of capital of 11 percent. Clearly, Projects F and G are acceptable since their IRRs exceed 11 percent. (Since they are independent projects, it is permissible to use the IRR method as a proxy for the NPV method.) The decision between Projects H and H* must be made according to the NPV rule. Since we do not know the project cash flows, we cannot calculate their NPVs. However, one of the two would be chosen since both will have positive NPVs. Thus, the optimal capital budget consists of Projects F and G, and either Project H or H*, and totals $600,000.

9. e. Since Project F is riskier than average, its cost of capital must be adjusted upward to $11\% + 2\% = 13\%$. However, its IRR is 18 percent so Project F remains acceptable. On the other hand, Project I's cost of capital is adjusted downward to 9 percent, and hence it becomes acceptable. Thus, the optimal capital budget increases to $700,000. Note that Braxton's MCC remains at 11 percent.

10. c. Recognize that (1) risky *outflows* must be discounted at lower rates and (2) since Project Risky is risky, it must be discounted at a rate of $12\% - 3\% = 9\%$. Project Average must be discounted at 12 percent. At these rates:

$$NPV_R = -\$1,680.34 \text{ and } NPV_A = -\$1,614.94.$$

Thus, Project Average is the better project because it has the lower PV of costs.

10-12

©1992 The Dryden Press
All rights reserved.

CHAPTER 11
CAPITAL STRUCTURE AND LEVERAGE

OVERVIEW

Capital structure theory suggests that some optimal capital structure exists which simultaneously maximizes a firm's stock price and minimizes its cost of capital. The use of debt tends to increase earnings per share, which will lead to a higher stock price; but, at the same time, the use of debt also increases the risk borne by stockholders, which lowers the stock price. The optimal capital structure strikes a balance between these risk and return effects. While it is difficult to determine the optimal capital structure with precision, it is possible to identify the factors that influence it. A firm's target capital structure is generally set equal to the estimated optimal structure. The target may change over time as conditions vary, but, at any given moment, a well-managed firm's management has a specific structure in mind; and financing decisions are made so as to be consistent with this target structure.

OUTLINE

I.   **Capital structure policy involves a tradeoff between risk and return: Using more debt raises the riskiness of the firm's earnings stream; however, a higher debt ratio generally leads to a higher expected rate of return.**

    A.   The optimal capital structure is the one that strikes the optimal balance between risk and return and thereby maximizes the price of the stock.

    B.   Four primary factors influence capital structure decisions:
       1. Business risk is the amount of risk in a firm's operations if no debt is used. The greater the firm's business risk, the lower its optimal debt ratio.
       2. A major reason for using debt is the fact that interest is tax deductible. Therefore, the higher a firm's tax rate, the more advantageous debt is to the firm.
       3. Financial flexibility, which is the ability to raise capital on reasonable terms under adverse conditions, is another consideration. The potential future availability of funds, and the consequences of a funds shortage, have a major influence on the target capital structure.
       4. Managerial conservatism or aggressiveness influences the target capital structures firms actually establish.

II. **Business risk is the uncertainty inherent in estimates of future returns on assets, or of returns on equity if the firm uses no debt, and is the single most important determinant of a firm's capital structure.**

    A.   Business risk varies from one industry to another and also among firms in a given industry. It can also change over time.

©1992 The Dryden Press
All rights reserved.

B. Business risk depends on the following factors: (1) Demand variability, (2) sales price variability, (3) input price variability, (4) ability to adjust output prices for changes in input prices, and (5) operating leverage (the extent to which costs are fixed).

C. Operating leverage is the degree to which a firm uses fixed costs in its production processes.
1. High operating leverage implies that a relatively small change in sales will result in a large change in operating income.
2. The higher a firm's degree of operating leverage, the higher its breakeven point tends to be.
   a. The breakeven point is defined as the volume of sales at which total costs equal total revenues, so profits equal zero.
   b. The breakeven point is calculated as fixed costs divided by the difference in sales price and variable cost per unit:

$$Q_{BE} = \frac{F}{P - V}.$$

3. The higher a firm's operating leverage, the higher its business risk, other things held constant.
4. Production technology limits control over the amount of fixed costs and operating leverage. However, firms do have some control over the type of production processes they employ, and so the firm's capital budgeting decisions will have an impact on its operating leverage and business risk.

III. **Financial leverage refers to the firm's use of fixed-income securities, such as debt and preferred stock, and financial risk is the additional risk placed on the common stockholders as a result of using financial leverage.**

A. The degree to which a firm employs financial leverage will affect its expected earnings per share (EPS) and the riskiness of these earnings. Financial leverage will cause EPS to rise if the return on assets is greater than the cost of debt. However, the degree of risk associated with the firm will also increase as leverage increases.

B. The optimal capital structure is the one that maximizes the price of the firm's stock, and this always calls for a debt ratio which is lower than the one that maximizes expected EPS.

C. The EPS indifference point is the level of sales at which EPS will be the same whether the firm uses debt or common stock financing.

D. At first, EPS will rise as the use of debt increases. Interest charges rise, but the number of outstanding shares will decrease as equity is replaced by debt. At some point EPS will peak. Beyond this point interest rates will rise so fast that EPS is depressed in spite of the fact that the number of shares outstanding is decreasing.

©1992 The Dryden Press
All rights reserved.

E. Risk, as measured by the standard deviation of EPS, rises continuously as the use of debt increases.

F. The expected stock price will at first increase with financial leverage, will then reach a peak, and finally it will decline as financial leverage becomes excessive due to the importance of potential bankruptcy costs.
  1. The optimal capital structure is found when the expected stock price is maximized.
  2. Management should set its target capital structure at this ratio of debt/assets.

G. The financial structure that maximizes EPS usually has more debt than the one which results in the highest stock price.

IV. Operating leverage and financial leverage are interrelated: A reduction in operating leverage would normally lead to an increase in the optimal amount of financial leverage, while an increase in operating leverage would lead to a decrease in the optimal amount of debt.

  A. The degree of operating leverage (DOL) is defined as the percentage change in operating income (EBIT) associated with a given percentage change in sales.
  1. The formula used to analyze the DOL for a single product is shown below:

  $$DOL = \frac{Q(P - V)}{Q(P - V) - F}.$$

  where Q = units of output, P = sales price per unit, V = variable cost per unit, and F = fixed operating costs.
  2. The formula to analyze the DOL for an entire firm is shown below:

  $$DOL = \frac{S - VC}{S - VC - F}.$$

  where S = sales in dollars, VC = total variable costs, and F = fixed operating costs.

  B. Financial leverage affects earnings after interest and taxes. The degree of financial leverage (DFL) is the percentage change in earnings available to common stockholders (EPS) associated with a particular percentage change in EBIT.
  1. The formula for DFL is:

  $$DFL = \frac{\%\Delta EPS}{\%\Delta EBIT} = \frac{EBIT}{EBIT - I}.$$

  2. To find the effects on income available to common stockholders, multiply the percentage change in EBIT by DFL. The greater the degree of financial leverage, the greater the impact of a given change in EBIT on EPS.

©1992 The Dryden Press
All rights reserved.

C. Degree of total leverage (DTL) combines DOL and DFL to show how a given change in sales will affect EPS.
   1. One formula for DTL is: DTL = DOL × DFL. Equivalent formulas include:

$$DTL = \frac{Q(P-V)}{Q(P-V) - F - I} = \frac{S-VC}{S-VC-F-I}.$$

   2. DTL shows the interrelationship between operating and financial leverage.

V. **There are problems with using the type of leverage analyses described in the text.**

A. It is extremely difficult to determine the relationships among financial leverage, P/E ratios, and cost of equity, k_s. Therefore, it is frequently difficult to use stock price analysis to determine a target capital structure.

B. Established management teams are often conservative; they may be more interested in survival than in maximizing expected stock prices.

C. Firms that provide vital services (utilities) must put long-run viability above short-run stock price maximization or cost of capital minimization.

D. Because of these factors, management may place considerable emphasis on the times-interest-earned ratio and the fixed charge coverage ratio when establishing the firm's financial structure. The higher these ratios, the less likely it is that a firm will be unable to meet all of its fixed charge obligations and thus face bankruptcy.

VI. **Capital structure theory has developed along two main lines: (1) tax benefit/bankruptcy cost trade-off theory and (2) signaling theory.**

A. Trade-off theory as set forth by Modigliani and Miller states that, due to the tax deductibility of interest on debt, a firm's value rises continuously as it uses more debt.
   1. This theory holds only under a very restrictive set of assumptions.
   2. These assumptions, however, do not hold true in the real world. For example, debt costs rise as the debt ratio rises, EBIT declines at extreme leverage, expected tax rates fall and reduce the value of the tax shelter, and the probability of bankruptcy increases as the debt level rises. Therefore, at some point, bankruptcy-related costs exceed the benefit of additional debt. This point denotes the target capital structure.

B. Signaling theory recognizes the fact that investors and managers do *not* have the same information regarding a firm's prospects, as was assumed by trade-off theory. This is called asymmetric information and it has an important effect on the optimal capital structure.

11-4

©1992 The Dryden Press
All rights reserved.

1. As a result, one would expect a firm with very favorable prospects to try to avoid selling stock and to attempt to raise any required new capital by other means, including using debt beyond the normal target capital structure.

2. The announcement of a stock offering by a mature firm that seems to have financing alternatives is taken as a signal that the firm's prospects as seen by its management are not bright.

VII. A firm's capital structure can change because of merger activity.

A. The acquiring firm may issue debt to purchase the target firm's stock. This action will then change the combined firm's capital structure.

B. This use of debt increases the firm's value sufficiently to cover the premium offered for the stock and to provide a profit for the acquiring firm.

VIII. The following factors will all have some influence on the firm's choice of a target capital structure.

A. *Sales stability.* If sales are stable, a firm will be more likely to take on increased debt and higher fixed charges.

B. *Asset structure.* Firms whose assets can readily be pledged as collateral for loans will tend to operate with a higher degree of financial leverage.

C. *Operating leverage.* Lower operating leverage generally permits a firm to employ more debt.

D. *Growth rate.* Firms that are growing rapidly generally need large amounts of external capital. The flotation costs associated with debt are generally less than those for common stock, so rapidly growing firms tend to use more debt.

E. *Profitability.* A high degree of profitability would indicate an ability to carry a high level of debt. However, many profitable firms are able to meet most of their financing needs with retained earnings, and do so.

F. *Taxes.* Interest charges are tax deductible, while dividend payments are not. This factor favors the use of debt over equity for firms in high tax brackets.

G. *Control.* Management may not wish to increase the shares of stock outstanding for fear of losing voting control of the company.

H. *Management attitudes.* Managements vary in their attitudes toward risk. More conservative managers will use stock rather than debt for financing, while less conservative managers will use more debt.

© 1992 The Dryden Press
All rights reserved.

I.   *Lender and rating agency attitudes.* This factor will penalize firms that go beyond the average for their industry in the use of financial leverage.

J.   *Market conditions.* At any point in time, securities markets may favor either debt or equity.

K.   *Firm's internal conditions.* Expected future earnings patterns and internal factors will influence management's choice of debt versus equity.

L.   *Financial flexibility.* Most treasurers have as a goal to always be in a position to raise the capital needed to support operations, even under bad conditions. Therefore, they want to always maintain some reserve borrowing capacity.

IX. **There are wide variations in the use of financial leverage both among industries and among individual firms within each industry.**

SELF-TEST QUESTIONS

Definitional

1.   Determination of an _____ capital structure requires consideration of both _____ and _____.

2.   A firm's _____ capital structure is generally set equal to the estimated optimal structure.

3.   Business risk refers to the uncertainty about expected _____ _____ _____, or of returns on equity, if the firm uses no debt.

4.   Some of the factors that influence a firm's business risk include: (1) _____ variability, (2) sales price variability, and (3) _____ leverage.

5.   Business risk represents the riskiness of the firm's operations if it uses no _____; financial risk represents the additional risk borne by common stockholders as a result of using _____.

6.   Common stockholders are compensated for bearing financial risk by a higher _____ _____.

7.   Expected EPS generally _____ as the debt/assets ratio increases.

8.   As financial leverage increases, the stock price will first begin to rise, but it will then decline as financial leverage becomes excessive because potential _____ _____ become increasingly important.

© 1992 The Dryden Press
All rights reserved.

9. Financial leverage refers to the use of _____ financing.

10. Difficulties in determining the relationship between ___ / ___ ratios, the cost of _____, and the degree of _____ _____ have made some managers reluctant to rely heavily on stock price analysis to help determine the optimal capital structure.

11. Conservative financial managers may try to maintain a target _____ _____ that does not maximize the firm's _____ _____.

12. Established management teams are often conservative; they may be more concerned with _____ than with maximizing stock prices.

13. The _____ ratio and the _____-_____-_____ ratio give some indication of a firm's risk of default on its fixed charges.

14. The _____ ___ _____ _____ is defined as the percentage change in EBIT associated with a given change in sales volume.

15. The _____ ___ _____ _____ is defined as the percentage change in EPS associated with a given change in EBIT.

16. The _____ ___ _____ _____ is defined as the percentage change in EPS associated with a given change in sales volume.

17. Debt has a _____ advantage over equity in that _____ is a deductible expense while _____ are not.

18. Management may prefer additional _____ as opposed to common stock in order to help maintain _____ of the company.

Conceptual

19. Firm A has a higher degree of business risk than Firm B. Firm A can offset this by increasing its operating leverage.

   a. True   b. False

20. Two firms operate in different industries, but they have the same expected EPS and the same standard deviation of expected EPS. Thus, the two firms must have the same financial risk.

   a. True   b. False

©1992 The Dryden Press
All rights reserved.

21. As a general rule, the capital structure that maximizes stock price also:

a. Maximizes the weighted average cost of capital.
b. Maximizes EPS.
c. Maximizes bankruptcy costs.
d. Minimizes the weighted average cost of capital.
e. Minimizes the required rate of return on equity.

22. A decrease in the debt ratio will normally have no effect on:

a. Financial risk.   b. Total risk.   c. Business risk.
d. Systematic risk.   e. Firm-unique risk.

23. Two firms could have identical financial and operating leverage yet have different degrees of business risk.

a. True   b. False

24. Which of the following statements is most *correct*?

a. The "pure MM" theory of capital structure, when income taxes are considered, suggests that the value of a firm rises as it uses more and more debt, and that this increase is due to tax savings. Thus, the optimal capital structure under MM theory calls for 100 percent debt.
b. When the "pure MM" theory is modified to include bankruptcy costs, an optimal capital structure with some debt, but less than 100 percent debt, is found for the "typical" firm.
c. Under the signaling, or asymmetric information theory, the issuance of new common stock by a mature company is taken by investors as bad news. As a result, new stock issues depress the stock price. This implies that firms should, under normal conditions, use less debt than they otherwise might so as to have a reserve borrowing capacity which would enable them to avoid issuing stock under most conditions.
d. The above statements are all true.
e. The above statements are all false.

25. Which of the following statements is most *correct*?

a. If a firm is exposed to a high degree of business risk as a result of its high operating leverage, then it probably should offset this risk by using a larger-than-average amount of financial leverage. This follows because debt has a lower after-tax cost than equity.
b. Financial risk can be reduced by replacing common equity with preferred stock.
c. As explained in the text, one of the advantages of the degree of leverage concept is that it takes account of market risk, so if a firm's stockholders hold diversified

11-8

©1992 The Dryden Press
All rights reserved.

portfolios of stocks, as opposed to holding only the stock of the one firm, this fact is accounted for by the use of the degree of total leverage.

d. In the text it was stated that the capital structure which minimizes the WACC also maximizes the firm's stock price and its total value, but generally not its expected EPS. One reason given for why debt is beneficial is that it shelters operating income from taxes, while it was stated that a disadvantage of excessive debt has to do with costs associated with bankruptcy and financial distress generally.

e. All of the above statements are false.

SELF-TEST PROBLEMS

1. The Fisher Company will produce 50,000 10-gallon aquariums next year. Variable costs will equal 40 percent of dollar sales, while fixed costs total $100,000. At what price must each aquarium be sold for the firm's EBIT to be $90,000?

   a. $5.00   b. $5.33   c. $5.50   d. $6.00   e. $6.33

2. Brown Products is a new firm just starting operations. The firm will produce backpacks which will sell for $22.00 each. Fixed costs are $500,000 per year, and variable costs are $2.00 per unit of production. The company expects to sell 50,000 backpacks per year, and its effective tax rate is 40 percent. Brown needs $2 million to build facilities, obtain working capital, and start operations. If Brown borrows part of the money, the interest charges will depend on the amount borrowed as follows:

Amount Borrowed	Percentage of Debt in Capital Structure	Interest Rate on Total Amount Borrowed
$ 200,000	10%	9.00%
400,000	20	9.50
600,000	30	10.00
800,000	40	15.00
1,000,000	50	19.00
1,200,000	60	26.00

Assume that stock can be sold at a price of $20 per share on the initial offering, regardless of how much debt the company uses. Then after the company begins operating, its price will be determined as a multiple of its earnings per share. The multiple (or the P/E ratio) will depend upon the capital structure as follows:

Debt/Assets	P/E	Debt/Assets	P/E
0.0	12.5	40.0	8.0
10.0	12.0	50.0	6.0
20.0	11.5	60.0	5.0
30.0	10.0		

©1992 The Dryden Press
All rights reserved.

What is Brown's optimal capital structure, which maximizes stock price, as measured by the debt/assets ratio?

    a. 10%   **b.** 20%   **c.** 30%   **d.** 40%   **e.** 50%

3. Refer to the previous problem. What is Brown's degree of operating leverage at the expected level of sales?

    a. 1.00   **b.** 1.08   **c.** 2.00   **d.** 2.16   **e.** 3.00

4. Refer to Self-Test Problem 2. What is Brown's degree of financial leverage at the expected level of sales?

    a. 1.00   **b.** 1.08   **c.** 2.00   **d.** 2.16   **e.** 3.00

5. Refer to Self-Test Problem 2. What is Brown's degree of total leverage at the expected level of sales and optimal capital structure?

    a. 1.00   **b.** 1.08   **c.** 2.00   **d.** 2.16   **e.** 3.00

6. Bicycles Inc. currently sells 75,000 units annually. At this sales level, its net operating income (EBIT) is $4 million and the degree of total leverage is 2.0. The firm's debt consists of $20 million in bonds with a 10 percent coupon. Bicycles is considering a new assembly line which would entail an increase in fixed costs, resulting in a degree of operating leverage of 1.8. However, the firm desires to maintain the degree of total leverage at 2.0. Assuming that EBIT remains at $4 million, what dollar amount of bonds must be retired to accomplish adding the assembly line yet retain the old degree of total leverage?

    a. $10 million **b.** $12 million **c.** $14 million **d.** $16 million **e.** $18 million

7. Tapley Dental Supplies Inc. is in a stable, no-growth situation. Its $1,000,000 of debt consists of perpetuities which have a 10 percent coupon and sell at par. Tapley's EBIT is $500,000, its cost of equity is 15 percent, it has 100,000 shares outstanding, all earnings are paid out as dividends, and its tax rate is 40 percent. Tapley could borrow an additional $500,000 at an interest rate of 13 percent without having to retire the original debt, and it would use the proceeds to repurchase stock *at the current price*, not at the new equilibrium price. The increased risk from the additional leverage will raise the cost of equity to 17 percent. If Tapley does recapitalize, what will the new stock price be?

    a. $17.20   **b.** $16.00   **c.** $16.50   **d.** $17.00   **e.** $16.75

©1992 The Dryden Press
All rights reserved.

ANSWERS TO SELF-TEST QUESTIONS

1. optimal; risk; return
2. target
3. returns on assets
4. demand; operating
5. debt; debt
6. expected return
7. increases
8. bankruptcy costs
9. debt (or fixed-charge)
10. P/E; equity; financial leverage

11. capital structure; stock price
12. survival
13. debt; times-interest-earned (or fixed charge coverage)
14. degree of operating leverage (DOL)
15. degree of financial leverage (DFL)
16. degree of total leverage (DTL)
17. tax; interest; dividends
18. debt; control

19. b. Increasing operating leverage will increase Firm A's business risk; therefore, Firm A should use less operating leverage.

20. b. The two firms would have the same total risk. However, they could have different combinations of business and financial risk.

21. d. The optimal capital structure balances risk and return to maximize the stock price. The structure that maximizes stock price also minimizes the firm's cost of capital.

22. c. Business risk measures the riskiness of the firm's operations assuming no debt is used.

23. a. Business risk consists of several elements in addition to operating leverage, for example, sales variability, and it does not depend on financial risk at all.

24. d. Statements a, b, and c are all correct; therefore, statement d is the proper choice.

25. d. Statement a is false; if a firm is exposed to a high degree of business risk this implies that it should offset this risk by using a lower amount of financial leverage. Statement b is false; preferred stock is a fixed-income security, and as such, would increase financial risk. Statement c is false; the degree of total leverage is equal to the DOL × DFL—which takes into account both business risk and financial risk. Statement d is correct.

SOLUTIONS TO SELF-TEST PROBLEMS

1. e.
$$EBIT = PQ - VQP - F$$
$$\$90,000 = P(50,000) - 0.4(50,000)P - \$100,000$$
$$30,000P = \$190,000$$
$$P = \$6.33.$$

©1992 The Dryden Press
All rights reserved.

2. b. The first step is to calculate EBIT:

Sales in dollars [50,000($22)]	$1,100,000
Less: Fixed costs	500,000
Variable costs [50,000($2)]	100,000
EBIT	$ 500,000

The second step is to calculate the EPS at each debt/assets ratio using the formula:

$$\text{EPS} = \frac{(\text{EBIT} - \text{I})(1 - \text{T})}{\text{Shares outstanding}}.$$

Recognize (1) that I = interest charges = (dollars of debt)(interest rate at each D/A ratio), and (2) that shares outstanding = (assets − debt)/initial price per share = ($2,000,000 − debt)/$20.00.

D/A	EPS	D/A	EPS
0%	$3.00	40%	$3.80
10	3.21	50	3.72
20	3.47	60	2.82
30	3.77		

Finally, the third step is to calculate the stock price at each debt/assets ratio using the following formula: Price = (P/E)(EPS).

D/A	Price	D/A	Price
0%	$37.50	40%	$30.40
10	38.52	50	22.32
20	39.91	60	14.10
30	37.70		

Thus, a debt/assets ratio of 20 percent maximizes stock price. This is the optimal capital structure.

3. c.
$$\text{DOL} = \frac{Q(P - V)}{Q(P - V) - F} = \frac{50,000(\$22 - \$2)}{50,000(\$22 - \$2) - \$500,000}$$

$$= \frac{\$1,000,000}{\$500,000} = 2.0.$$

©1992 The Dryden Press
All rights reserved.

4. b. $DFL = \dfrac{EBIT}{EBIT - I} = \dfrac{PQ - VQ - F}{PQ - VQ - F - I}$

$= \dfrac{\$1,100,000 - \$100,000 - \$500,000}{\$1,100,000 - \$100,000 - \$500,000 - \$38,000}$

$= \dfrac{\$500,000}{\$462,000} = 1.08.$

5. d. $DTL = \dfrac{PQ - VQ}{PQ - VQ - F - I}$

$= \dfrac{\$1,100,000 - \$100,000}{\$1,100,000 - \$100,000 - \$500,000 - \$38,000}$

$= \dfrac{\$1,000,000}{\$462,000} = 2.16,$

or $DTL = (DOL)(DFL) = (2.00)(1.08) = 2.16.$

6. d. $DOL = \dfrac{PQ - VQ}{PQ - VQ - F} = 1.8.$

But, $PQ - VQ - F = EBIT = \$4$ million. Therefore, $(PQ - VQ)/\$4$ million $= 1.8$, so $PQ - VQ = \$7.2$ million. Now,

$DTL = \dfrac{PQ - VQ}{PQ - VQ - F - I} = 2.0$

$\dfrac{\$7,200,000}{\$4,000,000 - I} = 2.0$

$I = \$400,000.$

Therefore, the new interest payment must be $0.40 million. The current interest payment is 0.10($20 million) = $2.0 million. Thus, the interest payment must be reduced by $1.60 million by retiring bonds. This would require that $1.60/0.10 = $16 million of bonds be retired.

7. a. Value of stock = [$500,000 − 0.1($1,000,000)](0.6)/0.15 = $1,600,000.

$P_0 = \$1,600,000/100,000 = \$16.$

After the recapitalization, value of stock is equal to [$500,000 − 0.1($1,000,000) − 0.13($500,000)](0.6)/0.17 = $1,182,353.

$P_0 = \$1,182,353/(100,000 - 500,000/16) = \$17.20.$

©1992 The Dryden Press
All rights reserved.

CHAPTER 12
DIVIDEND POLICY

OVERVIEW

Dividend policy involves the decision to pay out earnings as dividends or to retain and reinvest them in the firm. Any change in dividend policy has both favorable and unfavorable effects on the firm's stock price: higher dividends mean higher immediate cash flows to investors, which is good, but lower future growth, which is bad. The optimal dividend policy balances these opposing forces and maximizes stock price. Three theories regarding the relationship between dividend payout and stock price have been proposed: (1) *dividend irrelevance*, which states that dividend policy has no effect on the firm's stock price, (2) the *"bird-in-the-hand"* theory, which states that investors prefer dividends because they are less risky than potential capital gains, and (3) the *tax preference theory* which states that investors prefer to have companies retain earnings rather than pay them out as dividends because capital gains are subject to less taxes than dividends. In addition, the water is muddied because of the existence of *signaling* and *clientele* effects. It is simply not possible to state that any one dividend policy is correct, and hence it is impossible to develop a precise model for use in establishing dividend policy. Thus, financial managers must consider a number of factors when setting their firms' dividend policies.

OUTLINE

I.   **Dividend policy involves the decision to pay out earnings versus retaining them for reinvestment in the firm.**

   A.   The constant growth stock model, $P_0 = D_1/(k_s - g)$ shows that paying out more dividends will increase stock price. However, if this results in insufficient equity funds to meet investment needs, then the firm must sell new common stock and incur flotation costs, which will cause the price of the stock to decrease.

   B.   The optimal dividend policy strikes a balance between investors' desire for current cash flows (dividends) and future expected growth so as to maximize the value of the firm's stock.

II. **A number of theories have been proposed to explain how factors interact to determine a firm's optimal dividend policy. These theories include: (1) the dividend irrelevance theory, (2) the "bird-in-the-hand" theory, and (3) the tax preference theory.**

   A.   Modigliani and Miller (MM), the principal proponents of the *dividend irrelevance theory*, argue that the value of the firm depends only on the income produced by its assets, not on how this income is split between dividends and retained earnings (and hence growth).

12-1

©1992 The Dryden Press
All rights reserved.

1. MM prove their proposition, but only under a set of restrictive assumptions including (1) no personal taxes, (2) independence between dividend policy and equity costs, and (3) zero flotation costs.
2. Obviously, firms and investors do pay taxes and do incur flotation costs, and investors may apply a different required rate of return on equity (k_s) to firms that pay out more rather than less of their earnings. Thus, the MM conclusions on dividend irrelevance may not be valid under real-world conditions.

B. The most critical assumption of MM's dividend irrelevance theory is that dividend policy does not affect the required rate of return on equity, k_s.
   1. Myron Gordon and John Lintner argue that k_s increases as the dividend payout is reduced because investors are more sure of receiving dividend payments than income from capital gains that presumably result from retained earnings.
   2. MM call the Gordon-Lintner argument the *"bird-in-the-hand"* theory because Gordon and Lintner believe that investors view dividends in the hand as being less risky than capital gains in the bush. In MM's view, however, most investors are going to reinvest their dividends in the same or similar firms; and the riskiness of the firm's cash flows to investors in the long run is solely a function of the firm's asset cash flows.

C. The *tax preference theory* states that investors may prefer to have companies retain most of their earnings because of various tax advantages. Investors then would be willing to pay more for low payout companies than for otherwise similar high payout companies.

D. Empirical testing of these theories has not produced definitive results regarding which theory is correct.

III. **There are two other issues which have a bearing on optimal dividend policy: (1) the information content, or signaling, hypothesis and (2) the clientele effect.**

A. It has been observed that a dividend increase announcement is often accompanied by an increase in the price of the stock.
   1. This might be interpreted by some to mean that investors prefer dividends over capital gains, thus supporting the Gordon-Lintner hypothesis.
   2. However, MM argue that a dividend increase is a signal to investors that the firm's management forecasts good future earnings. Thus, MM argue that investors' reactions to dividend announcements do not necessarily show that investors prefer dividends to retained earnings. Rather, the fact that the stock price changes merely indicates that there is an important information content in dividend announcements. This is referred to as the *information content, or signaling, hypothesis.*

B. MM also suggest that a *clientele effect* might exist.

12-2

©1992 The Dryden Press
All rights reserved.

1. Some stockholders (for example, retirees) prefer current income; therefore, they would want the firm to pay out a high percentage of its earnings as dividends.
2. Other stockholders have no need for current income (for example, doctors in their peak earning years) and they would simply reinvest any dividends received, after first paying income taxes on the dividend income. Therefore, they would want the firm to retain most of its earnings.
3. Thus, a firm establishes a dividend policy and then attracts a specific clientele that is drawn to this dividend policy.

IV. **The theories offer conflicting advice, yet managers must take action. Here are the actual dividend policies that firms follow in practice:**

A. *Residual dividend policy* is based on the premise that investors prefer to have a firm retain and reinvest earnings rather than pay them out in dividends if the rate of return the firm can earn on reinvested earnings exceeds the rate of return investors can obtain for themselves on other investments of comparable risk. Further, it is less expensive for the firm to use retained earnings than it is to issue new common stock. A firm using the residual policy would follow these four steps:
1. Determine the optimal capital budget.
2. Determine the amount of equity required to finance the optimal capital budget, recognizing that the funds used will consist of both equity and debt to preserve the optimal capital structure.
3. To the extent possible, use retained earnings to supply the equity required.
4. Pay dividends only if more earnings are available than are needed to support the optimal capital budget.

B. A company's policy of *constant, or steadily increasing, dividends per share* implies to shareholders that the regular dividend will at least be maintained and, accordingly, that earnings will be sufficient to cover it. Some other features of this policy are as follows:
1. Dividends are increased only when earnings have increased and seem stable enough to maintain the new dividend level.
2. Dividend payments will be maintained, at least temporarily, even if earnings fall below the level of the dividend payment. Firms try very hard never to reduce the regular dividend.
3. Most corporations follow this type of policy.
   a. Stable dividends or a stable dividend growth rate will tend to stabilize a firm's stock price movements.
   b. Investors who rely on dividends for income normally prefer a stable dividend policy.
   c. A stable growth rate policy confirms investors' estimates of the growth factor, and hence reduces risk perceptions.
4. Because of these factors, many people think that a stable dividend policy (including a steady growth rate) will maximize the price of a firm's stock.

©1992 The Dryden Press
All rights reserved.

C. It would be possible for a firm to pay out a constant percentage of earnings, that is, a *constant payout ratio*. Only a few firms pay out a constant percentage of their yearly earnings. This would normally result in an unpredictable dividend stream and would not please most investors.

D. The policy of paying a *low regular dividend plus extras* is a compromise between a stable dividend (or stable growth rate) and a constant payout rate. It is often followed by firms with relatively volatile earnings from year to year. The low regular dividend can usually be maintained even when earnings decline, and "extra" dividends can be paid when excess funds are available.

V. **Firms usually pay dividends on a quarterly basis in accordance with the following payment procedures:**

A. *Declaration date.* This is the day on which the board of directors declares the dividend. At this time they set the amount of the dividend to be paid, the holder-of-record date, and the payment date.

B. *Holder-of-record date.* This is the date the stock transfer books of the corporation are closed. Those shareholders who are listed on the company's books on this date are the holders of record and they receive the announced dividend.

C. *Ex-dividend date.* This date is four days prior to the holder-of-record date. Shares purchased after the ex-dividend date are not entitled to the dividend. This practice is a convention of the brokerage business which allows sufficient time for stock transfers to be made on the books of the corporation.

D. *Payment date.* This is the day when dividend checks are actually mailed to the holders of record.

VI. **Many firms have instituted dividend reinvestment plans (DRPs) whereby stockholders can automatically reinvest dividends received in the stock of the paying corporation. Income taxes on the amount of the dividends must be paid even though stock rather than cash is received.**

VII. **Regardless of the debate on the relevancy of dividend policy, it is possible to identify several factors which influence dividend policy. These factors are grouped into four broad categories.**

A. Constraints: (1) Bond indentures, (2) impairment of capital rule, (3) availability of cash, and (4) penalty tax on improperly accumulated earnings.

B. Investment opportunities: (1) Location of the IOS schedule and (2) ability to accelerate or postpone projects.

©1992 The Dryden Press
All rights reserved.

C. Alternative sources of capital: (1) Cost of selling new stock, (2) ability to substitute debt for equity, and (3) control.

D. Effects of dividend policy on k_s: (1) Stockholders' desire for current versus future income, (2) perceived riskiness of dividends versus capital gains, (3) the tax advantage of capital gains over dividends, and (4) the information content of dividends (signaling).

VIII. **Stock dividends and stock splits are often used to lower a firm's stock price, and, at the same time, to conserve its cash resources.**

A. The effect of a stock split is an increase in the number of shares outstanding and a reduction in the par, or stated, value of the shares. For example, if a firm had 1,000 shares of stock outstanding with a par value of $100 per share, a 2-for-1 split would reduce the par value to $50 and increase the number of shares to 2,000.
   1. The total net worth of the firm remains unchanged.
   2. The stock split does not involve any cash payment, only additional certificates representing new shares.

B. A stock dividend requires an accounting entry transfer from retained earnings to the common stock and paid-in capital accounts and an accompanying pro-rata distribution of new shares to the existing stockholders.
   1. Dollars transferred from retained earnings = Number of shares outstanding × Percentage of the stock dividend × Market price of the stock.
   2. Again, no cash is involved with this "dividend." Net worth remains unchanged, and the number of shares is increased.

C. Unless the total amount of dividends paid on shares is increased, any upward movement in the stock price following a stock split or dividend is likely to be temporary. The price will normally fall in proportion to the dilution in earnings and dividends unless earnings and dividends rise.

IX. **Stock repurchases are an alternative to dividends for transmitting cash to stockholders.**

A. Stock repurchased by the issuing firm is called treasury stock.

B. Advantages of a repurchase include:
   1. The repurchase is often motivated by management's belief that the firm's shares are undervalued.
   2. The stockholder is given a choice of whether or not to sell his stock to the firm.
   3. The repurchase can remove a large block of stock overhanging the market.
   4. If an increase in cash flow is temporary, the cash can be distributed to stockholders as a repurchase rather than as a dividend, which could not be maintained in the future.
   5. Repurchases can be used to produce large-scale changes in capital structures.

©1992 The Dryden Press
All rights reserved.

C. Disadvantages of repurchase include:
   1. Repurchases are not as dependable as cash dividends; therefore, the price of the stock may benefit more from cash dividends. A dependable repurchase program may not be practical due to the improper accumulation tax.
   2. Selling stockholders may not be aware of all the implications of the repurchase; therefore, repurchases are usually announced in advance.
   3. If a firm pays too high a price for the repurchased stock, it is to the disadvantage of the remaining stockholders.

D. While repurchases on a regular basis do not appear feasible due to various uncertainties, occasional repurchases do offer some significant advantages over dividends, and repurchases can be valuable in making a major change in capital structure within a short period.

SELF-TEST QUESTIONS

Definitional

1. MM argue that a firm's dividend policy has ____ _____ on a stock's price.

2. Gordon and Lintner hypothesize that investors value a dollar of _____ more highly than a dollar of expected _____ _____.

3. A company may be forced to increase its _____ ratio in order to avoid a tax on retained earnings deemed to be unnecessary for the conduct of the business.

4. Some stockholders prefer dividends to _____ _____ because of a need for current _____.

5. If the _____ of a firm's stock increases with the announcement of an increase in dividends, it may be due to the _____ content in the dividend announcement rather than to a preference for dividends over capital gains.

6. A firm with _____ earnings is most appropriate for using the policy of "extra" dividends.

7. The stock transfer books of a corporation are closed on the _____-__-_____ date.

8. The ___-_____ date occurs four days prior to the _____-__-_____ date and provides time for stock transfers to be recorded on the books of the firm.

9. Actual payment of a dividend is made on the _____ date as announced by the _____ ___ _____.

©1992 The Dryden Press
All rights reserved.

10. Many firms have instituted _____ _____ plans whereby stockholders can use their dividends to purchase additional shares of the company's stock.

11. A stock dividend requires that an accounting transfer be made from _____ _____ to the _____ _____ and _____ - ____ _____ accounts.

12. A stock split involves a reduction in the _____ _____ of the common stock, but no accounting transfers are made between accounts.

13. The assumption that some investors prefer a high dividend payout while others prefer a low payout is called the _____ effect.

14. The residual dividend policy is based on the fact that new common stock is _____ _____ than retained earnings.

15. Stock repurchased by the firm which issued it is called _____ _____.

Conceptual

16. An increase in cash dividends will always result in an increase in the price of the common stock because D_1 will increase in the stock valuation model.

    a. True   b. False

17. A stock dividend will affect which of the following balance sheet accounts?

    a. Common stock   b. Paid-in capital
    c. Retained earnings   d. Cash
    e. The accounts in a, b, and c will all be affected.

18. A stock split will affect the amounts shown in which of the following balance sheet accounts?

    a. Common stock   b. Paid-in capital
    c. Retained earnings   d. Cash
    e. None of the above accounts

19. If investors prefer dividends to capital gains, then:

    a. The required rate of return on equity, k_s, will not be affected by a change in dividend policy.
    b. The cost of capital will not be affected by a change in dividend policy.
    c. k_s will increase as the payout ratio is reduced.
    d. k_s will decrease as the retention rate increases.
    e. A policy conforming to the residual theory of dividends will maximize stock price.

©1992 The Dryden Press
All rights reserved.

20. If investors are indifferent between dividends and capital gains, the farther to the left the IOS and MCC schedule intersect, the higher the dividend payout ratio should be.

    a. True   **b.** False

21. Which of the following statements is most correct?

    a. Modigliani and Miller's theory of the effect of dividend policy on the value of a firm has been called the "bird-in-the-hand" theory, because MM argued that a dividend in the hand is less risky than a potential capital gain in the bush. After extensive empirical tests, this theory is now accepted by most financial experts.
    b. According to proponents of the "dividend irrelevance theory," if a company's stock price rises after the firm announces a greater-than-expected dividend increase, the price increase occurs because of signaling effects, not because of investors' preferences for dividends over capital gains.
    c. If one drew a graph where the dividend yield was plotted on the vertical axis and the expected growth rate on the horizontal axis, the line setting forth the relationship would, if the irrelevance theory were correct, have a slope coefficient of -1.0, while if the bird-in-the-hand theory were correct, the slope coefficient would be less negative, say -0.7.
    d. Statements a, b, and c are all correct.
    e. Statements b and c are both correct.

22. Which of the following statements is most correct?

    a. The residual dividend policy calls for the establishment of a fixed, stable dividend (or dividend growth rate) and then for the level of investment each year to be determined as a residual equal to net income after taxes minus the established dividends.
    b. According to the residual dividend policy, for any given MCC schedule and level of earnings, the further to the right the IOS schedule cuts the MCC schedule, the lower the optimal dividend payout ratio.
    c. According to the text, a firm would probably maximize its stock price if it established a specific dividend payout ratio, say 40 percent, and then paid that percentage of earnings out each year, because stockholders would then know exactly how much dividend income to count on when they planned their spending for the coming year.
    d. If you buy a stock after the ex-dividend date but before the dividend has been paid, then you, and not the seller, will receive the next dividend check the company sends out.
    e. Each of the above statements is false.

©1992 The Dryden Press
All rights reserved.

SELF-TEST PROBLEMS

1. Express Industries' expected net income for next year is $1 million. The company's target and current capital structure is 40 percent debt and 60 percent common equity. The optimal capital budget for next year is $1.2 million. If Express uses the residual theory of dividends to determine next year's dividend payout, what is the expected payout ratio?

   a. 0%   **b.** 10%   **c.** 28%   **d.** 42%   **e.** 56%

2. Amalgamated Shippers has a current and target capital structure of 30 percent debt and 70 percent equity. This past year Amalgamated, which uses a residual theory dividend policy, had a dividend payout ratio of 47.5 percent and net income of $800,000. What was Amalgamated's capital budget?

   a. $400,000   **b.** $500,000   **c.** $600,000   **d.** $700,000   **e.** $800,000

ANSWERS TO SELF-TEST QUESTIONS

1. no effect
2. dividends; capital gains
3. payout
4. capital gains; income
5. price (or value); information
6. volatile (fluctuating)
7. holder-of-record
8. ex-dividend; holder-of-record
9. payment; board of directors
10. dividend reinvestment
11. retained earnings; common stock; paid-in capital
12. par value
13. clientele
14. more costly
15. treasury stock

16. b. A dividend increase could be perceived by investors as signifying poor investment opportunities and hence lower growth in future earnings, thus reducing g in the DCF model. The net effect on stock price is uncertain.

17. e. A stock dividend requires an accounting entry transfer from the retained earnings account to the common stock and paid-in capital accounts. There is no cash involved in a stock dividend.

18. e. A stock split will affect the par value and number of shares outstanding. However, no dollar values will be affected.

19. c. This is the Gordon-Lintner hypothesis. If investors view dividends as being less risky than potential capital gains, then the cost of equity is inversely related to the payout ratio.

20. a. If investors are indifferent, firms should follow the residual theory. Thus, the smaller the optimal capital budget, the higher the dividend payout ratio.

12-9

©1992 The Dryden Press
All rights reserved.

21. e. Statement a is false; the proponents of this theory were Gordon and Lintner and empirical tests have not proven any of the dividend theories. Both statements b and c are correct. Therefore, statement e is the proper choice.

22. b. Statement a is false; the residual dividend policy calls for the determination of the optimal capital budget and then the dividend is established as a residual of net income minus the amount of retained earnings necessary for the capital budget. Statement b is correct. Statement c is false; a constant payout policy would lead to uncertainty of dividends due to fluctuating earnings. Statement d is false; if a stock is bought after the ex-dividend the dividend remains with the seller of the stock.

SOLUTIONS TO SELF-TEST PROBLEMS

1. c. The $1,200,000 capital budget will be financed using 40 percent debt and 60 percent equity. Therefore, the equity requirement will be 0.6($1,200,000) = $720,000. Since the expected net income is $1,000,000, $280,000 will be available to pay as dividends. Thus, the payout ratio is expected to be $280,000/$1,000,000 = 0.28 = 28%.

2. c. Of the $800,000 in net income, 0.475($800,000) = $380,000 was paid out as dividends. Thus, $420,000 was retained in the firm for investment. This is the equity portion of the capital budget, or 70 percent of the capital budget. Therefore, the total capital budget was $420,000/0.7 = $600,000.

©1992 The Dryden Press
All rights reserved.

CHAPTER 13
COMMON STOCK AND THE
INVESTMENT BANKING PROCESS

OVERVIEW

This chapter is more descriptive than analytical, but financial managers do need a working knowledge of the issues covered. Common stock constitutes the ownership position in a firm. As owners, the common stockholders have certain rights and privileges, including (1) the right to control the firm through election of directors and (2) the right to the residual earnings of the firm. Firms generally begin their corporate life as closely held companies, with all the common stock held by the founding managers. Then, as the company grows, it is often necessary to sell stock to the general public (that is, go public) to raise more funds. At this point, the firm's managers must be familiar with securities markets, including their regulation by the Securities and Exchange Commission (SEC). Eventually, the firm may choose to list its stock on one of the organized exchanges.

OUTLINE

I. **Common stock represents the ownership of an incorporated business.**

    A. Legal and accounting terminology are important in analyzing the owners' position in a business firm.
        1. Shares of common stock are authorized by the owners of a business and issued by management.
        2. *Par value* is the minimum amount for which new shares can be issued.
        3. *Retained earnings* represent the net income earned over the years that has been reinvested in the business rather than paid out as dividends.
        4. Any difference between the par value and what stockholders paid for common stock is shown on the balance sheet as *additional paid-in capital*.
        5. The *book value* of each common share is equal to the net worth, or common equity (common stockholder's equity), consisting of the sum of common stock, retained earnings, and paid-in capital, divided by the number of shares of common stock outstanding.

    B. The corporation's common stockholders have certain rights and privileges.
        1. Common stockholders have control of the firm through their election of the firm's directors, who in turn select officers to manage the business.
          a. In a large, publicly owned firm, neither the managers nor any individual shareholders normally have the 51 percent necessary for absolute control of the company.

©1992 The Dryden Press
All rights reserved.

    b. Thus, stockholders must vote for directors, and the voting process is regulated by both state and federal laws.

    c. Stockholders who are unable to attend annual meetings may still vote by means of a *proxy*. Proxies can be solicited by any party seeking to control the firm.

2. The *preemptive right* gives the current shareholders the right to purchase any new shares issued in proportion to their current holdings.

    a. The preemptive right may or may not be required by state law.

    b. When granted, the preemptive right enables current owners to maintain their proportionate share of ownership and control of the business.

    c. It also prevents the sale of shares at low prices to new stockholders which would dilute the value of the previously issued shares.

C. Special classes of common stock are sometimes created by a firm to meet special needs and circumstances. If two classes of stock were desired, one would normally be called "Class A" and the other "Class B."

1. Class A might be entitled to receive dividends before dividends can be paid on Class B stock.

2. Class B might have the exclusive right to vote.

3. Note that Class A and Class B have no standard meanings.

4. *Founders' shares* are stock owned by the firm's founders that have sole voting rights but restricted dividends for a specified number of years.

D. Financing with common stock has the following advantages to the corporation:

1. Common stock does not obligate the firm to make fixed payments to stockholders.

2. Common stock carries no fixed maturity date.

3. Common stock increases the creditworthiness of the firm, thus increasing the future availability of debt at a lower cost.

4. Common stock can often be sold more easily than debt if the firm's prospects look potentially good but risky.

5. Financing with common stock serves as a reserve of borrowing capacity.

E. Financing with common stock has the following disadvantages to the corporation:

1. Issuing common stock extends voting rights, and perhaps even control, to new stockholders.

2. Common stock gives new stockholders the right to a percentage of profits rather than to a fixed payment in the case of creditors.

3. The cost of underwriting and distributing common stock is high.

4. If common stock is sold to the point where the equity ratio exceeds that in the optimal capital structure, a firm's average cost of capital will increase; and its stock price will not be maximized.

5. Dividends paid to stockholders are not tax deductible as is interest paid to creditors.

©1992 The Dryden Press
All rights reserved.

II. **Some companies are so small that their common stocks are not actively traded; they are owned by only a few people, usually the companies' managers. Such firms are said to be closely held corporations. In contrast, the stocks of most larger companies are owned by a large number of investors, most of whom are not active in management. Such companies are said to be publicly held corporations.**

A. Stock market transactions may be separated into three distinct categories.
1. The *secondary market* deals with trading in previously issued, or outstanding, shares of established, publicly owned companies. The company receives no new money when sales are made in the secondary market.
2. The *primary market* handles additional shares sold by established, publicly owned companies. Companies can raise additional capital by selling in this market.
3. The primary market also handles new public offerings of shares in firms that were formerly closely held. Capital for the firm can be raised by *going public*, and this market is often termed the *initial public offering (IPO) market*.

B. Most businesses begin life as proprietorships, partnerships, or closely held corporations. However, if the business prospers and grows, at some point the decision must be made as to whether to go public. There are advantages and disadvantages to public ownership.
1. Going public has the following advantages:
   a. The original owners are able to diversify their holdings by selling some of their stock in a public offering.
   b. Public ownership increases the liquidity of the stock.
   c. New corporate cash is more easily raised by a publicly owned company.
   d. Going public establishes the firm's value in the marketplace.
2. Going public has the following disadvantages:
   a. A publicly owned company must file quarterly and annual reports with various governmental agencies.
   b. Publicly owned firms must disclose operating and ownership data.
   c. The opportunities for owners/managers to engage in questionable, but legal, self-dealings are reduced.
   d. If a publicly held firm is very small, its shares will be traded very infrequently; therefore, a liquid market will not really exist.
   e. Managers of publicly owned firms with less than 50 percent control must be concerned about tender offers and proxy fights. This sometimes leads to operating decisions that are not in the best long-run interests of the shareholders.

C. Stocks traded on organized exchanges are called listed stocks. While the decision to go public is significant, the decision to list is not a major event. In order to have a listed stock, a company must apply to an exchange, pay a relatively small fee, and meet the exchange's minimum requirements.
1. The company will have to file a few new reports with an exchange.
2. It will have to abide by the rules of the exchange.

©1992 The Dryden Press
All rights reserved.

3. Firms benefit from listing their stock by gaining liquidity, status, and free publicity. These factors may cause the value of the stock to be increased.

D. Sales of new securities, as well as operations in the secondary markets, are regulated by the federal government through the Securities and Exchange Commission (SEC) and, to a lesser extent, by each of the 50 states.
   1. The SEC has jurisdiction over all interstate offerings to the public in amounts of $1.5 million or more.
   2. New issues must be registered at least 20 days before they are offered to the public. A *prospectus* describing the company and the securities to be offered must be sent to prospective purchasers of the new issue.
   3. The SEC has control over stock trades by corporate insiders. Officers, directors, and major stockholders must file monthly reports of changes in their holdings of the stock of the corporation.

E. The Federal Reserve Board controls the flow of credit that may be used in purchasing securities through the use of margin requirements, which stipulate the maximum percentage of the purchase price of a security that can be borrowed.

III. **The financial manager must have a knowledge of the investment banking process, the process by which new securities are issued. Investment banking decisions take place in two stages.**

A. At Stage I, the firm makes some preliminary decisions on its own.
   1. The dollar amount of new capital required is established.
   2. The type of securities to be offered is specified.
   3. The basis on which to deal with the investment bankers, either by a *competitive bid* or a *negotiated deal* is determined.
   4. Finally, the investment banking firm must be selected.

B. The Stage II decisions are made jointly by the firm and the selected investment banker.
   1. First, the two parties will reevaluate the Stage I decisions.
   2. The firm and its investment banker must decide whether the banker will work on a "best efforts" basis or will "underwrite" the issue.
      a. On a *best efforts sale*, the banker does not guarantee that the securities will be sold or that the company will get the cash it needs.
      b. On an *underwritten issue*, the company does get a guarantee. Essentially, the banker purchases the issue, then resells the securities at a higher price. The banker bears significant risks in underwritten offerings.
   3. The costs associated with a new security issue are termed *flotation costs*.
      a. These costs include compensation to the investment banker plus legal, accounting, printing, and other costs borne by the issuer.
      b. Flotation costs depend on the type of security issued and the size of the issue.
   4. Several factors must be considered when setting the offering price.

13-4

©1992 The Dryden Press
All rights reserved.

a. If the firm is already publicly owned, the offering price will be based upon the existing market price.

b. The investment banker will have an easier job if the issue is priced relatively low, while the issuer naturally wants as high a price as possible.

c. Investors must be attracted to new issues. This can be done by reducing the price or by "promoting" the issue.

d. If *pressure* from a new stock issue drives down the price of the stock, all shares outstanding are affected, not just the new shares. This loss in firm value is also a flotation cost. However, it may not be a permanent loss; however, if the company's prospects really were poorer than investors had thought, then most of the price decline would have occurred sooner or later.

C. Because of potential losses from price declines caused by a falling market, underwriters do not generally handle issues single-handedly. Groups of investment bankers form an *underwriting syndicate* to spread the risk and minimize individual losses. Syndicates are also useful because an individual banker's clients may not be able to absorb a large issue. In addition to a syndicate, a *selling group* may handle the distribution of securities to individual investors.

D. For new issues, the investment banker will normally maintain a market in the shares after the public offering. This is done in order to provide liquidity for the shares and to maintain a good relationship with both the issuer and the investors who purchased the shares.

SELF-TEST QUESTIONS

Definitional

1. Ownership interest in a corporation is reflected on the balance sheet by the _____ _____ accounts.

2. Amounts paid by stockholders in excess of the par value are shown as "additional _____-___ _____."

3. One of the fundamental rights of common stockholders is to elect a firm's _____, who in turn elect the firm's operating management.

4. If a stockholder cannot vote in person, participation in the annual meeting is still possible through a _____.

5. The preemptive right protects stockholders against loss of _____ of the corporation as well as _____ of market value from the sale of new shares below market value.

13-5

©1992 The Dryden Press
All rights reserved.

6. Firms may find it desirable to separate the common stock into different _____. Generally, this classification is designed to differentiate stock in terms of the right to receive _____ and the right to _____.

7. A _____ _____ or _____ _____ corporation is one whose stock is held by a small group, normally its management.

8. The trading of previously issued shares of a corporation takes place in the _____ market, while new issues are offered in the _____ market.

9. _____ _____ refers to the sale of shares of a closely held business to the general public.

10. Going public establishes the firm's _____ in the marketplace.

11. Securities traded on the organized exchanges are known as _____ securities.

12. Before an interstate issue of stock amounting to $1.5 million or more can be sold to the public, it must be _____ with and approved by the _____.

13. Setting the _____ price for an issue of stock may present a conflict of interest between the issuer and the _____ _____.

14. In order to spread the risk of underwriting a sizable common stock issue, investment bankers will form an _____ _____.

15. Credit used to buy stock is known as _____ credit, and its use is controlled by the _____ _____ _____.

Conceptual

16. A change in the dividend payout ratio will have the most direct, or most immediate, effect on a firm's

   a. Common stock account.
   b. Earnings per share.
   c. Paid-in capital account.
   d. Net operating income.
   e. Retained earnings account.

17. When stockholders assign their right to vote to another party, this is called

   a. A privilege.
   b. A preemptive right.
   c. An ex right.
   d. A proxy.
   e. A prospectus.

©1992 The Dryden Press
All rights reserved.

18. A firm may go public, yet the firm itself may not receive any additional funds in the process.

    a. True   **b.** False

19. Flotation costs are generally higher for bond issues than for stock issues.

    a. True   **b.** False

20. When new shares are being sold, if it appears that the investment bankers will be unable to sell the entire issue at the initial offering price, the only way the entire issue can be sold is to lower the price.

    a. True   **b.** False

21. Which of the following statements is most correct?

    a. The preemptive right gives current stockholders the right to purchase a pro rata share of any new stock that the firm decides to issue. This is a fundamental right, and all stockholders have it.

    b. Whenever a publicly-owned firm decides to issue new common stock, it must register the stock with the SEC, and prospective stockholders must be given a copy of the prospectus. The SEC must approve the prospectus, and one key aspect of this approval is that the SEC must agree that the price at which the shares are to be offered is fair to investors.

    c. Once a company "goes public," it must file periodic statements with the SEC. These periodic statements are called "prospectuses," or, sometimes, "red herring prospectuses."

    d. One important recent innovation is "shelf registration," whereby large companies can register securities in advance, in effect putting them "on the shelf" of an investment banking house, which can then sell them at any time, in whole or in part, when the market is receptive to the securities. Theoretically, either stock or bonds could be sold through shelf registrations, but, because of the preemptive right, as a practical matter, only bonds are involved.

    e. All of the above statements are false.

©1992 The Dryden Press
All rights reserved.

SELF-TEST PROBLEMS

(The following data apply to the next three Self-Test Problems.)

Pepple-Smith Company
Common Stockholders' Equity Accounts

Common stock (100,000 shares authorized, 80,000 shares outstanding, $1 par)	$ 80,000
Additional paid-in capital	720,000
Retained earnings	1,200,000
Total common stockholders' equity	$2,000,000

1. If all 80,000 shares outstanding were sold at one offering, how much did Pepple-Smith receive for each share?

    a. $1   **b.** $5   **c.** $10   **d.** $20   **e.** $25

2. What is the current book value per share?

    a. $1   **b.** $5   **c.** $10   **d.** $20   **e.** $25

3. Suppose the firm sold the remaining authorized shares and netted $20.00 per share from the sale. What is the new book value per share?

    a. $23   **b.** $24   **c.** $25   **d.** $26   **e.** $27

ANSWERS TO SELF-TEST QUESTIONS

1. common equity
2. paid-in capital
3. directors
4. proxy
5. control; dilution
6. classes; dividends; vote
7. closely held; privately owned
8. secondary; primary
9. Going public
10. value
11. listed
12. registered; SEC
13. offering; investment banker
14. underwriting syndicate
15. margin; Federal Reserve Board

16. e. Although a change in the dividend payout would, in the long run, affect every item listed, retained earnings would be affected most directly.

17. d. Recently, there has been a spate of proxy fights, whereby a dissident group of stockholders solicits proxies in competition with the firm's management. If the dissident group gets a majority of the proxies, then it can gain control of the board of directors and oust existing management.

©1992 The Dryden Press
All rights reserved.

18. a. An example, that of the Ford Foundation selling stock to the general public, is given in the text. Also, a firm may go public if its managers sell off a portion of their stock holdings. Then, the funds obtained go to the managers rather than the firm.

19. b. The investment banker normally must expend greater effort in selling stocks, thus must charge a higher fee.

20. b. The investment bankers may be able to increase the demand for the stock by "promoting" the issue. If not, then a price reduction may be required.

21. e. Statement a is false; stockholders *often* have this right, but not always. Statement b is false; the SEC is responsible for making sure the information in the registration and prospectus is adequate; however, it does not determine the fairness of the offering price. Statement c is false; prospectuses accompany any sales solicitations. Statement d is false; shelf registrations are also applicable to common stock. Thus, statement e is the correct choice.

SOLUTIONS TO SELF-TEST PROBLEMS

1. c. The offering of 80,000 shares resulted in the firm collecting $80,000 in par value and $720,000 in additional paid-in capital for a total of $800,000. Thus, each share must have brought Pepple-Smith $800,000/80,000 = $10.

2. e. The total common equity of $2,000,000 represents the total investment of the 80,000 shares outstanding. Thus, the book value per share is $2,000,000/80,000 = $25.

3. b. The firm now sells the remaining 20,000 shares and nets $20 per share for a total of $400,000. Thus, the new total common equity is $2,400,000, and 100,000 shares are outstanding. The new book value per share is $2,400,000/100,000 = $24. Note that selling new shares below book value results in a lower book value on all shares. The opposite holds if new shares are sold above book value.

©1992 The Dryden Press
All rights reserved.

CHAPTER 14
LONG-TERM DEBT

OVERVIEW

Most firms find it desirable to use long-term debt financing. The two most important classes of fixed income securities are term loans and bonds. These securities come in many types: secured and unsecured, zero-coupon and normal coupon, floating rate and fixed rate, and so on. The variety of types stems from the fact that different groups of investors favor different types of securities, and their tastes change over time. The astute financial manager knows how to "package" securities at a given point in time to attract the greatest number of potential investors, thereby keeping the firm's cost of capital to a minimum.

OUTLINE

I.   Long-term debt is often called funded debt. When a firm "funds" its short-term debt, this means that it replaces short-term debt with securities of longer maturity.

II.   A term loan is a contract under which a borrower agrees to make a series of interest and principal payments on specific dates to the lender.

    A.   The financial institution which lends the funds is usually a bank, an insurance company, or a pension fund.

    B.   The *maturity* of a term loan is generally from 3 to 15 years, but it may be as short as 2 or as long as 30 years.

    C.   Term loans have three major advantages over public offerings: speed, flexibility, and low issuance costs.

    D.   The interest rate on a term loan can either be fixed for the life of the loan or be variable.

III. A bond is a long-term contract under which a borrower agrees to make payments of interest and principal on specific dates to the holder of the bond.

    A.   Bonds differ from term loans in that they are generally offered to the public rather than to a single lender or a small group of lenders.

    B.   The interest rate is generally fixed, although in recent years there has been an increase in the use of various types of floating rate bonds.

    C.   Some of the more important types of bonds include the following:

©1992 The Dryden Press
All rights reserved.

1. Under a *mortgage bond*, the corporation pledges certain assets as security for the bond. All such bonds are written subject to an indenture, which is a legal document that spells out in detail the rights of both the bondholders and the corporation.

2. A *debenture* is an unsecured bond, and as such it provides no lien against specific property as security for the obligation. Debenture holders are, therefore, general creditors whose claims are protected by property not otherwise pledged.

3. *Subordinate debentures* have claims on assets, in the event of bankruptcy, only after senior debt as named in the subordinate debt's indenture has been paid off. Subordinated debentures may be subordinated to designated notes payable or to all other debt.

4. There are several other important types of bonds:
   a. *Convertible bonds* are securities that can be converted into a fixed number of shares of common stock at the option of the bondholder.
   b. Bonds issued with *warrants* provide the investor with an option to buy the common stock of the firm at a *stated price*. The warrants are detachable from the bonds, and the bonds remain outstanding even after the warrants have been exercised.
   c. *Income bonds* pay interest only when covered by the earnings of the firm.
   d. *Putable bonds* may be turned in and exchanged for cash at the holder's option.
   e. *Indexed, or purchasing power, bonds* have their coupon rates tied to an inflation index, such as the consumer price index.

IV. **A firm's managers are concerned with both the effective cost of debt and any restrictions in debt contracts which might limit the firm's future alternatives. There are a number of features which could affect either the cost of the firm's debt or the firm's future flexibility.**

   A. The *indenture* is the legal document which spells out the rights of both the bondholders and the issuing corporation. It contains the basic terms of the issue as well as any special provisions such as *restrictive covenants*, *call provisions*, and *sinking funds*. A *trustee*, assigned to represent the bondholders, makes certain that terms of the indenture are carried out.

   B. A *call provision* gives the issuing corporation the right to call the entire bond issue for redemption before its regular maturity.
      1. When a bond is called, the company must normally pay an amount greater than the par value. This extra payment is referred to as a *call premium*.
      2. Bonds are frequently called when the issuing firm can *refund* the issue at a lower interest rate. The call premium is thus a penalty for depriving investors of the higher interest rate.

   C. A *sinking fund* provision requires that a firm retire a portion of its bond issue each year.

©1992 The Dryden Press
All rights reserved.

1. Failure to make a sinking fund payment constitutes technical default, so lenders can require immediate payment on the entire issue and possibly force the firm into bankruptcy.
2. Generally, sinking funds permit the firm to call a specific number of bonds for redemption or to buy the required number of bonds in the open market. The firm will select whichever method is the least expensive.

V. **There have been several recent innovations in long-term financing.**

A. *Zero coupon bonds* pay no interest but are offered at a substantial discount below their par values and hence provide capital appreciation rather than interest income.
   1. The advantages to the issuer are that no cash outlays are required until maturity, and these bonds often have a lower required rate of return than coupon bonds.
   2. The advantages for investors are that there is little danger of a call, and zeros guarantee a "true" yield to maturity since there is no reinvestment rate risk.

B. When interest rates are volatile, lenders are reluctant to lend long term. Thus, they charge very high maturity risk premiums. On the other hand, borrowers, in general, would rather borrow long term so that they do not have to worry about having to continually refund their debt. The answer to the dilemma is *long-term floating rate debt*.
   1. The floating rate bond may have a 5- or 10-year maturity, but the interest rate changes periodically to reflect current market conditions.
   2. Floating rate debt is advantageous to lenders because it causes the market value of the debt to be stabilized, and it provides lenders with more income to meet their own obligations.
   3. Floating rate debt is also advantageous to corporations because they can obtain debt with a long maturity without committing themselves to paying an historically high rate of interest for the entire term of the loan. However, if interest rates rise, borrowers will face increasing interest expense.

C. Another new type of bond is the *junk bond*, a high-risk, high-yield bond issued to finance a leveraged buyout or merger, or by a troubled company.

VI. **Bond issues are normally assigned quality ratings by both Moody's Investors Service and Standard & Poor's Corporation. These ratings reflect the probability that a bond will go into default. Aaa (Moody's) and AAA (S&P) are the highest ratings.**

A. Rating assignments are based on qualitative and quantitative factors including the firm's debt/assets ratio, current ratio, and coverage ratios.

B. Bond ratings are important both to firms and to investors.

14-3

©1992 The Dryden Press
All rights reserved.

1. Because a bond's rating is an indicator of its default risk, the rating has a direct, measurable influence on the bond's interest rate and the firm's cost of debt capital.
2. Most bonds are purchased by institutional investors rather than individuals, and many institutions are restricted to investment-grade securities.

C. Rating agencies review outstanding bonds on a periodic basis, occasionally upgrading or downgrading a bond as the issuer's circumstances change. Also, if a company issues more bonds, this will trigger a review by the rating agencies.

VII. **Most firms use several types of long-term securities.**

A. The various types of securities offer different risk/return combinations to investors and hence have different costs to the firm.

B. In theory, a firm should be indifferent between different types of securities because each would have a cost commensurate with its risk.
1. However, changes in supply/demand conditions can cause some securities to be "cheaper" than others at times.
2. Additionally, innovative, or new, securities often offer firms a particular bargain rate until "pent-up demand" for them is satisfied.

VIII. **Long-term financing decisions are difficult because they are influenced by many factors, most of which are subjective. Additionally, these factors vary among firms at any point in time and for any given firm over time.**

A. One of the foremost considerations is the firm's *target capital structure*.
1. Over the long haul, firms try to maintain their target structures.
2. However, from year to year, a firm may stray from the target to minimize flotation costs, to take advantage of market conditions, or because of its own internal situation. As examples, a firm would not want to issue long-term debt if it was convinced interest rates were about to fall; and it would not want to issue stock if it felt that its earnings were about to rise sharply, and more than the public anticipated.

B. Firms also must consider the *maturity of the assets being financed*.
1. If a firm uses 30-year bonds to finance 10-year assets, the bond payments would continue long after the assets were retired.
2. If a firm uses 10-year bonds to finance 30-year assets, it would have to "roll over" the debt after 10 years.
3. Each of the above strategies involves significant risks. In general, the least risky strategy is to match the maturity of the debt to the maturity of the assets being financed.

C. *Current interest rate levels and forecasts of future interest rates* also play an important role in the financing decision.

©1992 The Dryden Press
All rights reserved.

1. If current rates are high and are expected to drop, it might be wise to use short-term financing until rates drop and then lock in the lower rates with long-term financing.
2. Conversely, if current rates are low and expected to rise, use long-term financing now to lock in the rates.
3. However, interest rates are difficult, if not impossible, to forecast. Thus, pursuing one of the above strategies could prove to be disastrous if the forecasts were wrong.

D. The firm's *current condition and earnings outlook* also have an effect on the choice of securities.
1. A firm may delay debt financing which would trigger a review by the rating agencies.
2. Debt issued when in a poor financial condition would probably cost more and have more severe restrictive covenants.

E. The *amount of financing required* and the *availability of assets which could be pledged as collateral* also impact the financing decision.

IX. **In the event of bankruptcy, debtholders have a prior claim over the claims of both common and preferred stockholders to a firm's income and assets.**

A. When a business becomes insolvent, it does not have enough cash to meet scheduled interest and principal payments. Thus, it must decide whether to dissolve the firm through liquidation or to permit it to reorganize and thus stay alive. These issues are discussed in Chapters 7 and 11 of the federal bankruptcy statutes.
1. In a reorganization, a plan may call for restructuring of the firm's debt, in which case the interest rate may be reduced, the term to maturity lengthened, or some of the debt may be exchanged for equity.
2. Liquidation occurs if the company is deemed to be too far gone to be saved. Upon liquidation, assets are distributed as specified in Chapter 7 of the Bankruptcy Act, beginning with highest priority to secured creditors and ending with lowest priority to common stockholders (assuming anything is left).

B. Appendix 14A discusses bankruptcy and reorganization in more detail.

X. **Bond refunding decisions involve two separate questions: (1) Would it be profitable to call an outstanding issue now, and to replace it with a new issue? (2) Even if refunding is currently profitable, would it be better to call now or to postpone the refunding to a later date?**

A. Refunding decisions are similar to capital budgeting decisions, and the net present value method is the primary tool. Thus, the costs of undertaking the refunding operation (the investment outlay) are compared to the present value of the interest that will be saved if the high interest rate bond is called and replaced with

14-5

©1992 The Dryden Press
All rights reserved.

a new, low interest rate bond. If the net present value of the refunding is positive, then the refunding should take place.

   B.   Appendix 14B examines the second issue of whether to call an issue now or to postpone to a later date.

SELF-TEST QUESTIONS

Definitional

1.   Long-term debt is sometimes referred to as _____ debt.

2.   A _____ loan is a contract to pay _____ and _____ on specific dates to a lender.

3.   Term loans are generally negotiated directly with a _____, an _____ _____, or a _____ _____. They are not sold to the _____ at large.

4.   A _____ is a long-term contract under which the _____ agrees to make payments of interest and principal to the holder.

5.   The legal document setting forth the terms and conditions of a bond issue is known as the _____.

6.   The _____ represents the bondholders and sees that the terms of the indenture are carried out.

7.   A bond secured by real estate is known as a _____ bond.

8.   Failure to make a sinking fund payment places the company in _____ _____, and could ultimately lead to _____.

9.   In meeting its sinking fund requirements, a firm may _____ the bonds or purchase them on the _____ _____.

10. Except when the call is for sinking fund purposes, when a bond issue is called, the firm must pay a _____ _____, or an amount in excess of the _____ value of the bond.

11. A restrictive _____ is a provision in the bond's _____ which requires the issuer to meet certain stated conditions.

12. A bond issue is most likely to be called if interest rates have _____ substantially since the time of issue.

©1992 The Dryden Press
All rights reserved.

13. Firms issue various securities because investors have different _____ /_____ trade-offs.

14. Over the long-run, a firm should finance in accordance with its _____ _____ _____.

15. The least risky financing strategy is to match the _____ of the debt with the _____ of the asset being financed.

Conceptual

16. There is a direct relationship between bond ratings and the required rate of return of bonds; that is, the higher the rating, the higher is the required rate of return.

    a. True   **b.** False

17. Which of the following would tend to increase the coupon interest rate on a bond that is to be issued?

    a. Adding a sinking fund   **b.** Adding a restrictive covenant
    c. Adding a call provision   **d.** A change in the bond's rating from Aa to Aaa
    e. Both a and c above

18. Zero coupon bonds have become quite popular over the last several years. These bonds are advantageous to the issuer because

    a. The bond is, in effect, not callable.
    b. These bonds generally have a higher yield to maturity than normal coupon bonds.
    c. The bond's cash outflows are spread over the life of the bond.
    d. The bonds are initially sold above par value.
    e. None of the above statements is correct.

19. The "penalty" for having a low bond rating is less severe when the Security Market Line is relatively steep than when it is not so steep.

    a. True   **b.** False

20. Which of the following statements is most correct?

    a. A first mortgage bond is secured by a company's assets, whereas a debenture is a type of bond that is secured by a second mortgage, meaning that it will only be paid off, in the event of bankruptcy, after the first mortgage bondholders have been paid in full.
    b. If a company were to issue a number of different types of securities on a given day, their coupon rates (or dividend yields) would in all likelihood be ranked as follows:

©1992 The Dryden Press
All rights reserved.

preferred stock > straight fixed rate debentures > floating rate debentures > convertible debentures.

c. Company X is planning to issue new bonds. If the bonds of a U. S. company have a sinking fund, this means that the company must deposit funds with a trustee, who invests the funds and lets the amount on deposit build up to an amount sufficient to pay off the bonds when they mature. Sinking funds are set up differently in Europe, where the funds in the sinking fund are used either to buy bonds on the open market or else to call in a small fraction of the issue each year. The results of both American and European sinking funds are the same, though-- the bond obligation is paid off systematically rather that in one lump sum at maturity.

d. Each of the above statements is true.

e. Each of the above statements is false.

21. Which of the following statements is most correct?

a. If a company decides to use callable bonds, the interest rate on the bonds will be higher than if it made the bonds noncallable. Therefore, only weak companies whose interest rate would be high anyway tend to issue callable bonds.

b. Sinking fund provisions as spelled out in the indenture normally give the firm the right to call bonds for sinking fund purposes at par. This is bad for bondholders if interest rates have fallen. Therefore, if a company insists on including a sinking fund provision on its new bond issue, the interest rate will be higher than if the issue does not have a sinking fund.

c. The primary advantage of zero coupon bonds to investors, especially to wealthy individual investors, is that the investor gets his or her returns in the form of capital gains rather than interest income. Since capital gains (1) are taxed at relatively low rates and (2) are deferred until the bond matures or is sold, zero coupon corporate bonds have a significant advantage over regular coupon bonds.

d. The bond refunding decision is analyzed like a capital budgeting decision. The investment cost consists of the call premium plus the flotation cost on the new issue, and the cash flow benefits consist of the interest saved each year as a result of substituting low rate debt for high rate debt. Rational companies constantly monitor the situation, and they call callable bonds immediately if the NPV on the refunding decision is positive.

e. The above statements are all false.

SELF-TEST PROBLEMS

1. J.C. Nickel is planning a zero coupon bond issue. The bond has a par value of $1,000, matures in 10 years, and will be sold at an 80 percent discount, or for $200. The firm's marginal tax rate is 40 percent. What is the annual after-tax cost of debt to Nickel on this issue? (Assume that the discount can be amortized over the life of the bond and deducted from taxable income.)

14-8

©1992 The Dryden Press
All rights reserved.

a. 9.59%   **b.** 10.00%   **c.** 11.62%   **d.** 14.79%   **e.** 17.46%

(The following data apply to Self-Test Problems 2 and 3.)

The Privy Company has just issued a 10-year bond with a 10 percent annual coupon. The $100,000 issue sold at its par value of $1,000 per bond. The indenture has a sinking fund provision which stipulates that one-tenth of the issue will be redeemed at the end of each year.

2. Assume that interest rates fall after the issue date, causing the market value of the bonds to rise, and that Privy exercises the sinking fund provision by calling one-tenth of the issue (10 bonds) each year. What is the effective before-tax cost of the issue?

    a. 8.0%   **b.** 9.2%   **c.** 10.0%   **d.** 11.2%   **e.** 12.0%

3. Now assume that interest rates rise after the issue date, causing the market value of bonds to fall, and that the firm retires the issue over time by buying 10 of the bonds outstanding each year on the open market. Further, assume that Privy can repurchase each bond (with a face value of $1,000) for $950, so its total expenditure to purchase 10 bonds is $9,500. Now what is the effective before-tax cost of the issue?

    a. 8.0%   **b.** 9.2%   **c.** 10.0%   **d.** 11.2%   **e.** 12.0%

4. Assume that the City of Miami sold an issue of $1,000 maturity value, tax exempt (muni), zero coupon bonds 10 years ago. The bonds had a 30-year maturity when they were issued, and the interest rate built into the issue was a nominal 12 percent, but with semiannual compounding. The bonds are now callable at a premium of 12 percent over the accrued value. What effective annual rate of return would an investor who bought the bonds when they were issued and who still owns them earn if they are called today?

    a. 13.33%   **b.** 12.00%   **c.** 12.37%   **d.** 11.76%   **e.** 13.64%

14-9

©1992 The Dryden Press
All rights reserved.

Appendix 14A

14A-1. The Stanton Marble Company has the following balance sheet:

Current assets	$15,120	Accounts payable	$ 3,240
Fixed assets	8,100	Notes payable (to bank)	1,620
		Accrued taxes	540
		Accrued wages	540
		Total current liabilities	$ 5,940
		First mortgage bonds	2,700
		Second mortgage bonds	2,700
		Total mortgage bonds	$ 5,400
		Subordinated debentures	3,240
		Total debt	$14,580
		Preferred stock	1,080
		Common stock	7,560
Total assets	$23,220	Total liabilities and equity	$23,220

The debentures are subordinated only to the notes payable. Suppose Stanton Marble goes bankrupt and is liquidated, with $5,400 being received from the sale of the fixed assets, which were pledged as security for the first and second mortgage bonds, and $8,640 received from the sale of current assets. The trustee's costs total $1,440. How much will the holders of subordinated debentures receive?

   a. $2,052   **b.** $2,448   **c.** $3,240   **d.** $2,709   **e.** $3,056

Appendix 14B

14B-1. The City of Tampa issued $1,000,000 of 12 percent coupon, 25-year, semiannual payment, tax-exempt muni bonds 10 years ago. The bonds had 10 years of call protection, but now Tampa can call the bonds if it chooses to do so. The call premium would be 11 percent of the face amount. New 15-year, 10 percent, semiannual payment bonds can be sold at par, but flotation costs on this issue would be 3 percent, or $30,000. What is the net present value of the refunding?

   a. $13,011   **b.** $12,262   **c.** $15,121   **d.** $13,725   **e.** $14,545

ANSWERS TO SELF-TEST QUESTIONS

1. funded
2. term; interest; principal
3. bank; insurance company; pension fund; public
4. bond; borrower
5. indenture
6. trustee
7. mortgage
8. technical default; bankruptcy
9. call; open market
10. call premium; par
11. covenant; indenture

©1992 The Dryden Press
All rights reserved.

12. fallen
13. risk/return

14. target capital structure
15. maturity; maturity

16. b. The relationship is inverse. The higher the rating, the lower is the default risk, and hence the lower is the required rate of return. Aaa/AAA is the highest rating, and as we go down the alphabet, the ratings are lower.

17. c. Sinking funds, restrictive covenants, and an improvement in the bond rating all indicate lower risk for the bond, and hence would lower the coupon rate.

18. e. The primary advantages to the issuer are (1) that zero coupons have a lower required rate of return, and (2) that annual interest payments are avoided.

19. b. A steeper SML implies a higher risk premium on risky securities, and thus a greater "penalty" on lower-rated bonds.

20. e. Statement a is false; a debenture is unsecured. Statement b is false; the before-tax yield of the preferred stock would be below those on the debentures because of their tax treatment. Statement c is false; sinking funds are used either to buy bonds on the open market or to call in a small fraction of the issue each year. Therefore, the correct choice is statement e.

21. e. Statement a is false; the second sentence of this statement is incorrect. Statement b is false; sinking fund provisions make a bond issue less risky, and thus, lower the coupon rate on the issue. Statement c is false; investors must impute interest income in each year on zero coupon bonds even though the interest is not received until maturity. The advantage to investors is that there is no reinvestment rate risk with zeros. Statement d is false; companies do not necessarily call callable bonds immediately if the NPV on the refunding decision is positive because if interest rates decrease further it may be beneficial to wait awhile. Therefore, the correct choice is statement e.

SOLUTIONS TO SELF-TEST PROBLEMS

1. a. Look at the cash flows to the firm. At Year 0, the firm receives $200. At Year 10, the firm must pay out $1,000. For each of the 10 years, Nickel is declaring a ($1,000 - $200)/10 = $80 interest expense, even though it is not actually paying interest in the interim period. The tax benefit of that expense is 0.40($80) = $32. Putting these cash flows on a time line, we get the following:

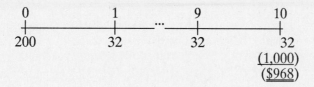

©1992 The Dryden Press
All rights reserved.

The cost of debt to the firm is that discount rate which equates the present values of the cash inflows and outflows, or the IRR.

Financial calculator solution: Input the cash flows into the cash flow register and solve for IRR = 9.59%.

2. c. Each year, Privy will retire $10,000 face value in bonds. Thus, its interest expense would also decrease by one-tenth each year:

Year	Debt Outstanding at Beginning of Year	Interest Expense
1	$100,000	$10,000
2	90,000	9,000
--	--------	--------
9	20,000	2,000
10	10,000	1,000

Thus, Privy pays 10 percent on the outstanding balance throughout the life of the issue and it is being retired at par value. Its effective before-tax cost is also 10 percent.

3. b. To answer this, you must lay out the cash flows over the life of the issue:

Year	Debt Outstanding at Beginning of Year	Interest Expense	Sinking Fund Expense	Total Service Requirement
1	$100,000	$10,000	$9,500	$19,500
2	90,000	9,000	9,500	18,500
3	80,000	8,000	9,500	17,500
4	70,000	7,000	9,500	16,500
5	60,000	6,000	9,500	15,500
6	50,000	5,000	9,500	14,500
7	40,000	4,000	9,500	13,500
8	30,000	3,000	9,500	12,500
9	20,000	2,000	9,500	11,500
10	10,000	1,000	9,500	10,500

Now, the firm receives $100,000 at Time 0, and pays out the cash flows shown above in the righthand column. The IRR of this cash flow stream, 9.2 percent, is Privy's before-tax cost of debt. The ability to repurchase the bonds at less than par reduces the cost of the issue. (Note that Privy would not actually be able to repurchase the final $10,000 worth of bonds for $9,500. The market value of the bonds would equal par value at maturity.)

©1992 The Dryden Press
All rights reserved.

4. e.

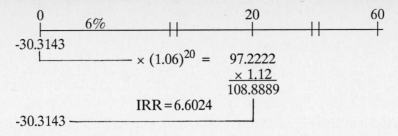

$$0 \qquad\qquad 6\% \qquad\qquad\qquad 20 \qquad\qquad\qquad 60$$

-30.3143

$$\times (1.06)^{20} = \quad 97.2222$$
$$\underline{\times 1.12}$$
$$108.8889$$

$$IRR = 6.6024$$

-30.3143

Periodic rate = 6.6024%.

EAR $= (1.066024)^2 - 1 = 0.1364 = 13.64\%$.

Appendix 14A

14A-1. a.

Claimant	Claim Amount (1)	Priority Distribution and General Creditor (2)	Subordinate Adjustment (3)	Percent of Claim (4)
Accounts payable	$3,240	$2,448	$2,448	75.56%
Notes payable	1,620	1,224	1,620	100.00
Accrued taxes	540	540	540	100.00
Accrued wages	540	540	540	100.00
1st mortgage bonds	2,700	2,700	2,700	100.00
2nd mortgage bonds	2,700	2,700	2,700	100.00
Subordinated debentures	3,240	2,448	2,052	63.33
Preferred stock	1,080	0	0	0.00
Common stock	7,560	0	0	0.00
Trustee	1,440	1,440	1,440	100.00
Total	$24,660	$14,040	$14,040	56.93%

Explanation of the columns:
(1) Values are taken from the balance sheet.
(2) Since the firm's total debt is $16,020 and only $14,040 is received from the sale of assets, the preferred and common stockholders are wiped out. These stockholders receive nothing.

The $5,400 from the sale of fixed assets is immediately allocated to the mortgage bonds. The holders of the first mortgage bonds are paid off first, so they receive $2,700. The remaining $2,700 from the sale of fixed assets is allocated to the second mortgage bonds, so these bondholders are also paid off.

By law, trustee expenses have first claim on the remaining available funds, wages have second priority, and taxes have third priority. Thus, these claims are paid in full.

14-13

©1992 The Dryden Press
All rights reserved.

We now have $6,120 remaining and claims of $8,100, so the general creditors will receive 75.56 cents on the dollar:

$$\frac{\text{Funds available}}{\text{Unsatisfied debt}} = \frac{\$1,040 - \$5,400 - \$1,080 - \$1,440}{\$3,240 + \$1,620 + \$3,240} = 0.7556.$$

General creditors are now initially allocated 75.56 percent of their original claims.

(3) This column reflects a transfer of funds from the subordinated debentures to the notes payable to the bank. Since subordinated debentures are subordinate to bank debt, notes payable to the bank must be paid in full before the debentures receive anything. The notes are paid in full by transferring the difference between their book value and initial allocation ($1,620 − $1,224 = $396) from subordinated debentures to notes payable. This reduces the allocation to subordinated debentures and increases the allocation to notes payable by $396.

Appendix 14B

14B-1.   d.   Interest on old bond per 6 months: $120,000/2 = $60,000
             Interest on new bond per 6 months: $100,000/2 =   50,000
             Savings per six months $10,000

             Cost: Call premium = 11% = $110,000
                        Flotation cost = 3% =   30,000
                                          $140,000

$k = 10\%/2 = 5\%$ per 6 months.

$$\text{NPV} = \sum_{t=1}^{30} \frac{\$10,000}{(1 + k)^t} - \$140,000 = \$153,725 - \$140,000 = \$13,725.$$

Alternatively, input the cash flows into the cash flow register, I = 5, and then solve for NPV = $13,725.

©1992 The Dryden Press
All rights reserved.

CHAPTER 15
HYBRID FINANCING:
PREFERRED STOCK, LEASING, AND OPTIONS

OVERVIEW

Firms can use different types of long-term financing other than common stock and debt. Other types of securities include (1) preferred stock, which is a hybrid security that represents a cross between debt and equity; (2) leasing, which is an alternative to borrowing; and (3) options, especially warrants and convertibles, which allow debtholders to share in the capital gains if a business is especially successful. All of these methods are widely used today, and an understanding of them is essential for the financial manager.

OUTLINE

I.   **Preferred stock is a hybrid type of long-term financing. It is called a hybrid because it represents an equity investment in a business, yet it has many of the characteristics associated with debt.**

    A.   If an analysis is being made by a common stockholder, preferred is treated like debt because it entails fixed charges which must be paid ahead of common stock dividends. However, if the analysis is being made by a creditor studying a firm's vulnerability to failure, preferred stock is viewed as part of the equity base.

    B.   Preferred stock has the following important features:
        1. Preferred stockholders have priority over common stockholders with regard to earnings and assets.
        2. Unlike common stock, preferred stock always has a par value.
        3. Most preferred stock provides for *cumulative dividends*; that is, all preferred dividends in arrears must be paid before common dividends can be paid.
        4. Some preferred stock is *convertible* into common stock.

    C.   There are advantages and disadvantages to financing with preferred stock:
        1. Preferred stock is a fixed cost form of financing, yet the firm avoids the danger of bankruptcy if earnings are too low to pay the preferred dividend. Preferred also allows a firm to avoid sharing control, as it must do when selling common stock.
        2. Although advantageous to a firm, preferred stock does have a higher after-tax cost of capital than debt, mainly because preferred dividends are not tax deductible.
        3. For the investor, preferred stock provides reasonably assured income. Also, for corporate investors, 70 percent of preferred dividends received are not taxable.

©1992 The Dryden Press
All rights reserved.

4. The disadvantages to the investors are (a) that returns are limited on preferred stock even though a substantial portion of ownership risk is borne by the preferred stockholders, and (b) that there are no legal rights to dividends even if a company earns a profit.

II. **The ownership of assets is not as important as the ability to use them in a profitable manner. Leasing provides the same ability to use capital assets as outright ownership. Leasing is similar to borrowing, and it provides the same type of financial leverage.**

A. Historically, land and buildings were the types of assets most often leased, but today it is possible to lease almost any kind of fixed asset.
 1. The *lessor* is the owner of the leased property and receives such tax benefits of ownership as the depreciation write-offs and, when they apply, investment tax credits.
 2. The *lessee* buys the right to use the property by making lease payments to the lessor.

B. There are three common types of leasing arrangements.
 1. Under a *sale and leaseback*, a firm owning an asset sells the property and simultaneously leases it back for a specified period at specific terms. This arrangement provides an alternative to simply borrowing against the property on a mortgage loan basis.
 2. *Operating leases* provide for both financing and maintenance. Ordinarily, these leases call for the lessor to maintain and service the leased equipment, and the cost of maintenance is built into the lease payments. These leases are frequently not fully amortized; that is, the payments required under the lease contract are not sufficient to recover the full cost of the equipment.
 3. *Financial, or capital, leases* are fully amortized; however, they do not provide for maintenance and are not cancelable. They differ from a sale-leaseback only in that new equipment is purchased by the lessor from a manufacturer rather than from the user-lessee.

C. Leasing is often referred to as *off balance sheet financing* because often neither the leased assets nor the lease liabilities appear on the firm's balance sheet.
 1. A firm with extensive lease arrangements would have both its assets and its liabilities understated in comparison with a firm which borrowed to purchase the assets. The firm that leases would show a lower debt ratio.
 2. FASB #13 requires firms to *capitalize* certain financial leases and thus to restate their balance sheets to report leased assets as fixed assets and the present value of future lease payments as debt.

D. Any prospective lease must be evaluated by both the lessee and the lessor. The lessee must determine whether leasing an asset is less costly than buying it, and the lessor must decide whether or not the lease will provide a reasonable rate of return.

©1992 The Dryden Press
All rights reserved.

E. For the lessee, leasing is a substitute for debt financing. In an NPV-type analysis, the lessee estimates the cost of leasing and the cost of owning. If the PV cost of leasing is less than the PV cost of owning, the asset should be leased.

    1. All cash flows must reflect tax effects.

    2. Since leasing is a substitute for debt financing and since lease cash flows have approximately the same risk as debt cash flows, the *appropriate discount rate is the after-tax cost of debt*.

F. Other factors often arise in leasing decisions.

    1. The value of the asset at lease termination is called its *residual value*.

        a. It might first appear that assets with large residual values would most likely be owned since the owner gets the residual value.

        b. However, competition among leasing companies forces lease contracts to reflect expected residual values. Thus, large residual value assets do not necessarily imply that firms should buy them rather than lease them.

    2. It is sometimes argued that firms which lease can get more favorable debt terms than firms which do not lease. That is, since some leases do not appear on the balance sheet, a firm may be able to use more leverage than if it did not lease.

III. An option is a contract which gives its holder the right to buy (or sell) an asset at some predetermined price within a specified period of time.

A. There are many types of options and option markets.

    1. Call options convey the right to buy a share of stock at a set price called the *exercise*, or *striking*, *price*.

    2. Put options give the holder the right to sell the stock at the striking price.

    3. An option, whether a call or a put, has both a buyer and a seller.

        a. The buyer has the right to exercise the option.

        b. The seller, who is called the writer, must execute the transaction if the option is exercised.

        c. A seller who writes call options on stock he or she holds is said to write *covered options*. A similar option written by someone who does not hold the stock is called a *naked option*.

    4. Corporations on whose stock options are written have nothing to do with the options market—they do not raise money in this market nor have any direct transactions in it.

B. The *formula value* of an option is defined as follows: Formula value = Current price of the stock - Striking price. The formula value can be thought of as the value of the option if it expired today.

    1. For example, if a stock sells for $25 and the option's exercise price is $20, the option's formula value is $25 - $20 = $5.

    2. However, the actual price as set in the options market will be higher than the formula value.

©1992 The Dryden Press
All rights reserved.

3. An option's market price is higher than its formula value because options offer investors greater leverage and less loss potential than do the underlying stocks.

C. In addition to the stock price and the striking price, the value of an option also depends on the following:
1. *Time to maturity*. The longer the option period, the greater its market value over its formula value.
2. *Stock price variability*. The greater the volatility of the underlying stock's price, the greater the premium.

IV. **A warrant is an option issued by a company which gives the holder the right to buy a stated number of shares of common stock at a specified price. Thus, warrants are essentially company-issued call options.**

A. Often warrants are attached to debt instruments as an incentive for investors to buy the combined issue at a lower interest rate than would otherwise be the case. Additionally, warrants may eliminate the need for extremely restrictive indenture provisions.

B. Warrants were originally used as "sweeteners" by small, risky firms to help sell either debt or preferred stocks. However, some strong firms have also used warrants.

C. The price paid for a bond with warrants is determined as follows: Price paid for bond with warrants = Straight-debt value of bond + Value of warrants.

D. Most warrants are *detachable* and can be traded separately from the bond or preferred stock with which they were issued.

E. There are three conditions which encourage holders to exercise their warrants:
1. Warrant holders will surely exercise warrants and buy stock if the warrants are about to expire with the market price of the stock above the exercise price.
2. Warrant holders will tend to exercise voluntarily and buy stock if the company raises the dividend on the common stock by a sufficient amount.
3. Warrants sometimes have *stepped-up exercise prices*, which prod owners into exercising them.

F. Warrants generally produce additional funds if a company is successful and grows, for then the stock price will increase over the exercise price.

V. **Convertible securities are bonds or preferred stocks that are exchanged for common stock at the option of the holder.**

A. Conversion of a bond or preferred stock, unlike exercise of a warrant, does not produce additional funds for the firm. However, conversion does lower the debt ratio.

©1992 The Dryden Press
All rights reserved.

B. The *conversion ratio* (CR) specifies the number of common shares that will be received for each bond or share of preferred stock that is converted.

C. The *conversion price*, P_c, is the effective price paid for the common stock when conversion occurs. For example, if a bond is issued at its par value of $1,000 and can be converted into 40 shares of common stock, the conversion price would be

$$\text{Conversion price} = P_c = \frac{\text{Par value of bond}}{CR} = \frac{\$1,000}{40} = \$25.$$

Someone buying the bond for $1,000 and then converting it would, in effect, be paying $25 per share for the stock.

D. The conversion price is typically set at about 10 to 30 percent above the market price of common stock when the bond is sold. Thus, if the common stock is selling for $20.83 at the time the convertible is issued, the conversion price might be set at 1.2($20.83) = $25. This would produce a *conversion ratio* of CR = 40:

$$CR = \frac{\$1,000}{P_c} = \frac{\$1,000}{\$25} = 40 \text{ shares.}$$

E. The bond's conversion value, C_t, is the value of common stock obtained by converting a convertible security. The actual market price of the bond must always be equal to or greater than the higher of its pure-debt value or its conversion value.

F. Convertibles have certain advantages and disadvantages to the issuing corporation:
   1. By giving investors an opportunity to realize capital gains, a firm can sell debt with a lower interest rate.
   2. The sale of a convertible issue may be thought of as having the effect of selling common stock at a higher-than-market price at the time the convertible is issued.
   3. If earnings do not rise and pull the stock price up, and hence conversion does not occur, the company could be saddled with debt in the face of low earnings.

VI. **If warrants or convertibles are outstanding, a firm can theoretically report earnings per share in one of three ways:**

A. *Simple EPS.* Earnings available to common stockholders are divided by the average number of shares actually outstanding during the period.

B. *Primary EPS.* The earnings per share are divided by the average number of shares that would have been outstanding if warrants and convertibles likely to be converted in the near future had actually been exercised or converted.

©1992 The Dryden Press
All rights reserved.

C. *Fully diluted EPS.* This is similar to primary EPS except that all warrants and convertibles are assumed to be exercised or converted, regardless of the likelihood of either occurring.

SELF-TEST QUESTIONS

Definitional

1. Preferred stock is referred to as a hybrid because it is similar to _____ in some respects and to _____ _____ in others.

2. The dividend on a share of _____ stock may be indicated as a _____ of the par value or in dollars.

3. Most preferred stock dividends are _____ and thus must be paid before dividends can be paid to common stockholders.

4. Preferred stocks are attractive to _____ investors because of the 70 percent dividend exclusion.

5. Issuing preferred stock decreases the danger of _____ if operating income is low.

6. Conceptually, leasing is similar to _____, and it provides the same type of financial _____.

7. Under a _____-____-_____ arrangement, the seller receives the purchase price of the asset but retains the _____ of the property.

8. _____ leases include both financing and maintenance arrangements.

9. A _____, or _____, lease is similar to a sale-and-leaseback arrangement, but financial leases generally apply to the purchase of _____ equipment directly from a manufacturer.

10. If the IRS allows the lease, then the _____ _____ are fully deductible.

11. Capitalizing a lease requires that the asset be listed under _____ _____, and that the _____ _____ of the future lease payments be shown as _____.

12. _____ among leasing companies will tend to force leasing rates down to the point where expected _____ values are fully reflected in the lease rates.

13. Since some leases do not appear on the _____ _____, a firm may be able to use more _____ than if it did not lease.

©1992 The Dryden Press
All rights reserved.

14. A firm with low profits may be able to transfer the depreciation write-off to another firm and be compensated in the form of lower _____ _____.

15. The leasing decision is normally a _____ decision rather than a _____ _____ decision.

16. _____ are the dominant factors behind most nonoperating leases.

17. Warrants and convertible securities may make a company's securities more attractive to a broader range of _____ and lower its _____ ___ _____.

18. A _____ is an option sold with a bond or preferred stock permitting the owner to buy a stated number of shares of _____ _____ at a specified _____.

19. The formula value of an option equals the _____ price minus the _____, or _____, price.

20. When they are exercised, warrants add additional _____ _____ to a firm's capital structure.

21. Warrants will certainly be exercised if the stock price is above the _____ price and the warrant is about to _____.

22. Holders of warrants will have an extra incentive to exercise if the company sharply increases the _____ on its common shares.

23. Almost all warrants are _____ and can be traded separately from the debt or preferred stock with which they were issued.

24. Convertible bonds or preferred stocks may be exchanged for _____ _____ at the option of the _____.

25. The _____ _____ specifies the number of shares of common stock that will be received for each bond that is converted.

26. Selling a convertible issue may be thought of as selling _____ _____ at a price higher than the market price prevailing at the time the convertible is issued.

27. If a firm's stock price does increase, the company can force _____ of the convertible bonds by including a _____ _____ in the bond indenture.

28. In reporting its earnings, a firm with warrants and convertible securities must report both _____ EPS and _____ _____ EPS.

©1992 The Dryden Press
All rights reserved.

Conceptual

29. When one is evaluating a lease proposal, cash flows should be discounted at a relatively high rate because lease flows are fairly certain.

    a. True **b.** False

30. Generally, operating leases are fully amortized, and the lease is written for the expected life of the asset.

    a. True **b.** False

31. A firm which uses extensive lease financing and does not capitalize its leases will have a substantially lower debt ratio than an otherwise similar firm which borrows to finance its assets.

    a. True **b.** False

32. Firms may or may not capitalize a financial lease, at their own option.

    a. True **b.** False

33. The coupon interest rate on convertible bonds is generally higher than the rate on nonconvertible bonds of the same riskiness and rating.

    a. True **b.** False

34. Primary EPS shows what EPS would have been if all warrants and convertibles outstanding had been converted prior to the reporting date.

    a. True **b.** False

35. Investors are willing to accept lower interest (or dividend) yields on convertible securities in the hopes of later realizing capital gains.

    a. True **b.** False

36. The conversion of a convertible bond replaces debt with common equity on a firm's balance sheet, but it does not bring in any additional capital.

    a. True **b.** False

37. Which of the following statements is most correct?

    a. Floating rate preferred stocks, whose dividends are indexed to some market rate, are often used by strong, profitable corporations for two reasons: (1) the fact that the

©1992 The Dryden Press
All rights reserved.

dividend is indexed means that the stock will generally sell at a price close to par, which makes it safe to the purchaser, so its cost to the issuer will be low, and (2) the fact that 70 percent of preferred dividends can be deducted by the issuer for tax purposes lowers the cost even further.

b. Some years ago leasing was called "off balance sheet financing" because the leased asset and the corresponding lease obligation did not appear directly on the balance sheet. Today, though, that situation has changed materially, because *all leases* must be capitalized and reported on the balance sheet, along with the value of the leased asset.

c. In a lease versus purchase analysis, cash flows should generally be discounted at the weighted average cost of capital (WACC).

d. Each of the above statements is true.

e. Each of the above statements is false.

SELF-TEST PROBLEMS

(The following data apply to the next three Self-Test Problems.)

Treadmill Trucking Company is negotiating a lease for five new tractor/trailer rigs with International Leasing. Treadmill has received its best offer from Betterbilt Trucks for a total price of $900,000. The terms of the lease offered by International Leasing call for 4 payments of $260,000, with each payment occurring at the beginning of each year. As an alternative to leasing, the firm can borrow from a large insurance company and buy the trucks. The $900,000 would be borrowed on an amortized term loan at a 10 percent interest rate for 4 years. Assume the trucks fall into the MACRS 3-year class and have an expected residual value of $100,000. Maintenance costs would be included in the lease. If the trucks are owned, a maintenance contract would be purchased at the beginning of each year for $10,000 per year. Treadmill plans to buy a new fleet of trucks at the end of the fourth year. Treadmill Trucking has an effective tax rate of 20 percent.

1. What is Treadmill's present value of the cost of owning?

    a. $715,225   **b.** $710,354   **c.** $707,189   **d.** $691,717   **e.** $714,675

2. What is Treadmill's present value of the cost of leasing?

    a. $702,468   **b.** $705,265   **c.** $744,036   **d.** $729,668   **e.** $735,419

3. Treadmill should lease the trucks.

    a. True   **b.** False

©1992 The Dryden Press
All rights reserved.

4. The Clayton Corporation has warrants outstanding that permit the holder to purchase one share of common stock per warrant at $30. What is the formula value of Clayton's warrants if the common stock is currently selling at $20 per share?

   a. -$20   **b.** -$10   **c.** $5   **d.** $10   **e.** $20

5. Refer to the previous problem. Calculate the formula value if the common stock is now selling at $40 per share.

   a. -$20   **b.** -$10   **c.** $0   **d.** $10   **e.** $20

6. White Corporation has just sold a bond issue with 10 warrants attached to each bond. The bonds have a 20-year maturity, an annual coupon rate of 12 percent, and they sold at the $1,000 initial offering price. The current yield to maturity on bonds of equal risk, but without warrants, is 15 percent. What is the value of each warrant?

   a. $22.56   **b.** $21.20   **c.** $20.21   **d.** $19.24   **e.** $18.78

(The following data apply to the next three Self-Test Problems.)

Central Food Brokers is considering issuing a 20-year convertible bond that will be priced at its par value of $1,000 per bond. The bonds have a 12 percent annual coupon interest rate, and each bond could be converted into 40 shares of common stock. The stock currently sells at $20 per share, has an expected annual dividend of $3.00, and is growing at a constant 5 percent rate per year. The bonds are callable after 10 years at a price of $1,050, with the price declining by $5 per year. If, after 10 years, the conversion exceeds the call price by at least 20 percent, management will probably call the bonds.

7. What is the conversion price?

   a. $20   **b.** $25   **c.** $33   **d.** $40   **e.** $50

8. If the yield to maturity on nonconvertible bonds of similar risk is 16 percent, what is the straight-debt value?

   a. $1,000.00   **b.** $907.83   **c.** $812.22   **d.** $762.85   **e.** $692.37

9. If an investor expects the bond issue to be called in Year 10, and he plans on converting it at that time, what is the investor's expected rate of return upon conversion?

   a. 12.0%   **b.** 12.2%   **c.** 13.6%   **d.** 14.4%   **e.** 15.3%

©1992 The Dryden Press
All rights reserved.

ANSWERS TO SELF-TEST QUESTIONS

1. debt; common stock
2. preferred; percentage
3. cumulative
4. corporate
5. bankruptcy
6. borrowing; leverage
7. sale-and-leaseback; use
8. Operating
9. financial; capital; new
10. lease payments
11. fixed assets; present value; debt
12. Competition; residual
13. balance sheet; leverage
14. lease payments
15. financing; capital budgeting
16. Taxes
17. investors; cost of capital
18. warrant; common stock; price
19. market; striking; exercise
20. common equity
21. exercise (striking); expire
22. dividend
23. detachable
24. common stock; holder
25. conversion ratio
26. common stock
27. conversion; call provision
28. primary; fully diluted

29. b. The cash flows are fairly certain, so they should be discounted at a relatively low rate, generally, the after-tax cost of debt.

30. b. Operating leases are frequently not fully amortized. The lessor expects to recover all costs either in subsequent leases or through the sale of the used equipment at its residual value.

31. a. However, analysts would recognize that leases are as risky as debt financing, and thus include the impact of lease financing on the firm's debt costs and capital structure. Also, if the company which leases capitalizes the leases, then the debt ratios will be similar.

32. b. FASB #13 spells out in detail the conditions under which leases must be capitalized for an unqualified audit opinion.

33. b. The coupon interest rate is lower because investors expect some capital gains return upon conversion. Note, however, that the overall required rate of return is probably higher for the convertible issue than the straight debt issue because the capital gains portions of the convertible's total return is more risky.

34. b. Primary EPS includes only those shares from warrants and convertibles *likely to be converted* in the near future. Fully diluted EPS includes all shares.

35. a. However, the investor is including the expected capital gain as part of his required return, so the total required return on convertibles is higher than on a straight security.

36. a. The bond is turned in to the company and replaced with common stock. No cash is exchanged. When a warrant is exercised, the firm gets additional capital.

©1992 The Dryden Press
All rights reserved.

37. e. Statement a is false; preferred dividends are not tax deductible to the issuer. Statement b is false; only certain leases that meet the FASB #13 criteria for capitalization have to be reported on the balance sheet. Statement c is false; the discount rate in a borrow-versus-lease decision is the after-tax cost of debt because the cash flows are fairly certain. Therefore, statement e is the correct choice.

SOLUTIONS TO SELF-TEST PROBLEMS

1. e. Place the cash flows associated with ownership on a time line:

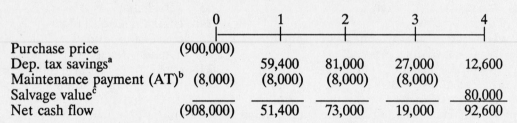

	0	1	2	3	4
Purchase price	(900,000)				
Dep. tax savings[a]		59,400	81,000	27,000	12,600
Maintenance payment (AT)[b]	(8,000)	(8,000)	(8,000)	(8,000)	
Salvage value[c]					80,000
Net cash flow	(908,000)	51,400	73,000	19,000	92,600

PV cost of owning at 8 percent after-tax cost of debt is $714,675.

[a]Depreciable basis = $900,000.

Year	Factor	Depreciation Expense	Tax Savings
1	0.33	$297,000	$ 59,400
2	0.45	405,000	81,000
3	0.15	135,000	27,000
4	0.07	63,000	12,600
		$900,000	$180,000

[b]After-tax maintenance cash flow = $10,000(1 − T) = $10,000(0.8) = $8,000.

[c]After-tax residual value = $100,000(1 − T) = ($100,000)(0.8) = $80,000.

2. c. Place the cash flows associated with leasing on a time line:

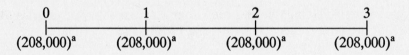

0	1	2	3
(208,000)[a]	(208,000)[a]	(208,000)[a]	(208,000)[a]

[a]$260,000(1 − T) = ($260,000)(0.8) = $208,000.

PV cost of leasing at 8 percent after-tax cost of debt is $744,036.

© 1992 The Dryden Press
All rights reserved.

3. b. The PV cost of leasing is \$744,036 − \$714,675 = \$29,361 more than the cost of owning.

4. b. Formula value = Market price − Exercise price. When P_0 = \$20, Formula value = \$20 − \$30 = -\$10. Note that negative prices cannot actually exist, so the formula value would be considered to be zero.

5. d. When P_0 = \$40, Formula value = \$40 − \$30 = \$10.

6. e. First, find the straight-debt value:

$$V_B = INT(PVIFA_{k_d,N}) + M(PVIF_{k_d,N})$$

$$= \$120(PVIFA_{15\%,20}) + \$1,000(PVIF_{15\%,20}) = \$812.22.$$

Alternatively, input N = 20, I = 15, PMT = 120, FV = 1,000, and solve for PV = \$812.22.

Thus the value of the attached warrants is \$1,000 − \$812.22 = \$187.78. Since each bond has 10 warrants, each warrant must have a value of \$18.78.

7. b. P_c = Par value/Shares received = \$1,000/40 = \$25.00.

8. d. $V_B = INT(PVIFA_{k_d,N}) + M(PVIF_{k_d,N})$

$$= \$120(PVIFA_{16\%,20}) + \$1,000(PVIF_{16\%,20}) = \$762.85.$$

Alternatively, input N = 20, I = 16, PMT = 120, FV = 1,000, and solve for PV = \$762.85.

9. c. This is solved by finding the value of k_c in the equation:

$$\frac{\text{Price}}{\text{paid}} = INT(PVIFA_{k_c,N}) + \frac{\text{Stock's expected}}{\text{market value}}(PVIF_{k_c,N}).$$

Stock's expected market value = $(1.05)^{10} \times \$20 \times 40$ shares = \$1,303.12.

Therefore, find the value of k_c for the following:

$$\$1,000 = \$120(PVIFA_{k_c,10}) + \$1,303.12(PVIF_{k_c,10}),$$

so k_c = 13.6%.

©1992 The Dryden Press
All rights reserved.

CHAPTER 16
FINANCIAL FORECASTING

OVERVIEW

Managers are vitally concerned with *future financial statements* and with the effects of alternative assumptions and policies on these *projected*, or *pro forma*, statements. The construction of pro forma statements begins with a *sales forecast*. On the basis of the sales forecast, the amount of assets necessary to support this sales level is determined. Although some liabilities will increase *spontaneously* with increased sales, if the sales growth rate is rapid, then external capital will be required to support the growth in sales.

Pro forma statements are important for two reasons. First, if projected operating results look poor, management can reformulate its plans for the coming year. Second, it is desirable to plan the acquisition of funds well in advance to insure that funds will be available when they are needed.

OUTLINE

I. **Well run companies generally base their operating plans on a set of forecasted financial statements. A sales forecast for the next five years or so is developed, the assets required to meet the sales target are determined, and a decision is made concerning how to finance the required assets. These forecasts represent the "base case" and are a standard by which to judge alternate forecasts.**

   A. The sales forecast generally begins with a review of sales for the past 5 to 10 years.

   B. If the sales forecast is off, the consequences can be serious. Thus, an accurate sales forecast is critical to the well-being of the firm.

II. **The projected balance sheet method is a way to estimate the external financial requirements of a firm.**

   A. The methodology involves projecting the asset requirements for the coming period, then projecting the liabilities and equity that will be generated under normal operations, and subtracting the projected liabilities/capital from the required assets to estimate the *Additional Funds Needed (AFN)*.

   B. The first step is to forecast next year's income statement.
      1. A sales forecast is needed.
      2. Assumptions about the operating cost ratio, the tax rate, interest charges, and the dividend payout ratio are made.
      3. In the simplest case, costs are assumed to increase at the same rate as sales; in more complicated situations, cost changes are forecasted separately.

16-1

©1992 The Dryden Press
All rights reserved.

4. The objective is to determine how much income the company will earn and then retain for reinvestment in the business during the forecasted year.

C. The second step is to forecast next year's balance sheet.
1. All asset accounts can be assumed to vary directly with sales unless the firm is operating at less than full capacity. If the firm is not operating at full capacity, then fixed assets will not vary directly with sales, but the cash, receivables, and inventory accounts will increase in proportion to the increase in sales.
2. Liabilities, equity, or both must also increase if assets increase--asset expansions must be financed in some manner.
3. Certain liability accounts, such as accounts payable and accruals, will increase *spontaneously* with sales. Retained earnings will increase, but not proportionately with sales. The new retained earnings is determined from the projected income statement.
4. Other financing accounts, such as short-term debt, long-term debt, and common stock, are not directly related to sales. Changes in these accounts result from managerial decisions; they do not increase spontaneously as sales increase.
5. The difference between projected total assets and projected liabilities and capital is the amount of additional funds needed.

D. The third step is the decision on how to finance the additional funds required. Sometimes contractual agreements, such as a limit on the debt ratio, will restrict the firm's financing decisions.

E. One complexity that arises in financial forecasting relates to *financing feedbacks*, which are the effects on the income statement and balance sheet of actions taken to finance increases in assets. Financing feedbacks are incorporated into the pro forma financial statements through additional calculations, or *passes*, of the projected income statement and balance sheet.

F. Once the pro forma financial statements have been developed, the key ratios can be analyzed.

III. **Although forecasts of capital requirements are always made by constructing pro forma financial statements as described above, an approximation can be obtained by using a simple forecasting formula.**

A. The formula is as follows: Additional funds needed = Required increase in assets — Spontaneous increase in liabilities — Increase in retained earnings, or

$$AFN = A^*/S(\Delta S) - L^*/S(\Delta S) - MS_1(1 - d).$$

Here, A^*/S = assets that must increase if sales are to increase, expressed as a percentage of sales, or the required dollar increase in assets per \$1 increase in sales; L^*/S = liabilities that increase spontaneously with sales as a percentage of sales, or spontaneously generated financing per \$1 increase in sales; S_1 = total

©1992 The Dryden Press
All rights reserved.

expected sales for the year in question (note that S_0 = last year's sales); ΔS = change in sales = $S_1 - S_0$; M = profit margin, or rate of profits after taxes per \$1 of sales; and d = the percentage of earnings paid out in dividends (dividend payout ratio).

B. Inherent in the formula is the assumption that each asset item must increase in direct proportion to sales increases and that designated liability accounts also grow at the same rate as sales. Obviously, these assumptions do not always hold, so its results are not always reliable. Thus, the formula is often used as a supplement to the forecasted balance sheet method.

C. The faster a firm's growth rate in sales, the greater its need for additional financing.
   1. Dividend policy as reflected in the payout ratio also affects external capital requirements: the higher the payout ratio, the smaller the addition to retained earnings, and hence the greater the requirements for external capital. Dividend policy may be changed to satisfy internal financing requirements, but this may have a negative impact on stock price and may be met with resistance from investors.
   2. The amount of assets required per dollar of sales, A*/S, is often called the *capital intensity ratio*. This factor has a major effect on capital requirements per unit of sales growth. If the capital intensity ratio is low, then sales can grow rapidly without much outside capital. However, if a firm is capital intensive, even a small growth in output will require a great deal of outside capital.
   3. Profit margin, M, also has an effect on capital requirements. The higher the profit margin, the lower the funds requirement, and the lower the profit margin, the higher the requirement. Thus, highly profitable firms can raise most of their capital internally.

IV. **The forecasting process is greatly complicated if the ratios of balance sheet items to sales are not constant at all levels of sales.**

   A. Where economies of scale occur in asset use, the ratio of that asset to sales will change as the size of the firm increases.

   B. Technological considerations sometimes dictate that fixed assets be added in large, discrete units, often referred to as *lumpy assets*. This automatically creates excess capacity immediately after a plant expansion.

   C. *Cyclical changes* can cause the actual asset/sales ratio for a given period to be quite different from the planned ratio. This situation can result in excess capacity.

V. **If any of the above conditions apply (economies of scale, lumpy assets, or excess capacity), the A*/S ratio will not be a constant, and the constant growth forecasting method should not be used. Rather, other techniques must be used to forecast asset levels to determine additional financing requirements. Two of these methods include simple linear regression and excess capacity adjustments.**

© 1992 The Dryden Press
All rights reserved.

A. If one assumes that the relationship between a certain type of asset and sales is linear, then one can use simple linear regression techniques to estimate the requirements for that type of asset for any given sales increase. An estimated regression equation is determined which provides an estimated relationship between a given asset account and sales.

B. Since excess capacity may exist in fixed assets, projected sales levels need to be adjusted downward since they were estimated on the assumption of full capacity of fixed assets.

1. The target fixed assets to sales ratio is equal to the current year's fixed assets divided by full capacity sales:

$$\text{Target FA/sales ratio} = \frac{\text{Current year's fixed assets}}{\text{Full capacity sales}}.$$

2. The required level of fixed assets is equal to the target fixed assets to sales ratio times projected sales.

$$\text{Required level of FA} = \frac{\text{Target FA}}{\text{Sales}}(\text{Projected sales}).$$

VI. Although the type of financial forecasting described in this chapter can be done with a hand calculator, virtually all corporate forecasts are made using computerized forecasting models. Most models are based on a spreadsheet program, such as Lotus 1-2-3. Spreadsheet programs are easy to construct for forecasts extending over several years, and they are useful for instantaneously recomputing projected statements and ratios when one of the input variables is changed.

SELF-TEST QUESTIONS

Definitional

1. The most important element in financial planning is the forecast of _sales_.

2. Those asset items that typically increase proportionately with higher sales are _cash_, _A/R_, and _inv_. _Fixed_ assets are frequently not used to full capacity and hence do not increase in proportion to sales.

3. If various asset categories increase, _liabs_ and/or _equity_ must also increase.

4. Typically, certain liabilities will rise _spont_ with sales. These include accounts _payable_ and _accruals_.

5. _notes_ and _l-t debt_ are examples of accounts that do not increase automatically with higher levels of sales.

©1992 The Dryden Press
All rights reserved.

6. As the dividend _____ _____ is increased, the amount of earnings available to finance new assets is _____ .

7. Retained earnings depend not only on next year's sales level and dividend payout ratio but also on the _____ _____ .

8. The amount of assets required per dollar of sales, A*/S is often called the _____
_____ _____ .

9. A capital intensive industry will require large amounts of _____ capital to finance increased growth.

10. The projected balance sheet method assumes that the _____ of balance sheet items to _____ is _____ at all levels of sales.

11. The assumption of constant percentage of sales ratios may not be accurate when assets must be added in discrete amounts, called "_____" assets, or when _____ of scale are considered.

Conceptual

12. An increase in a firm's inventories will call for additional financing unless the increase is offset by an equal or larger *decrease* in some other asset account.

    a. True   b. False

13. If the capital intensity ratio of a firm actually decreases as sales increase, use of the formula method will typically *overstate* the amount of additional funds required, other things held constant.

    a. True   b. False

14. If the dividend payout ratio is 100 percent, all ratios are held constant, and the firm is operating at full capacity, then any increase in sales will require additional financing.

    a. True   b. False

15. Which of the following would *reduce* the additional funds required if all other things are held constant?

    a. An increase in the dividend payout ratio.
    b. A decrease in the profit margin.
    c. An increase in the capital intensity ratio.
    d. An increase in the expected sales growth rate.
    e. A decrease in the firm's tax rate.

16-5

©1992 The Dryden Press
All rights reserved.

16. One of the first steps in the projected balance sheet method of forecasting is to identify those asset and liability accounts which increase spontaneously with retained earnings.

   a. True   **b.** False

17. Which of the following statements is most correct?

   a. Suppose economies of scale exist in a firm's use of assets. Under this condition, the firm should use the regression method of forecasting asset requirements rather than the projected balance sheet method.
   b. If a firm must acquire assets in lumpy units, it can avoid errors in forecasts of its need for funds by using the linear regression method of forecasting asset requirements, because all the points will lie on the regression line.
   c. If economies of scale in the use of assets exist, then the AFN formula rather than the projected balance sheet method should be used to forecast additional funds requirements.
   d. Notes payable to banks are included in the AFN formula, along with a projection of retained earnings.
   e. One problem with the AFN formula is that it does not take account of the firm's dividend policy.

SELF-TEST PROBLEMS

1. United Products Inc. has the following balance sheet:

Current assets	$ 5,000	Accounts payable	$ 1,000
		Notes payable	1,000
Net fixed assets	5,000	Long-term debt	4,000
		Common equity	4,000
Total assets	$10,000	Total liabilities and equity	$10,000

Business has been slow, therefore, fixed assets are vastly underutilized. Management believes it can double sales next year with the introduction of a new product. No new fixed assets will be required, and management expects that there will be no earnings retained next year. What is next year's additional funding requirement?

   a. $0   **b.** $4,000   **c.** $6,000   **d.** $13,000   **e.** $19,000

2. The 1991 balance sheet for American Pulp and Paper is shown below (millions of dollars):

©1992 The Dryden Press
All rights reserved.

Cash	$ 3.0	Accounts payable	$ 2.0
Accounts receivable	3.0	Notes payable	1.5
Inventory	5.0		
Current assets	$11.0	Current liabilities	$ 3.5
Fixed assets	3.0	Long-term debt	3.0
		Common equity	7.5
Total assets	$14.0	Total liabilities and equity	$14.0

In 1991, sales were $60 million. In 1992, management believes that sales will increase by 20 percent to a total of $72 million. The profit margin is expected to be 5 percent, and the dividend payout ratio is targeted at 40 percent. No excess capacity exists. What is the additional funding requirement (in millions) for 1992 using the formula method?

a. $0.36   **b.** $0.24   **c.** $0   **d.** -$0.24   **e.** -$0.36

3. Refer to the previous problem. How much can sales grow above the 1992 level of $60 million without requiring any additional funds?

a. 12.28%   **b.** 14.63%   **c.** 15.75%   **d.** 17.65%   **e.** 18.14%

4. Smith Machines Inc. has a net income this year of $500 on sales of $2,000 and is operating its fixed assets at full capacity. Management expects sales to increase by 25 percent next year and is forecasting a dividend payout ratio of 30 percent. The profit margin is not expected to change. If spontaneous liabilities are $500 this year, and no excess funds are expected next year, what is Smith's total assets this year?

a. $1,000   **b.** $1,500   **c.** $2,250   **d.** $3,000   **e.** $3,500

(The following data apply to the next three Self-Test Problems.)

Crossley Products Company's 1991 financial statements are shown below:

Crossley Products Company
Balance Sheet as of December 31, 1991
(Thousands of Dollars)

Cash	$ 600	Accounts payable	$ 2,400
Receivables	3,600	Notes payable	1,157
Inventories	4,200	Accruals	840
Total current assets	$8,400	Total current liabilities	$ 4,397
		Mortgage bonds	1,667
		Common stock	667
Net fixed assets	7,200	Retained earnings	8,869
Total assets	$15,600	Total liabilities and equity	$15,600

©1992 The Dryden Press
All rights reserved.

Crossley Products Company
Income Statement for December 31, 1991
(Thousands of Dollars)

Sales	$12,000
Operating costs	10,261
Earnings before interest and taxes	$ 1,739
Interest	339
Earnings before taxes	$ 1,400
Taxes (40%)	560
Net income	$ 840
Dividends (60%)	$504
Addition to retained earnings	$336

5. Assume that the company was operating at full capacity in 1991 with regard to all items except fixed assets; fixed assets in 1991 were being utilized to only 75 percent of capacity. By what percentage could 1992 sales increase over 1991 sales without the need for an increase in fixed assets?

   a. 33%   b. 25%   c. 20%   d. 44%   e. 50%

6. Now suppose 1992 sales increase by 25 percent over 1991 sales. How much additional external capital (in thousands) will be required? Assume that Crossley cannot sell any fixed assets. (Hint: Use the projected balance sheet method to develop a pro forma balance sheet and income statement.) Assume that any required financing is borrowed as notes payable. Do not include any financing feedbacks, and use a pro forma income statement to determine the addition to retained earnings.

   a. $825   b. $925   c. $750   d. $900   e. $850

7. Use the financial statements developed in Self-Test Problem 6 to incorporate the financing feedback which results from the addition of notes payable. (That is, do the next financial statement iteration.) For purposes of this part, assume that the notes payable interest rate is 12 percent. What is the AFN (in thousands) for this iteration?

   a. $28   b. $30   c. $20   d. $24   e. $36

©1992 The Dryden Press
All rights reserved.

(The following data apply to the next two Self-Test Problems.)

Taylor Technologies Inc.'s 1991 financial statements are shown below:

Taylor Technologies Inc.
Balance Sheet as of December 31, 1991

Cash	$ 90,000	Accounts payable	$ 180,000
Receivables	180,000	Notes payable	78,000
Inventories	360,000	Accruals	90,000
Total current assets	$ 630,000	Total current liabilities	$ 348,000
		Common stock	900,000
Net fixed assets	720,000	Retained earnings	102,000
Total assets	$1,350,000	Total liabilities and equity	$1,350,000

Taylor Technologies Inc.
Income Statement for December 31, 1991

Sales	$1,800,000
Operating costs	1,639,860
EBIT	$ 160,140
Interest	10,140
EBT	$ 150,000
Taxes (40%)	60,000
Net income	$ 90,000
Dividends (60%)	$54,000
Addition to retained earnings	$36,000

8. Suppose that in 1992 sales increase by 10 percent over 1991 sales. Construct the pro forma financial statements using the projected balance sheet method. How much additional capital will be required? Assume the firm operated at full capacity in 1991. Do not include financing feedbacks.

   a. $72,459   **b.** $70,211   **c.** $68,157   **d.** $66,445   **e.** $63,989

9. Now assume that 50 percent of the additional capital required will be financed by selling common stock and the remainder by borrowing as notes payable. Assume that the interest rate on notes payable is 13 percent. Do the next iteration of financial statements incorporating financing feedbacks. What is the AFN for this iteration?

   a. $1,063   **b.** $957   **c.** $1,124   **d.** $927   **e.** $1,185

©1992 The Dryden Press
All rights reserved.

ANSWERS TO SELF-TEST QUESTIONS

1. sales
2. cash; receivables; inventories; Fixed
3. liabilities; equity
4. spontaneously; payable; accruals
5. Bonds; common stock (or preferred stock, or retained earnings)
6. payout ratio; decreased
7. profit margin
8. capital intensity ratio
9. external
10. ratio; sales; constant
11. "lumpy"; economies

12. a. When an increase in one asset account is not offset by an equivalent decrease in another asset account, then financing is needed to reestablish equilibrium on the balance sheet. Note, though, that this additional financing may come from a spontaneous increase in accounts payable or from retained earnings.

13. a. A decreasing capital intensity ratio, A*/S, means that less assets are required, proportionately, as sales increase. Thus, the external funding requirement is overstated. Always keep in mind that the formula method assumes that the asset/sales ratio is constant regardless of the level of sales.

14. a. With a 100 percent payout ratio, there will be no retained earnings. When operating at full capacity, *all* assets are spontaneous, but *all* liabilities cannot be spontaneous since a firm must have common equity. Thus, the growth in assets cannot be matched by a growth in spontaneous liabilities, so additional financing will be required in order to keep the financial ratios (the debt ratio in particular) constant.

15. e. Answers a through d would increase the additional funds required, but a decrease in the tax rate would raise the profit margin and thus increase the amount of available retained earnings.

16. b. The first step is to identify those accounts which increase spontaneously with sales.

17. a. Statement a is correct; economies of scale cause the ratios to change over time, which violates the assumption of the projected balance sheet method. Statement b is false; the points will not all lie on the regression line. Statement c is false; the AFN formula requires constant ratios over time. Statement d is false; the AFN formula includes only spontaneous liabilities and notes payable do not spontaneously increase with sales. Statement e is false; the AFN formula includes the dividend payout, so dividend policy is included.

SOLUTIONS TO SELF-TEST PROBLEMS

1. b. Look at next year's balance sheet:

©1992 The Dryden Press
All rights reserved.

		Accounts payable	$ 2,000
		Notes payable	1,000
Current assets	$10,000	Current liabilities	$ 3,000
Net fixed assets	5,000	Long-term debt	4,000
		Common equity	4,000
			$11,000
		AFN	4,000
Total assets	$15,000	Total liabilities and equity	$15,000

With no retained earnings next year, the common equity account remains at $4,000. Thus, the additional financing requirement is $15,000 - $11,000 = $4,000.

2. b. None of the items on the right side of the balance sheet rises spontaneously with sales except accounts payable. Therefore,

$$AFN = (A^*/S)(\Delta S) - (L^*/S)(\Delta S) - MS_1(1 - d)$$
$$= (\$14/\$60)(\$12) - (\$2/\$60)(\$12) - (0.05)(\$72)(0.6)$$
$$= \$2.8 - \$0.4 - \$2.16 = \$0.24 \text{ million.}$$

The firm will need $240,000 in additional funds to support the increase in sales.

3. d. Note that g = sales growth = $\Delta S/S$, and $S_1 = S(1 + g)$. Then,

$$AFN = A^*g - L^*g - M[(S)(1 + g)](1 - d) = 0$$
$$\$14g - \$2g - 0.05[(\$60)(1 + g)](0.6) = 0$$
$$\$12g - 1(\$3 + \$3g)(0.60) = 0$$
$$\$12g - \$1.8 - \$1.8g = 0$$
$$\$10.20g = \$1.80$$
$$g = 0.1765 = 17.65\%.$$

4. c.
$$0 = (A^*/S)(\Delta S) - (L^*/S)(\Delta S) - MS_1(1 - d)$$
$$0 = (A^*/\$2,000)(\$500) - (\$500/\$2,000)(\$500)$$
$$\quad - (\$500/\$2,000)(\$2,500)(1 - 0.3)$$
$$0 = (\$500A^*/\$2,000) - \$125 - \$437.50$$
$$0 = (\$500A^*/\$2,000) - \$562.50$$
$$\$562.50 = 0.25A^*$$
$$A^* = \$2,250.$$

5. a.
$$\text{Full capacity sales} = \frac{\text{Current sales}}{\% \text{ of capacity at which FA were operated}} = \frac{\$12,000}{0.75} = \$16,000.$$

$$\text{Percent increase} = \frac{\text{New sales} - \text{Old sales}}{\text{Old sales}} = \frac{\$16,000 - \$12,000}{\$12,000} = 0.33 = 33\%.$$

©1992 The Dryden Press
All rights reserved.

Therefore, sales could expand by 33 percent before Crossley Products would need to add fixed assets.

6. e.

Crossley Products Company
Pro Forma Income Statement
December 31, 1992
(Thousands of Dollars)

	1991	(1 + g)	Pro Forma 1992
Sales	$12,000	(1.25)	$15,000
Operating costs	10,261	(1.25)	12,826
EBIT	$ 1,739		$ 2,174
Interest	339		339
EBT	$ 1,400		$ 1,835
Taxes (40%)	560		734
Net income	$ 840		$ 1,101
Dividends (60%)	$504		$661
Addition to RE	$336		$440

Crossley Products Company
Pro Forma Balance Sheet
December 31, 1992
(Thousands of Dollars)

	1991	(1 + g)	Additions	1992	AFN	1992 After AFN
Cash	$ 600	(1.25)		$ 750		$ 750
Receivables	3,600	(1.25)		4,500		4,500
Inventories	4,200	(1.25)		5,250		5,250
Total current assets	$ 8,400			$10,500		$10,500
Net fixed assets	7,200			*7,200		7,200
Total assets	$15,600			$17,700		$17,700
Accounts payable	$ 2,400	(1.25)		$ 3,000		$ 3,000
Notes payable	1,157			1,157	+850	2,007
Accruals	840	(1.25)		1,050		1,050
Total current liabilities	$ 4,397			$ 5,207		$ 6,057
Mortgage bonds	1,667			1,667		1,667
Common stock	667			667		667
Retained earnings	8,869		440**	9,309		9,309
Total liabilities and equity	$15,600			$16,850		$17,700
AFN =				$850		

©1992 The Dryden Press
All rights reserved.

*From Part a we know that sales can increase by 33 percent before additions to fixed assets are needed.
**See income statement.

7. d.

Crossley Products Company
Pro Forma Income Statement
December 31, 1992
(Thousands of Dollars)

	1st Pass 1992	Financing Feedback	2nd Pass 1992
Sales	$15,000		$15,000
Operating costs	12,826		12,826
EBIT	$ 2,174		$ 2,174
Interest	339	+ 102*	441
EBT	$ 1,835		$ 1,733
Taxes (40%)	734		693
Net income	$ 1,101		$ 1,040
Dividends (60%)	$661		$624
Addition to RE	$440		$416

*Change in interest = $850(0.12) = $102.

	1st Pass 1992	Financing Feedback	2nd Pass 1992
Total assets	$17,700		$17,700
Accounts payable	$ 3,000		$ 3,000
Notes payable	2,007		2,007
Accruals	1,050		1,050
Total current liab.	$ 6,057		$ 6,057
Mortgage bonds	1,667		1,667
Common stock	667		667
Retained earnings	9,309	-24*	9,285
Total liabilities and equity	$17,700		$17,676
AFN =			$24

*Change in RE addition = $416 − $440 = -$24.

8. c. The first pass balance sheet indicates that the AFN = $68,157. This AFN ignores financing feedbacks.

©1992 The Dryden Press
All rights reserved.

	1991	(1 + g)	Addi-tions	1st Pass 1992	AFN Effects	2nd Pass
Sales	$1,800,000	(1.10)		$1,980,000		$1,980,000
Operating costs	1,639,860	(1.10)		1,803,846		1,803,846
EBIT	$ 160,140			$ 176,154		$ 176,154
Interest	10,140			10,140	+4,430*	14,570
EBT	$ 150,000			$ 166,014		$ 161,584
Taxes (40%)	60,000			66,406		64,634
Net income	$ 90,000			$ 99,608		$ 96,950
Dividends (60%)	$54,000			$59,765		$58,170
Addition to RE	$36,000			$39,843		$38,780

*Change in interest = $34,079(0.13) = $4,430.
Change in addition to RE = $38,780 − $39,843 = -$1,063.

Taylor Technologies Inc.
Pro Forma Balance Sheet
December 31, 1992

	1991	(1 + g)	Addi-tions	1st Pass 1992	AFN Effects	2nd Pass
Cash	$ 90,000	(1.10)		$ 99,000		$ 99,000
Receivables	180,000	(1.10)		198,000		198,000
Inventories	360,000	(1.10)		396,000		396,000
Total current assets	$ 630,000			$ 693,000		$ 693,000
Fixed assets	720,000	(1.10)		792,000		792,000
Total assets	$1,350,000			$1,485,000		$1,485,000
Accts. payable	$ 180,000	(1.10)		$ 198,000		$ 198,000
Notes payable	78,000			78,000	+34,079	112,079
Accruals	90,000	(1.10)		99,000		99,000
Total current liabilities	$ 348,000			$ 375,000		$ 409,079
Common stock	900,000			900,000	+34,078	934,078
Ret. earnings	102,000		39,843*	141,843	-1,063**	140,780
Total liabilities and equity	$1,350,000			$1,416,843		$1,483,937
AFN =				$68,157		$1,063

©1992 The Dryden Press
All rights reserved.

*See 1st pass income statement.
**See 2nd pass income statement.

9. a. See the AFN line in the final column of the projected balance sheet above. This AFN is the result of the change to retained earnings due to the increased interest expense from the addition of notes payable.

©1992 The Dryden Press
All rights reserved.

CHAPTER 17
WORKING CAPITAL POLICY
AND SHORT-TERM CREDIT

OVERVIEW

Working capital policy involves decisions relating to current assets, including decisions about financing them. Since about half of the typical firm's capital is invested in current assets, working capital policy and management are important to the firm and its shareholders. In fact, about 60 percent of a financial manager's time is devoted to working capital policy and management, and many finance students' first assignment on the job will involve working capital. For these reasons, working capital policy is a vitally important topic.

OUTLINE

I. **It is useful to begin by reviewing some basic definitions and concepts.**

   A. *Working capital*, sometimes called *gross working capital*, is defined as current assets, while *net working capital* is current assets minus current liabilities.

   B. The *current ratio*, which is current assets divided by current liabilities, is intended to measure a firm's liquidity. The *quick ratio*, which also attempts to measure liquidity, is current assets less inventories, divided by current liabilities.

   C. The most comprehensive picture of a firm's liquidity is obtained by examining its *cash budget*, which forecasts a firm's cash inflows and outflows, and thus focuses on what really counts, the firm's ability to generate the cash inflows required to meet its required cash outflows.

   D. *Working capital policy* refers to the firm's basic policies regarding target levels for each category of current assets and how current assets will be financed.

   E. *Working capital management* involves the administration of current assets and current liabilities.

II. **A firm's current asset levels and financing requirements rise and fall with business cycles and seasonal trends. At the peak of such cycles, businesses carry their maximum amounts of current assets. Similar fluctuations in financing needs can occur over these cycles, typically, financing needs contract during recessions, and they expand during booms.**

©1992 The Dryden Press
All rights reserved.

III. **The cash conversion cycle focuses on the conversion of operating events to cash flows.**

    A. The following terms and definitions are used:

        1. *Inventory conversion period*, which is the average length of time required to convert materials into finished goods, and then to sell these goods.

$$\text{Inventory conversion period} = \frac{\text{Inventory}}{\text{Sales per day}}.$$

        2. *Receivables collection period*, which is the average length of time required to convert the firm's receivables into cash, that is, to collect cash following a sale.

$$\text{Receivables collection period} = \frac{\text{Receivables}}{\text{Sales}/360}.$$

        3. *Payables deferral period*, which is the average length of time between the purchase of raw materials and labor and the payment of cash for them.

        4. *Cash conversion cycle*, which nets out the three periods just defined, and which therefore equals the average length of time between the firm's actual cash expenditures on productive resources and its own cash receipts from the sale of its products. Thus, the cash conversion cycle equals the average length of time the firm has funds tied up in current assets.

    B. Using these definitions, the cash conversion cycle is defined as follows:

Inventory conversion period	+	Receivables collection period	−	Payables deferral period	=	Cash conversion cycle.

    C. To illustrate, suppose it takes a firm an average of 72 days to convert raw materials and labor to widgets and to sell them, and it takes another 24 days to collect on receivables, while 30 days normally lapse between receipt of materials (and work done) and payments for materials and labor. In this case, the cash conversion cycle is 72 days + 24 days - 30 days = 66 days.

    D. A firm should shorten its cash conversion cycle as much as possible without increasing costs or depressing sales. This would maximize profits, because the longer the cash conversion cycle, the greater the need for external financing--and such financing has a cost.

IV. **Working capital policy involves two basic decisions: (1) What is the appropriate level for current assets and (2) how should current assets be financed?**

    A. There are three alternative policies regarding the total amount of current assets carried. Each policy differs in that different amounts of current assets are carried to support a given level of sales.

©1992 The Dryden Press
All rights reserved.

1. A *relaxed current asset investment policy* is one in which large amounts of cash, marketable securities, and inventories are carried, and where sales are stimulated by the use of a liberal credit policy.
2. A *restricted current asset investment policy* is one in which holdings of cash, securities, and inventories, and receivables are minimized.
3. A *moderate current asset investment policy* is between the two extremes.
4. Generally, the decision on current assets level involves a risk/return tradeoff. The relaxed policy minimizes risk, but it also has the lowest expected return. On the other hand, the restricted policy offers the highest expected return coupled with the highest risk.

B. The second short-term financial decision is how to finance current assets.
1. The *maturity matching, or "self-liquidating," approach* matches asset and liability maturities. Defined as a moderate current asset financing policy, this would use permanent financing for permanent assets (permanent current assets and fixed assets), and use short-term financing to cover seasonal and/or cyclical temporary assets (fluctuating current assets).
2. The *aggressive approach* is used by a firm which finances all of its fixed assets with long-term capital but part of its permanent current assets with short-term, nonspontaneous credit.
3. A *conservative approach* would be to use permanent capital to meet some of the cyclical demand, and then hold the temporary surpluses as marketable securities at the trough of the cycle. Here, the amount of permanent financing exceeds permanent assets.

V. **There are advantages and disadvantages to the use of short-term financing.**

A. A short-term loan can be obtained much faster than long-term credit.

B. Short-term debt is more flexible since it may be repaid if the firm's financing requirements decline. Long-term debt can be retired, but this will probably involve a prepayment penalty.

C. Short-term interest rates are normally lower than long-term rates. Therefore, financing with short-term credit usually results in lower interest costs.

D. Short-term debt is generally more risky than long-term debt for two reasons.
1. Short-term interest rates fluctuate widely while long-term rates tend to be more stable and predictable, and hence the interest rate on short-term debt could increase dramatically in a short period.
2. Short-term debt comes due every few months. If a firm does not have the cash to repay debt when it comes due, and if it cannot refinance the loan, it may be forced into bankruptcy.

VI. **Different types of short-term funds have different characteristics. One source of short-term funds is accrued wages and taxes, which increase and decrease**

©1992 The Dryden Press
All rights reserved.

spontaneously as a firm's operations expand and contract. This type of debt is "free" in the sense that no interest is paid on funds raised through accruals.

VII. Accounts payable, or trade credit, is the largest single category of short-term debt. Trade credit is a spontaneous source of funds in that it arises from ordinary business transactions. Most firms make purchases on credit, recording the debt as an account payable.

A. An increase in sales will be accompanied by an increase in inventory purchases, which will automatically generate additional financing.

B. The cost of trade credit is made up of discounts lost by not paying invoices within the discount period.
   1. For example, if credit terms are 2/10, net 30, the cost of 20 additional days credit is 2 percent of the dollar value of the purchases made.
   2. The following equation may be used to calculate the approximate annual percentage cost, on an annual basis, of not taking discounts:

$$\text{Approximate percentage cost} = \frac{\text{Discount \%}}{100 - \text{Discount \%}} \times \frac{360}{\text{Days credit is} - \text{Discount}} .$$
$$\text{outstanding} \quad \text{period}$$

   3. For example, the approximate cost of not taking the discount when the credit terms are 2/10, net 30, is

$$\text{Approximate percentage cost} = \frac{2}{98} \times \frac{360}{30 - 10} = 0.0204(18) = 0.367 = 36.7\%.$$

   4. In effective annual interest terms, the rate is even higher. Note that the first term on the right-hand side of the approximation equation is the periodic cost, and the second term is the number of periods per year. Thus, the effective annual rate is $(1.0204)^{18} - 1.0 = 1.438 - 1.0 = 43.8\%$.

C. Trade credit can be divided into two components: *Free trade credit* is that credit received during the discount period. *Costly trade credit* is obtained by foregoing discounts. This costly component should be used only when it is less expensive than funds obtained from other sources.
   1. Financial managers should always use the free component, but they should use the costly component only after analyzing the cost of this capital to make sure that it is less than the cost of funds which could be obtained from other sources.
   2. Competitive conditions may permit firms to do better than the stated credit terms by taking discounts beyond the discount period or by simply paying late. Such practices, called *stretching accounts payable*, reduce the cost of trade credit, but they also result in poor relationships with suppliers.

©1992 The Dryden Press
All rights reserved.

VIII. **Bank loans appear on a firm's balance sheet as notes payable and represent another important source of short-term financing. Bank loans are not generated spontaneously but must be negotiated and renewed on a regular basis.**

  A. About two-thirds of all bank loans mature in a year or less, although banks do make longer-term loans.

  B. When a firm obtains a bank loan, a promissory note specifying the following items is signed: the amount borrowed, the percentage interest rate, the repayment schedule, any collateral offered as security, and other terms of the loan.

  C. Banks normally require regular borrowers to maintain *compensating balances* equal to 10 to 20 percent of the face value of loans. Such required balances generally increase the effective interest rate on the loan.

  D. A *line of credit* is an informal understanding between the bank and the borrower concerning the maximum loan balance the bank will allow.

  E. A *revolving credit agreement* is a formal line of credit often used by large firms. Normally, the borrower will pay the bank a commitment fee to compensate the bank for guaranteeing that the funds will be available. This fee is paid in addition to the regular interest charge on funds actually borrowed.

IX. **The interest cost of loans will vary for different types of borrowers and for all borrowers over time. Rates charged will vary depending on economic conditions, the risk of the borrower, and the size of the loan. Interest charges on bank loans can be calculated in several ways:**

  A. *Regular, or simple, interest.* The interest payment is determined by multiplying the loan amount, or face value, by the stated interest rate. Principal and interest are then paid at the end of the loan period.

$$\text{Effective annual rate}_{\text{Simple}} = \frac{\text{Interest}}{\text{Amount received}}.$$

  1. On a simple interest loan of less than one year the effective annual rate will be higher due to the compounding effect.

$$\text{Effective annual rate}_{\text{Simple}} = \left(1 + \frac{k_{\text{Nom}}}{m}\right)^m - 1.0.$$

  2. Here k_{Nom} is the nominal, or stated, interest rate expressed as a decimal and m is the number of compounding periods per year (four for a quarterly loan or twelve for a monthly loan).

17-5

©1992 The Dryden Press
All rights reserved.

B. *Discount interest.* Under this method, the bank deducts interest in advance. The effective annual rate of interest is higher than the nominal, or stated, rate.

$$\text{Effective annual rate}_{\text{Discount}} = \frac{\text{Interest}}{\text{Face value} - \text{Interest}}.$$

1. Alternatively,

$$\text{Effective annual rate}_{\text{Disount}} = \frac{\text{Nominal rate (\%)}}{1.0 - \dfrac{\text{Nominal rate}}{\text{(fraction)}}}.$$

2. Effective annual rates on discount loans for less than one year have higher effective discount rates and are found using this formula:

$$\text{Effective annual rate}_{\text{Discount}} = \left(1.0 + \frac{\text{Interest}}{\text{Face value} - \text{Interest}}\right)^{m} - 1.0 .$$

3. Here interest and face value are in dollars. A $1,000 loan at 12 percent for one month, discount interest, would have an effective annual rate of 12.82 percent.

$$\text{Effective annual rate}_{\text{Discount}} = \left(1.0 + \frac{\$10}{\$1,000 - \$10}\right)^{12} - 1.0 = 12.82\%.$$

C. *Installment loans: add-on interest.* Interest charges are calculated and then added on to the funds received to determine the face value of the note, which is paid off in equal installments. The borrower has use of the full amount of the funds received only until the first installment is paid. The effective rate is approximately double the stated rate, because the average amount of the loan outstanding is only about half the face amount borrowed.

$$\text{Approximate effective annual rate}_{\text{Add-on}} = \frac{\text{Interest}}{(\text{Amount received})/2}.$$

D. Compensating balances tend to raise the effective interest rate on bank loans.
  1. In general, this formula is used to find the effective annual interest rate when compensating balances apply and interest is paid at the end of the period:

$$\text{Effective annual rate}_{\text{Simple/CB}} = \frac{\text{Nominal rate (\%)}}{1.0 - \dfrac{\text{Compensating balance}}{\text{(fraction)}}}.$$

  2. The analysis can be extended to the case where compensating balances are required and the loan is based on discount interest:

© 1992 The Dryden Press
All rights reserved.

$$\text{Effective annual rate}_{\text{Discount/CB}} = \frac{\text{Nominal rate (\%)}}{1.0 - \dfrac{\text{Nominal}}{\text{rate}} - \dfrac{\text{Compensating}}{\text{balance}}}.$$
$$\phantom{=\frac{1}{1.0 -}}\quad\text{(fraction)}\quad\text{(fraction)}$$

3. It should be noted that when compensating balances or discount interest or both apply, the borrower must borrow a face amount significantly greater than the funds actually received. For a discount loan with a compensating balance, the face amount is calculated as follows:

$$\text{Face value} = \frac{\text{Funds required}}{1.0 - \dfrac{\text{Nominal}}{\text{interest rate}} - \dfrac{\text{Compensating}}{\text{balance}}}.$$
$$\phantom{=\frac{1}{1.0 -}}\quad\text{(dec. fraction)}\quad\text{(dec. fraction)}$$

X. Choosing a bank involves an analysis of the following variables:

A. *Willingness to assume risks.* Some banks are quite conservative, while others are more willing to make risky loans.

B. *Advice and counsel.* A bank's ability to provide counsel is particularly important to firms in their formative years.

C. *Loyalty to customers.* This variable deals with a bank's willingness to support customers during difficult economic times.

D. *Specialization.* A bank may specialize in making loans to a particular type of business. Firms should seek out a bank which is familiar with their particular type of business.

E. *Maximum loan size.* This is an important consideration for large companies when establishing a borrowing relationship because most banks cannot lend to a single customer more than 15 percent of the total amount of the bank's capital.

F. *Merchant banking.* Originally the term applied to banks which not only loaned depositors' money but also provided its customers with equity capital and financial advice. In recent years, commercial banks have been attempting to get back into merchant banking, in part because of their foreign competitors.

G. *Other services.* The availability of services such as lockbox systems should also be taken into account when selecting a bank.

XI. Commercial paper, another source of short-term credit, is an unsecured promissory note. It is generally sold to other business firms, to insurance companies, to banks,

© 1992 The Dryden Press
All rights reserved.

and to money market mutual funds. Only large, financially strong firms are able to tap the commercial paper market.

    A. Maturities of commercial paper range from a few days to nine months, with an average of about five months.

        1. Interest rates on prime commercial paper generally range from 1 ½ to 2 ½ percentage points below the stated prime rate, and about ½ of a percentage point above the T-bill rate. However, rates fluctuate daily with supply and demand conditions in the marketplace, and since no compensating balance is required, the effective cost is even lower in comparison to bank loans.

        2. A disadvantage of the commercial paper market vis-a-vis bank loans is that the impersonal nature of the market makes it difficult for firms to use commercial paper at times when they are in temporary financial distress.

XII. For a strong firm, borrowing on an unsecured basis is generally cheaper and simpler than on a secured loan basis because of the administrative costs associated with the use of security. However, lenders will refuse credit without some form of collateral if a borrower's credit standing is questionable.

XIII. Appendix 17A discusses procedures for using accounts receivable and inventories as security for short-term loans. Accounts receivable financing involves either the pledging of receivables or the selling of receivables (factoring). Credit can also be secured by business inventories. Blanket liens, trust receipts, and warehouse receipts are methods for using inventories as security.

SELF-TEST QUESTIONS

Definitional

1. Current assets are also referred to as _____ _____.

2. _____ working capital is defined as _____ assets minus current _____.

3. The _____ _____ _____ is the average length of time the firm has funds tied up in current assets.

4. In the maturity matching approach to working capital financing, permanent assets should be financed with _____ capital, while _____ assets should be financed with short-term credit.

5. Some firms use short-term financing to finance permanent assets. This approach maximizes _____ _____, but also has the _____ _____.

6. Short-term borrowing provides more _____ for firms that are uncertain about their _____ borrowing needs.

© 1992 The Dryden Press
All rights reserved.

7. Short-term borrowing will be less expensive than borrowing long-term if the yield curve is _____ sloping.

8. Short-term interest rates fluctuate _____ than long-term rates.

9. _____ wages and taxes are a common source of short-term credit. However, most firms have little control over the _____ of these accounts.

10. Accounts payable, or _____ _____, is the largest single source of short-term credit for most businesses.

11. Trade credit is a _____ source of funds in the sense that it automatically increases when sales increase.

12. Trade credit can be divided into two components: _____ trade credit and _____ trade credit.

13. Free trade credit is that credit received during the _____ period.

14. _____ trade credit should only be used when the cost of the trade credit is less than the cost of _____ sources.

15. The instrument signed when bank credit is obtained is called a _____ _____.

16. Many banks require borrowers to keep _____ _____ on deposit with the bank equal to 10 or 20 percent of the face value of the loan.

17. Maturities on commercial paper generally range from _____ to _____ months, with interest rates set about two percentage points _____ the _____ rate.

18. A _____ loan is one where collateral such as _____ or _____ have been pledged in support of the loan.

19. A _____ ___ _____ is an understanding between a bank and a borrower as to the maximum loan that will be permitted.

20. The fee paid to a bank to secure a revolving credit agreement is known as a _____ fee.

21. If interest charges are deducted in advance, this is known as _____ interest, and the effective rate is higher than the _____ interest rate.

22. With an _____ loan, the average amount of the usable funds during the loan period is equal to approximately _____ - _____ of the face amount of the loan.

23. Commercial paper can only be issued by _____, _____ _____ firms.

© 1992 The Dryden Press
All rights reserved.

24. _____ occurs when accounts receivable are sold, and the buyer has no recourse against the firm selling the receivables.

25. An _____ _____ lien gives the lender a lien against all inventories of the borrower.

Conceptual

26. The matching of asset and liability maturities is considered desirable because this strategy minimizes interest rate risk.

    a. True   **b.** False

27. Accruals are "free" in the sense that no interest must be paid on these funds.

    a. True   **b.** False

28. The effect of compensating balances is to decrease the effective interest rate of a loan.

    a. True   **b.** False

29. Which of the following statements concerning commercial paper is correct?

    a. Commercial paper is secured debt of large, financially strong firms.
    b. Commercial paper is sold primarily to individual investors.
    c. Maturities of commercial paper generally exceed nine months.
    d. Commercial paper interest rates are typically 1.25 to 1.50 percentage points above the stated prime rate.
    e. None of the above statements is correct.

30. Which of the following statements is most correct?

    a. If you had just been hired as Working Capital Manager for a firm with but one stockholder, and that stockholder told you that she had all the money she could possibly use, hence that her primary operating goal was to avoid even the remotest possibility of bankruptcy, then you should set the firm's working capital financing policy on the basis of the "Maturity Matching, or Self-Liquidating, Approach."
    b. Due to the existence of positive maturity risk premiums, at most times short-term debt carries lower interest rates than long-term debt. Therefore, if a company finances primarily with short-term as opposed to long-term debt, its expected TIE ratio, hence its overall riskiness, will be lower than if it finances with long-term debt. Therefore, the more conservative the firm, the greater its reliance on short-term debt.
    c. If a firm buys on terms of 2/10, net 30, and pays on the 30th day, then its accounts payable may be thought of as consisting of some "free" and some "costly" trade credit. Since the percentage cost of the costly trade credit is lowered if the

© 1992 The Dryden Press
All rights reserved.

payment period is reduced, the firm should try to pay earlier than on Day 30, say on Day 25.

d. Suppose a firm buys on terms of 2/10, net 30, but it normally pays on Day 60. Disregarding any "image" effects, it should, if it can borrow from the bank at an effective rate of 14 percent, take out a bank loan and start taking discounts.

e. Each of the above statements is false.

SELF-TEST PROBLEMS

(The following data apply to the next three Self-Test Problems.)

A firm buys on terms of 2/10, net 30, but generally does not pay until 40 days after the invoice date. Its purchases total $1,080,000 per year.

1. How much "non-free" trade credit does the firm use on average each year?

   a. $120,000   **b.** $90,000   **c.** $60,000   **d.** $30,000   **e.** $20,000

2. What is the approximate cost of the "non-free" trade credit?

   a. 16.2%   **b.** 19.4%   **c.** 21.9%   **d.** 24.5%   **e.** 27.4%

3. What is the effective cost rate of the costly credit?

   a. 16.2%   **b.** 19.4%   **c.** 21.9%   **d.** 24.5%   **e.** 27.4%

4. Lawton Pipelines Inc. has developed plans for a new pump that will allow more economical operation of the company's oil pipelines. Management estimates that $2,400,000 will be required to put this new pump into operation. Funds can be obtained from a bank at 10 percent discount interest, or the company can finance the expansion by delaying payment to its suppliers. Presently, Lawton purchases under terms of 2/10, net 40, but management believes payment could be delayed 30 additional days without penalty; that is, payment could be made in 70 days. Which means of financing should Lawton use? (Use the approximate cost of trade credit.)

   a. Trade credit, since the cost is about 12.24 percent.
   b. Trade credit, since the cost is about 3.13 percentage points less than the bank loan.
   c. Bank loan, since the cost is about 1.13 percentage points less than trade credit.
   d. Bank loan, since the cost is about 3.13 percentage points less than trade credit.
   e. The firm could use either since the costs are the same.

(The following data apply to the next four Self-Test Problems.)

You plan to borrow $10,000 from your bank, which offers to lend you the money at a 10 percent nominal, or stated, rate on a 1-year loan.

© 1992 The Dryden Press
All rights reserved.

5. What is the effective interest rate if the loan is a discount loan?

   a. 11.1%   b. 13.3%   c. 15.0%   d. 17.5%   e. 20.0%

6. What is the approximate effective interest rate if the loan is an add-on interest loan with 12 monthly payments?

   a. 11.1%   b. 13.3%   c. 15.0%   d. 17.5%   e. 20.0%

7. What is the effective interest rate if the loan is a discount loan with a 15 percent compensating balance?

   a. 11.1%   b. 13.3%   c. 15.0%   d. 17.5%   e. 20.0%

8. Under the terms of the previous problem, how much would you have to borrow to have the use of $10,000?

   a. $10,000   b. $11,111   c. $12,000   d. $13,333   e. $15,000

9. Gibbs Corporation needs to raise $1,000,000 for one year to supply working capital to a new store. Gibbs buys from its suppliers on terms of 4/10, net 90, and it currently pays on the 10th day and takes discounts, but it could forego discounts, pay on the 90th day, and get the needed $1,000,000 in the form of costly trade credit. Alternatively, Gibbs could borrow from its bank on a 15 percent discount interest rate basis. What is the effective annual cost rate of the lower cost source?

   a. 20.17%   b. 18.75%   c. 17.65%   d. 18.25%   e. 19.50%

Appendix 17A

(The following data apply to the next two Self-Test Problems.)

Douglas Industries needs an additional $500,000, which it plans to obtain through a factoring arrangement. The factor would purchase Douglas's accounts receivable and advance the invoice amount, minus a 4 percent commission, on the invoices purchased each month. Douglas sells on terms of net 30 days. In addition, the factor charges a 14 percent annual interest rate on the total invoice amount, to be deducted in advance.

17A-1. What amount of accounts receivable must be factored to net $500,000?

   a. $527,241   b. $515,464   c. $530,441   d. $525,367   e. $518,989

17A-2. If Douglas can reduce credit expenses by $10,000 per month and avoid bad debt losses of 3.5 percent on the factored amount, what is the total annual dollar cost of the savings that results from the use of the factoring arrangement?

© 1992 The Dryden Press
All rights reserved.

a. $12,353   **b.** $11,076   **c.** $14,544   **d.** $13,767   **e.** $11,841

ANSWERS TO SELF-TEST QUESTIONS

1. working capital
2. Net; current; liabilities
3. cash conversion cycle
4. permanent (long-term); temporary
5. expected return; greatest risk
6. flexibility; future
7. upward
8. more
9. Accrued; size (amount)
10. trade credit
11. spontaneous
12. free; costly
13. discount
14. Costly; alternative
15. promissory note
16. compensating balances
17. one; nine; below; prime
18. secured; receivables; inventories
19. line of credit
20. commitment
21. discount; simple (or nominal or stated)
22. installment; one-half
23. large; financially strong
24. Factoring
25. inventory blanket

26. b. The matching of maturities minimizes default risk, or the risk that the firm will be unable to pay off its maturing obligations, and reinvestment rate risk, or the risk that the firm will have to roll over the debt at a higher rate.

27. a. Neither workers nor the IRS require interest payments on wages and taxes that are not paid as soon as they are earned.

28. b. Compensating balances increase the effective rate because the firm is required to maintain excess non-interest-bearing balances.

29. e. Commercial paper is the unsecured debt of strong firms. It generally has a maturity from one to nine months and is sold primarily to other corporations and financial institutions. Rates on commercial paper are typically below the prime rate.

30. d. Statement a is false; the conservative approach would be the safest current asset financing policy. Statement b is false; short-term debt fluctuates more than long-term debt, thus, the greater the firm's reliance on short-term debt, the riskier the firm. Statement c is false; it makes no difference in the cost if the firm pays on Day 25 versus Day 30 in this instance. Statement d is true; if the firm can "stretch" its payables the approximate cost is 14.69% (the effective cost is 15.66%). Thus, the firm should obtain the 14% bank loan to take discounts as this is the lowest cost to the firm.

© 1992 The Dryden Press
All rights reserved.

SOLUTIONS TO SELF-TEST PROBLEMS

1. b. $1,080,000/360 = $3,000 in purchases per day. Typically, there will be $3,000(40) = $120,000 of accounts payable on the books at any given time. Of this, $3,000(10) = $30,000 is "free" credit, while $3,000(30) = $90,000 is "non-free" credit.

2. d.

$$\text{Approximate cost} = \frac{\text{Discount \%}}{100 - \text{Discount \%}} \times \frac{360}{\substack{\text{Days credit is}\\\text{outstanding}} - \substack{\text{Discount}\\\text{period}}}$$

$$= \frac{2}{100 - 2} \times \frac{360}{40 - 10} = \frac{2}{98} \times \frac{360}{30} = 24.5\% .$$

3. e. The periodic rate is 2/98 = 2.04%, and there are 360/30 = 12 periods per year. Thus, the effective annual rate is 27.4 percent:

$$\left(1 + \frac{k_{Nom}}{m}\right)^{12} - 1.0 = (1.0204)^{12} - 1.0$$

$$= 1.2742 - 1.0 = 0.2742 = 27.4\%.$$

4. c.

$$\substack{\text{Effective rate on}\\\text{the discount loan}} = \frac{\text{Interest}}{\text{Face value} - \text{Interest}}$$

$$= \frac{(\$2,400,000)(0.10)}{\$2,400,000 - (\$2,400,000)(0.10)}$$

$$\frac{\$240,000}{\$2,160,000} = 0.1111 = 11.11\%.$$

Credit terms are 2/10, net 40, but delaying payments 30 additional days is the equivalent of 2/10, net 70. Assuming no penalty, the approximate cost is as follows:

$$\text{Approximate cost} = \frac{\text{Discount \%}}{100 - \text{Discount \%}} \times \frac{360}{\substack{\text{Days credit is}\\\text{outstanding}} - \substack{\text{Discount}\\\text{period}}}$$

$$= \frac{2}{100 - 2} \times \frac{360}{70 - 10}$$

$$= \frac{2}{98} \times \frac{360}{60} = 0.0204(6) = 12.24\% .$$

Therefore, the loan cost is 1.13 percentage points less than trade credit.

©1992 The Dryden Press
All rights reserved.

5. a. Effective rate $= \dfrac{\$10,000(0.10)}{\$10,000 - \$10,000(0.10)} = \dfrac{\$1,000}{\$9,000} = 11.1\%$.

6. e. Approximate effective rate $= \$1,000/\$5,000 = 20.0\%$.

7. b. Effective rate $= \dfrac{10\%}{1 - 0.15 - 0.10} = 13.3\%$.

8. d. $\dfrac{\$10,000}{1 - 0.15 - 0.10} = \$13,333$.

$0.15(\$13,333) = \$2,000$ is required for the compensating balance, and $0.10(\$13,333) = \$1,333$ is required for the immediate interest payment.

9. c. Accounts payable:

Approximate cost $= (4/96)(360/80) = 0.04167(4.5) = 18.75\%$.

EAR cost $= (1.04167)^{4.5} - 1.0 = 20.17\%$.

Notes payable: $0.15/0.85 = 17.65\%$.

Appendix 17A

17A-1. a. $\begin{array}{l}\text{Accounts receivable}\\\text{needed to factor}\end{array} = \dfrac{\$500,000}{1 - \left(\dfrac{0.14}{12} + 0.04\right)} = \$527,241$.

17A-2. c. Monthly costs:

Commission $= \$527,241(0.04) =$	\$21,090
Interest $= \$527,241(0.14/12) =$	6,151
	\$27,241

Monthly savings:

Credit expense	\$10,000
Bad debt losses $= \$527,241(0.035) =$	18,453
	\$28,453

The factoring arrangement will result in a savings of $\$28,453 - \$27,241 = \$1,212$ per month, or $\$1,212(12) = \$14,544$ per year.

©1992 The Dryden Press
All rights reserved.

CHAPTER 18
CASH AND MARKETABLE SECURITIES

OVERVIEW

Approximately 1.5 percent of the average industrial firm's assets are held as cash, which is defined as demand deposits plus currency. In addition, sizable holdings of near-cash short-term marketable securities such as Treasury bills are often reported on corporations' financial statements. However, cash and marketable securities balances vary widely both across industries and among firms within a given industry. In this chapter, we analyze the factors that determine firms' cash and marketable securities balances, and we describe the most commonly used types of marketable securities. The lessons to be learned from this chapter apply to the cash holdings of individuals and nonprofit organizations, including government agencies.

OUTLINE

I. **Cash is a nonearning asset. Excessive cash balances reduce the rate of return on equity and hence the value of a firm's stock. Thus, the goal of cash management is to minimize the amount of cash the firm must hold in order to conduct its normal business.**

    A. Firms hold cash for two primary reasons:
       1. Transactions balances are held to provide the cash needed to conduct normal business operations.
       2. Compensating balances are often required by banks for providing loans and services.

    B. Two secondary reasons are also cited:
       1. Precautionary balances are held in reserve for random fluctuations in cash inflows and outflows.
       2. Speculative balances are held to enable the firm to take advantage of bargain purchases.

    C. Most firms do not segregate funds for each of these motives, but they do consider them in setting their overall cash positions.

    D. An ample cash balance should be maintained to take advantage of trade discounts and favorable business opportunities, to help the firm maintain its credit rating, and to meet emergency needs.

II. **A cash budget projects cash inflows and outflows over some specified period of time.**

18-1

©1992 The Dryden Press
All rights reserved.

A. The basis for a cash budget is the sales forecast and the level of fixed assets and inventories that will be required to meet the forecasted sales level.

B. Cash budgets can be created for any interval, but firms typically use a monthly cash budget for the coming year, a weekly budget for the coming month, and a daily budget for the coming week, or something similar.

C. A typical cash budget consists of three sections.
1. The *collections and purchases worksheet* summarizes the firm's cash collections from sales and cash purchases for materials.
2. The *cash gain or loss section* lays out the cash inflows and outflows, and the "bottom line" of this section is the net cash gain or loss.
3. The *cash surplus or loan requirement section* summarizes the firm's cumulative need for loans and cumulative surplus cash.

D. If the firm's inflows and outflows are not uniform over the budget interval, say monthly, the cash budget will overstate or understate the firm's cash needs.

E. The cash budget can be used to help set the firm's target cash balance. This is accomplished by incorporating uncertainty into the budget, and then setting a target balance which provides a cushion against adverse conditions.

F. Computer programs, especially spreadsheet programs such as *Lotus 1-2-3*, are particularly well suited for preparing and analyzing the cash budget.

G. Note that the cash budget focuses on the physical movement of cash, and hence depreciation cash flow does not appear directly on the budget. It does, however, affect the amount of taxes shown.

III. **Cash management has changed significantly over the last two decades as a result of interest rates and new technology.**

A. Interest rates have, for the most part, been trending up, pushing up the opportunity cost of holding cash and forcing financial managers to search for more efficient ways of managing the firm's cash.

B. New technology, particularly computerized electronic funds transfer mechanisms, has provided a means to optimize cash transactions on a real-time basis.

C. Cash management techniques fall generally into five categories: (1) cash flow synchronization, (2) using float, (3) accelerating collections, (4) determining where and when funds are needed, and (5) controlling disbursements.

D. Synchronizing cash inflows and outflows permits a reduction in the firm's cash balances, decreases its bank loans, lowers its interest expense, and increases profits.

©1992 The Dryden Press
All rights reserved.

E. Float is the difference between the balance shown in a firm's checkbook and the balance on the bank's records. A firm's net float is a function of its ability to speed up collections on checks received (*collections float*) and to slow down collections on checks written (*disbursement float*).

IV. **Several techniques are now used to speed collections and to get funds where they are needed.**

A. A *lockbox plan* can reduce mail-time float and processing float.
1. In a lockbox system, customers mail checks to a post office box in a specified city. A local bank then collects the checks, deposits them, starts the clearing process and notifies the selling firm that payment has been received.
2. Processing time is further reduced because it takes less time for banks to collect local checks.

B. A *pre-authorized debit* allows funds to be automatically transferred from a customer's account to the firm's account on specified days.

C. *Concentration banking* mobilizes funds from decentralized receiving locations into one or more central cash pools. The cash manager then uses the pools for short-term investing or reallocation among the firm's other banks. Concentration banking allows firms to take maximum advantage of economies of scale in cash management and investment. Two commonly used transfer tools are *depository transfer checks* and *electronic depository transfers*.

V. **Accelerated collections represent one side of cash management, and the other side is controlling funds outflow.**

A. No single action controls cash outflows more effectively than *centralization of payables*, which permits the financial manager to evaluate the payments coming due for the entire firm and to schedule cash transfers to meet these needs on a company-wide basis.

B. *Zero-balance accounts (ZBAs)* are special disbursement accounts having a zero-dollar balance on which disbursement checks are written. Typically, a firm establishes several zero-balance accounts in their concentration bank, and then fund ZBAs from a master account.

C. *Controlled disbursement accounts* are similar to ZBAs, except that controlled disbursement accounts can be set up at any bank. Typically, these accounts are established at remote locations.

VI. **Firms often maintain bank balances in excess of transactions needs as a means of compensating the bank for various services. These balances are called compensating balances. The banks in turn earn income on these funds by lending them to their borrowing customers.**

©1992 The Dryden Press
All rights reserved.

A. Compensating balances also are required by some bank loan agreements. Compensating balances may be established as an absolute minimum or as a minimum average balance over some time period, generally a month.

B. Many banks in countries other than the United States use overdraft systems in which depositors write checks in excess of their actual balances. These banks then automatically extend loans to cover the shortages. Overdraft systems are becoming increasingly popular in the United States.

VII. Marketable securities typically provide lower yields than a firm's operating assets, yet they are often held in sizable amounts.

A. Marketable securities are held as a substitute for cash balances. The securities are sold when cash is needed for transactions.

B. A second use of marketable securities is as a temporary investment.
   1. Seasonal or cyclical operations may generate surplus cash at some times and deficits at other times. Marketable securities may be built up during one phase of the cycle and then liquidated to cover forecasted deficits.
   2. Marketable securities may be used to accumulate funds for a known financial requirement such as a bond redemption or a major tax payment.

C. A wide variety of marketable securities, differing in terms of risk and expected rate of return, are available.
   1. Default risk is the risk that an issuer will not be able to make promised interest payments or to repay principal amounts on schedule.
   2. The probability that some event, such as a recapitalization or leveraged buyout (LBO), will occur which suddenly increases a firm's credit risk, and hence lowers the value of its outstanding bonds, is called *event risk*.
   3. Interest rate risk involves the changes in security prices that occur with changes in interest rates.
   4. Inflation risk is the risk that inflation will reduce the purchasing power of a given sum of money.
   5. Liquidity, or marketability, risk refers to whether an asset can be quickly sold at or near its current market value.
   6. Most firms emphasize safety in their marketable securities portfolios even though such an investment policy requires a sacrifice in terms of the *rates of return* earned on the portfolios.

D. Many types of securities are available for investment of surplus cash. Among those most suitable for holding as near-cash reserves are U.S. Treasury bills, commercial paper, negotiable certificates of deposit, money market mutual funds, and Eurodollar time deposits.

VIII. One of the key elements in a firm's cash budget is the target cash balance. The target cash balance is normally set as the larger of the firm's transactions balances plus

18-4

©1992 The Dryden Press
All rights reserved.

precautionary balances or its required compensating balances. The Baumol model applies inventory methodology (EOQ model) to cash balances.

A. The optimal cash holdings to be transferred from marketable securities or to be borrowed, C*, can be found by the equation:

$$C* = \sqrt{\frac{2(F)(T)}{k}}.$$

Here, F = fixed costs of borrowing or of converting marketable securities into cash, T = total amount of net new cash needed for transactions over the entire period, usually a year, and k = the opportunity cost of holding cash.

B. Assuming no precautionary balances, the optimal average cash balance is C*/2.

C. The Baumol model is simplistic in many respects, but it can provide a useful starting point for establishing a target cash balance.

SELF-TEST QUESTIONS

Definitional

1. The goal of cash management is to _____ the amount of _____ the firm must hold in order to conduct its normal business activities.

2. Precautionary balances are maintained in order to allow for random, unforeseen fluctuations in cash _____ and _____.

3. The _____ _____, which is similar to the EOQ inventory model, is used to establish the target cash balance.

4. _____ balances are maintained to pay banks for services they perform.

5. The most important tool in cash management is the _____ _____.

6. Efficient cash management is often concerned with speeding up the _____ of checks received and slowing down the _____ of checks issued.

7. One method for speeding the collection process is the use of a _____ system.

8. The most effective method of controlling cash outflows is _____ _____ _____.

9. The difference between a firm's balance on its own books and its balance as carried on the bank's books is known as _____.

©1992 The Dryden Press
All rights reserved.

10. In a cash-gathering system, local depository banks channel funds to a regional _____ bank.

11. Three mechanisms by which firms transfer funds between accounts at different banks are _____ _____ _____, _____ depository transfer checks, and _____ _____.

12. As a general rule, a firm should invest in cash management operations so long as the marginal _____ on the cash saved exceeds the marginal _____ of freeing this cash.

13. Business firms subject to _____ patterns of cash flows may invest _____ funds in short-term securities and then liquidate them when cash _____ occur.

14. _____ risk refers to an issuer's inability to make interest payments or to repay the _____ at maturity.

15. The prices of _____ - _____ bonds are much more sensitive to changes in interest rates than are the prices of _____ - _____ bonds.

Conceptual

16. Money market mutual funds are suitable vehicles for investment of surplus cash, especially for small firms.

    a. True   b. False

17. Which of the following actions would not be consistent with good cash management?

    a. Increasing the synchronization of cash flows.
    b. Using ZBA accounts in disbursing funds.
    c. Using lock-boxes in funds collection.
    d. Maintaining an average cash balance equal to that required as a compensating balance or that which minimizes total cost.
    e. Minimizing the use of float.

18. Which of the following investments is not likely to be a proper investment for temporarily idle cash?

    a. Commercial paper.
    b. Treasury bills.
    c. Recently issued long-term AAA corporate bonds.
    d. Treasury bonds due within one year.
    e. AAA corporate bonds due within one year.

©1992 The Dryden Press
All rights reserved.

19. The term "interest rate risk" refers to the probability that a firm will be unable to continue making interest payments on its debt.

   a. True   **b.** False

SELF-TEST PROBLEMS

1. The Mill Company has a daily average collection of checks of $250,000. It takes the company 4 days to convert the checks to cash. Assume a lockbox system could be employed which would reduce the cash conversion period to 3 days. The lockbox system would have a net cost of $25,000 per year, but any additional funds made available could be invested to net 8 percent per year. Should Mill adopt the lockbox system?

   a. Yes; the system would free $250,000 in funds.
   b. Yes; the benefits of the lockbox system exceed the costs.
   c. No; the benefit is only $10,000.
   d. No; the firm would lose $5,000 per year if the system were used.
   e. The benefits and costs are equal; hence the firm is indifferent toward the system.

2. The Ryder Company has been practicing cash management for some time by using the Baumol model to determine cash balances. Recently, when the interest rate on marketable securities was 10 percent, the model called for an average cash balance of $1,000. A rapid increase in interest rates has driven this rate up to 15 percent. The firm incurs a cost of $20 per transaction. Ryder does not carry any precautionary balances. What is the appropriate average cash balance now?

   a. $596.97   **b.** $604.73   **c.** $816.50   **d.** $1,632.99   **e.** $1,333.33

3. Matthew and Sarah Weisner recently leased space in the Plaza Shopping Center and opened a new business, Weisner's Ice Cream Shop. Business has been good but the Weisners frequently run out of cash. This has necessitated late payment on certain ice cream orders, which in turn is beginning to cause a problem with suppliers. The Weisners plan to borrow from a bank to have cash ready as needed, but first they need to forecast how much cash will be needed. Therefore, they have decided to prepare a cash budget for June, July, and August to determine their cash needs.

   Ice cream sales are made on a cash basis only. The Weisners must pay for their ice cream orders 1 month after the purchase. Rent is $1,000 per month, and they pay themselves a combined salary of $2,400 per month. In addition, they must make a tax payment of $6,000 in June. The current cash on hand (June 1) is $200, but the Weisners have decided to maintain an average balance of $3,000. Estimated ice cream sales and purchases for June, July, and August are given below. May purchases amounted to $70,000.

©1992 The Dryden Press
All rights reserved.

	Sales	Purchases
June	$80,000	$20,000
July	20,000	20,000
August	30,000	20,000

What amount of money must be borrowed in each of the months in the budget period (June, July, and August)?

a. $2,200; $5,600; ($1,000)*
b. $2,700; $5,600; ($1,000)*
c. $2,200; $9,400; ($1,000)*
d. ($1,000)*; $4,700; $500
e. $2,200; $5,600; $2,000

*The firm projects a cash surplus in this month.

ANSWERS TO SELF-TEST QUESTIONS

1. minimize; cash
2. inflows; outflows
3. Baumol model
4. Compensating
5. cash budget
6. collection; payment
7. lockbox
8. centralization of payables
9. float
10. concentration
11. depository transfer checks; electronic; wire transfers
12. return; cost
13. seasonal; surplus; shortages
14. Default; principal
15. long-term; short-term

16. a. They offer safety and liquidity, the two most important factors in choosing marketable securities.

17. e. Management should try to maximize float.

18. c. Long-term bonds have too much interest rate risk for the firm's liquid asset portfolio.

19. b. Interest rate risk stems from the loss of a security's value if interest rates rise. Default risk refers to the probability of missing interest payments.

SOLUTIONS TO SELF-TEST PROBLEMS

1. d. Currently, Mill has 4($250,000) = $1,000,000 in unavailable collections. If lockboxes were used, this could be reduced to $750,000. Thus, $250,000 would be available to invest at 8 percent, resulting in an annual return of 0.08($250,000) = $20,000. If the system costs $25,000, Mill would lose $5,000 per year by adopting the system.

©1992 The Dryden Press
All rights reserved.

2. c. The model is

$$C* = \sqrt{\frac{2(F)(T)}{k}}\ .$$

Initially, the average cash balance, C*/2, is $1,000, thus C* = $2,000. Therefore,

$$\$2,000 = \sqrt{\frac{2(\$20)(T)}{0.10}}$$

$$\$4,000,000 = \frac{2(\$20)(T)}{0.10}$$

$$\$4,000,000 = \$400T$$

$$\$10,000 = T\ .$$

Therefore, the new average cash balance is

$$C* = \sqrt{\frac{2(\$20)(\$10,000)}{0.15}}$$

$$C* = \$1,632.99$$

$$C*/2 = \$816.50\ .$$

3. a. **Collections and Purchases Worksheet**

	June	July	August
Sales	$80,000	$20,000	$30,000
Purchases	20,000	20,000	20,000
Payments for purchases	70,000	20,000	20,000
Cash Gain or Loss for Month			
Receipts from sales	$80,000	$20,000	$30,000
Payments:			
Purchases	$70,000	$20,000	$20,000
Salaries	2,400	2,400	2,400
Rent	1,000	1,000	1,000
Taxes	6,000	---	---
Total payments	$79,400	$23,400	$23,400
Net cash gain (loss)	$ 600	($ 3,400)	$ 6,600
Cash Surplus or Loan Requirement			
Cash at start of month	$ 200	$ 800	($ 2,600)
Cash at end of month	$ 800	($ 2,600)	$ 4,000
Less: Target cash balance	$ 3,000	$ 3,000	$ 3,000
Total surplus cash or loans to			
maintain $3,000 target cash balance	($ 2,200)	($ 5,600)	$1,000

© 1992 The Dryden Press
All rights reserved.

CHAPTER 19
ACCOUNTS RECEIVABLE AND INVENTORY

OVERVIEW

Firms would, in general, rather sell for cash than on credit, but competitive pressures force most firms to offer credit. Thus, goods are shipped, inventories are reduced, and an account receivable is created. Eventually, the customer will pay the account, at which time the firm will receive cash and its receivables will decline. Managing receivables has both direct and indirect costs, but it also has an important benefit—granting credit will increase sales. The optimal credit policy is the one which maximizes the firm's net cash flows over time, giving consideration to the risk assumed. Inventory management techniques are covered in depth in production management courses. Still, most firms typically have about 25 percent of their assets in inventories, which represents a significant investment. Since financial managers have a responsibility both for raising the capital needed to carry inventories and for the overall profitability of the firm, it is essential that finance students understand the basics of inventory management.

OUTLINE

I.   **Carrying receivables has both direct and indirect costs, but it also has an important benefit—granting credit will increase sales.**

   A. *Accounts receivable* are created when a firm sells goods or performs services on credit rather than on a cash basis. When cash is received, accounts receivable are reduced by the same amount.

   B. The total amount of accounts receivable outstanding is determined by (1) the volume of credit sales and (2) the average length of time between sales and collections.

   C. The investment in receivables, like any asset, must be financed in some manner.

II. **Receivables must be actively managed to insure that the firm's receivables policy is effective. There are two commonly used methods to monitor a firm's receivables.**

   A. The *days sales outstanding (DSO)*, also sometimes called the average collection period (ACP), measures the average length of time it takes a firm's customers to pay off their credit purchases.
   1. The DSO is calculated by dividing the receivables balance by average daily credit sales.
   2. The DSO can be compared with the industry average and the firm's own credit terms to get an indication of how well customers are adhering to the terms

©1992 The Dryden Press
All rights reserved.

prescribed and how customers' payments, on average, compare with the industry average.

B. An *aging schedule* breaks down a firm's receivables by the ages of the accounts, and it points out the percentage of receivables due that are attributable to late paying customers.

C. Both the DSO and aging schedule can be distorted if sales are seasonal or if a firm is growing rapidly. A deterioration in either the DSO or the aging schedule should be taken as a signal to investigate further, but not necessarily as a sign that the firm's credit policy has weakened.

III. **The major controllable variables that affect sales are sales price, product quality, advertising, and the firm's credit policy. The credit policy consists of (1) the credit period, (2) credit standards, (3) collection policy, and (4) discounts.**

A. The *credit period* is the length of time for which credit is granted. Increasing the credit period often stimulates sales, but there is a cost involved in carrying the increased receivables.

B. *Credit standards* refer to the strength and creditworthiness a customer must exhibit in order to qualify for credit.
1. *Credit scoring systems* use multiple discriminant analysis (MDA) to assess credit quality in a quantitative manner. A major advantage of an MDA credit-scoring system is that a customer's credit quality is expressed in a single numeric value, rather than as a subjective assessment.
2. Two major sources of external credit information are available: credit associations and credit-reporting agencies such as Dun & Bradstreet and TRW.
3. The traditional method of measuring credit quality is to investigate potential credit customers with respect to five factors called the *five Cs of credit*. These include (a) *character*, or the probability that customers will try to honor their obligations, (b) *capacity*, or the customers' ability to pay, (c) *capital*, or the general financial condition of the firm, (d) *collateral*, and (e) *conditions*.

C. *Collection policy* refers to the procedures the firm follows to collect past-due accounts. The collection process can be expensive in terms of both direct costs and lost goodwill, but at least some firmness is needed to prevent an undue lengthening of the collection period and to minimize outright losses.

D. The last variable in the credit policy decision is the firm's *cash discount policy*. Cash discounts attract customers and encourage early payment but reduce the dollar amount received on each discount sale.

E. Other conditions may also influence a firm's overall credit policy.

©1992 The Dryden Press
All rights reserved.

1. It is sometimes possible to sell on credit and assess a carrying charge on the receivables that are outstanding, making credit sales more profitable than cash sales.
2. It is illegal for a firm to charge prices or to set credit terms that discriminate between customers unless these differential prices are cost-justified.
3. When offering credit, a seller can choose from a variety of credit instruments based on the type of trade and one's confidence in the buyer's ability to pay.
    a. An *open account* is used for most credit. With this instrument, the only formal evidence of credit is an invoice which accompanies the shipment and which the buyer signs to indicate that goods have been received.
    b. A *promissory note* may be used as evidence of the credit obligation and is useful when the order is large, when the seller anticipates having trouble collecting, or when the buyer wants a longer than usual time to pay for the order.
    c. A *draft* is a cross between a check and promissory note. A specific type of draft is chosen based on the seller's objectives. The common types are as follows: commercial draft, sight draft, time draft, trade acceptance, and banker's acceptance.
4. With a *conditional sales contract*, the seller retains legal ownership of the goods until the buyer has completed payment.

IV. **Changes in credit policy must be analyzed. For example, easing the credit policy normally stimulates sales. As sales rise, costs also rise (1) to produce the extra required goods, (2) to carry the additional receivables outstanding, and (3) because bad debt expenses may rise.**

A. The question to answer when considering a credit policy change, therefore, is whether sales revenues will rise more than costs.

B. One way to answer this question is to compare projected income statements, and hence focus on the incremental changes in expected sales revenues and costs that would result from a proposed change in the credit policy.
1. In this analysis, determine the firm's cost of carrying receivables before and after the change in credit policy.
2. The cost of carrying receivables is the product of the days sales outstanding, sales per day, the variable cost ratio, and the cost of funds.

$$\text{Cost of carrying receivables} = \text{DSO} \times \frac{\text{Sales}}{\text{per day}} \times \frac{\text{Variable}}{\text{cost ratio}} \times \frac{\text{Cost of}}{\text{funds}} .$$

3. Only variable costs are considered because only this portion needs to be financed; the remainder is profit.
4. The change in the level of bad debt losses and the dollar value of the discounts taken must also be determined.
5. If expected sales revenues less expected expenses are greater after the proposed change in credit policy than before, the change in credit policy should be

©1992 The Dryden Press
All rights reserved.

undertaken, unless the riskiness of the change is disproportionate to the benefits.

C. There is quite a bit of uncertainty in credit policy change analysis because the variables are very difficult to estimate. Further, the end result depends on the reactions of competitors. Thus, the final decision is based on the quantitative analysis plus a great deal of informed judgment.

V. **Inventories, which may be classified as raw materials, work-in-process, and finished goods, are essential to the operation of most businesses.**

A. Inventories are greatly influenced by the level of sales. Since inventories are acquired before sales can take place, an accurate sales forecast is critical to effective inventory management.

B. Proper inventory management requires close coordination among the sales, purchasing, production, and finance departments. The sales/marketing department is generally the first to spot changes in demand. These changes must be worked into the company's purchasing and manufacturing schedules, and the financial manager must arrange any financing that will be needed to support the inventory buildup. Improper coordination among departments, poor sales forecasts, or both, can lead to disaster.

VI. **The goal of inventory management is to provide the inventories required to sustain operations at the lowest total cost. The first step in developing an inventory model is to identify the costs involved in purchasing and maintaining inventories.**

A. *Carrying costs* generally rise in direct proportion to the average amount of inventory carried.
   1. Carrying costs associated with inventory include cost of the capital tied up, storage and handling costs, insurance, property taxes, and depreciation and obsolescence.
   2. The annual total carrying cost (TCC) is equal to the product of C = percentage carrying cost, P = price per unit, and A = average number of units. Thus, TCC = (C)(P)(A).

B. *Ordering costs*, which are considered to be fixed costs, decline as average inventories increase, that is, as the number of orders decrease.
   1. Ordering costs include the costs of placing and receiving orders.
   2. Total ordering cost (TOC) is the product of F = fixed cost associated with placing and receiving an order and N = the number of orders placed per year. Thus, TOC = (F)(N).
C. Total inventory costs (TIC) equal the sum of total carrying cost and total ordering cost: TIC = TCC + TOC = (C)(P)(A) + (F)(N).
   1. Now recognize that if Q units are ordered each time an order is placed, and assuming that inventories are used evenly over the year and inventory levels are

©1992 The Dryden Press
All rights reserved.

run down to zero immediately prior to receipt of the next order, then the average inventory level is one-half the number ordered: A = Q/2.

2. Further, if Q units are ordered each time, and S units are required over the year, then N = S/Q.

3. Using these relationships for A and N, the total inventory cost equation can be rewritten as

$$TIC = (C)(P)\left(\frac{Q}{2}\right) + (F)\left(\frac{S}{Q}\right).$$

VII. **Inventories are obviously necessary, but it is equally obvious that inventory levels that are too high or too low are costly to the firm. The economic ordering quantity (EOQ) model can determine the optimal inventory level.**

A. The model, which is derived by minimizing total inventory costs, is

$$EOQ = \sqrt{\frac{2(F)(S)}{(C)(P)}},$$

where EOQ is the optimal quantity to be ordered each time an order is placed, F = fixed costs of placing and receiving an order, S = annual sales in units, C = annual carrying cost expressed as a percentage of average inventory value, and P = purchase price the firm must pay per unit of inventory.

B. The assumptions of the EOQ model are as follows: (1) Sales can be forecasted perfectly, (2) sales are evenly distributed throughout the year, and (3) orders are received without delay.

VIII. **The basic EOQ model was derived under several restrictive assumptions. By relaxing some of the assumptions, the model can be extended to make it more useful.**

A. Because production sales do change, and because production and shipping delays do occur, the firm must carry additional inventories, or *safety stocks*.
1. The *reorder point* is determined by multiplying the lead time between order and delivery by the weekly usage.
2. The reorder point should be adjusted downward for goods in transit, which are goods which have been ordered but have not been received.

B. Suppliers often offer discounts for ordering large quantities; such discounts are called *quantity discounts*. To evaluate taking or not taking a quantity discount, the savings of the quantity discount are compared against the increased costs of ordering (and holding) a nonoptimal amount.

C. Inflation impacts the EOQ both by raising carrying costs and by increasing the value of the inventory, and hence, on average, has minimal impact on optimal holdings.

©1992 The Dryden Press
All rights reserved.

D. For most firms, it is unrealistic to assume that demand for an inventory item is uniform throughout the year. Thus, the EOQ model cannot be used on an annual basis, but it can be used on a seasonal basis, with inventories either run down or built up during the transition between seasons.

IX. **The EOQ model, plus safety stocks, can be used to establish the proper inventory levels, but inventory management also involves the establishment of an inventory control system. These systems vary from the extremely simple to the very complex.**

A. One simple control procedure is the *redline method*. A red line is drawn inside the bin where the inventory is stocked. When the red line shows, an order is placed.

B. The *two-bin method* has inventory items stocked in two bins. When the working bin is empty, an order is placed and inventory is drawn from the second bin.

C. Large companies employ much more sophisticated *computerized inventory control systems*. The computer starts with an inventory count in memory. As withdrawals are made, they are recorded by the computer, and the inventory balance is revised. Orders are automatically placed once the reorder point is reached.

D. The *just-in-time system* coordinates a manufacturer's production with suppliers' so that raw materials arrive from suppliers just as they are needed in the production process.

E. Another important development related to inventories is *out-sourcing*, which is the practice of purchasing components rather than making them in-house. Out-sourcing is often combined with just-in-time systems to reduce inventory levels.

F. A final point relating to inventory levels is the relationship between production scheduling and inventory levels. Inventory policy must be coordinated with the firm's manufacturing and procurement policies, because the ultimate goal is to minimize total production and distribution costs, and inventory costs are just one part of the picture.

X. **Because a firm's inventory usage rates change over time, a good inventory management system must respond promptly to such changes. One system that is used to monitor inventory EOQs and levels is the ABC system.**

A. Under this system, the firm analyzes each inventory item on the basis of its cost, frequency of usage, seriousness of a stock-out, reorder lead time, and other criteria.

B. Each item is then prioritized as A, B, or C, depending on the seriousness of the consequences should a stock-out occur. Then, inventory managers can focus more on the high-priority items, and devote less resources to the low-priority items.

19-6

©1992 The Dryden Press
All rights reserved.

SELF-TEST QUESTIONS

Definitional

1. _____ _____ are created when goods are sold or services are performed on credit.

2. A firm's outstanding accounts receivable will be determined by the _____ of credit sales and the length of time between _____ and _____.

3. Sales volume and the collection period will be affected by a firm's _____ _____.

4. Extremely strict credit standards will result in lost _____.

5. Effective credit standards require a balance between the _____ costs of credit and the marginal _____ on increased sales.

6. Credit terms generally specify the _____ for which credit is granted and any _____ _____ that is offered for early payment.

7. The optimal credit terms involve a tradeoff between increased _____ and the cost of carrying additional _____ _____.

8. _____ policy refers to the manner in which a firm tries to obtain payment from past-due accounts.

9. Two popular methods for monitoring receivables are _____ _____ and the _____ _____ _____.

10. Credit sales may be especially profitable if a _____ charge is assessed on accounts receivable.

11. _____ _____ are local groups which meet to exchange credit information.

12. Most credit is offered on _____ _____, which means that the only formal evidence of credit is the invoice.

13. If a seller wants a stronger legal claim against a creditor, the seller will require the buyer to sign a _____ _____.

14. Inventories are usually classified as _____ _____, _____ - __ - _____, and _____ _____.

15. The goal of inventory management is to provide the inventories needed for operations at the _____ _____.

©1992 The Dryden Press
All rights reserved.

16. Storage costs, obsolescence, and other costs that _____ with larger inventories are known as _____ costs.

17. Ordering and receiving costs are _____ related to average inventory size.

18. The _____ _____ quantity minimizes the total costs of ordering and holding inventories.

19. When the level of inventories reaches the _____ _____, the EOQ amount should be ordered.

20. _____ _____ must be maintained in order to allow for shipping delays and uncertainty in the rate of _____.

21. Running out of an item of inventory is called a _____ - ____.

22. Inventory control systems that require suppliers to deliver items as they are needed are called _____ - ___ - _____ systems.

23. The optimal ordering quantity should be thought of more as a _____ than as a point value.

Conceptual

24. A firm changes its credit policy from 2/10, net 30, to 3/10, net 30. The change is to meet competition, so no increase in sales is expected. The firm's average investment in accounts receivable will probably increase as a result of the change.

    a. True   b. False

25. An aging schedule is constructed by a firm to keep track of when its accounts payable are due.

    a. True   b. False

26. The goal of credit policy is to

    a. Minimize bad debt losses.
    b. Minimize DSO.
    c. Maximize sales.
    d. Minimize collection expenses.
    e. Extend credit to the point where marginal profits equal marginal costs.

27. If a credit policy change increases the firm's accounts receivable, the entire increase must be financed by some source of funds.

©1992 The Dryden Press
All rights reserved.

a. True   b. False

28. The costs of a stock-out do *not* include

    a. Disruption of production schedules.
    b. Loss of customer goodwill.
    c. Depreciation and obsolescence.
    d. Loss of sales.
    e. Answers c and d above.

29. The economic ordering quantity is the order quantity that provides the minimum total cost; that is, both the ordering and carrying cost components are minimized.

    a. True   b. False

30. The addition of a safety stock to the EOQ model

    a. Increases the EOQ proportionately.
    b. Raises the reorder point.
    c. Lowers the reorder point.
    d. Does not change the total inventory costs.
    e. Results in greater variability in the time required to receive deliveries.

SELF-TEST PROBLEMS

(The following data apply to the next three Self-Test Problems.)

Simmons Brick Company sells on terms of 3/10, net 30. Gross sales for the year are $1,200,000 and the collections department estimates that 30 percent of the customers pay on the tenth day and take discounts; 40 percent pay on the thirtieth day; and the remaining 30 percent pay, on average, 40 days after the purchase. Assume 360 days per year.

1. What is the days sales outstanding?

    a. 10 days   b. 13 days   c. 20 days   d. 27 days   e. 40 days

2. What is the current receivables balance?

    a. $60,000   b. $70,000   c. $75,000   d. $80,000   e. $90,000

3. What would be the new receivables balance if Simmons toughened up on its collection policy, with the result that all nondiscount customers paid on the thirtieth day?

    a. $60,000   b. $70,000   c. $75,000   d. $80,000   e. $90,000

©1992 The Dryden Press
All rights reserved.

(The following data apply to the next three Self-Test Problems.)

Furston Inc., a retail firm, currently has sales of $1 million. Its credit period and days sales outstanding are both 30 days, and 1 percent of its sales end up as bad debts. Furston's credit manager estimates that if the firm extends its credit period to 45 days, sales will increase by $100,000, but its bad debt losses on the incremental sales would be 3 percent. Variable costs are 40 percent, and the cost of carrying receivables, k, is 15 percent. Assume a tax rate of 40 percent and 360 days per year.

4. What would be the incremental investment in receivables if the change were made?

    a. $3,250   **b.** $41,667   **c.** $21,667   **d.** $50,000   **e.** $56,667

5. What would be the incremental cost of carrying receivables?

    a. $5,000   **b.** $3,250   **c.** $8,250   **d.** $10,000   **e.** $0

6. What would be the incremental change in profits?

    a. $32,250   **b.** $26,875   **c.** $20,000   **d.** $10,550   **e.** $15,875

(The following data apply to the next two Self-Test Problems.)

Hodes Furniture currently has annual sales of $2,000,000. Its days sales outstanding is 40 days, and bad debts are 5 percent of sales. The credit and collection manager is considering instituting a stricter collection policy, whereby bad debts would be reduced to 2 percent of total sales, and the days sales outstanding would fall to 30 days. However, sales would also fall by an estimated $250,000 annually. Variable costs are 60 percent of sales and the cost of carrying receivables is 12 percent. Assume a tax rate of 40 percent and 360 days per year.

7. What would be the incremental change in receivables investment if the change were made?

    a. -$16,667   **b.** -$27,167   **c.** -$48,611   **d.** -$45,833   **e.** -$72,431

8. What would be the incremental change in profits?

    a. -$16,667   **b.** -$17,700   **c.** -$20,250   **d.** -$25,750   **e.** -$15,000

(The following data apply to the next four Self-Test Problems.)

The South Florida Lawn Supply Company is reviewing its inventory policy regarding lawn seed. The following relationships and conditions exist:

©1992 The Dryden Press
All rights reserved.

(1) Orders must be placed in multiples of 100 bags.
(2) Requirements for the year are 16,200 bags.
(3) The purchase price per bag is $5.00.
(4) The carrying cost is 20 percent of inventory value.
(5) The fixed costs per order are $25.
(6) The desired safety stock is 300 units; this amount is on hand initially.
(7) Five days are required for delivery.
(8) Assume 360 days per year.

9. What is the economic ordering quantity?

   a. 600 bags   **b.** 700 bags   **c.** 800 bags   **d.** 900 bags   **e.** 1,000 bags

10. How many orders should South Florida Lawn Supply place each year?

   a. 22   **b.** 20   **c.** 18   **d.** 16   **e.** 14

11. What is the reorder point?

   a. 750 bags   **b.** 525 bags   **c.** 345 bags   **d.** 300 bags   **e.** 225 bags

12. What is the average inventory level?

   a. 750 bags   **b.** 525 bags   **c.** 345 bags   **d.** 300 bags   **e.** 225 bags

(The following data apply to the next six Self-Test Problems.)

The Magnuson Company is trying to determine its optimal inventory policy. The
following relationships and conditions exist for the firm:

(1) Annual sales are 120,000 units.
(2) The purchase price per unit is $500.
(3) The carrying cost is 20 percent of inventory value.
(4) The fixed costs per order are $600.
(5) The optimal safety stock is 500 units, which are already on hand.
(6) Assume 360 days per year.

13. What is the economic ordering quantity?

   a. 600 units   **b.** 800 units   **c.** 1,000 units   **d.** 1,200 units   **e.** 1,400 units

14. What is the maximum inventory the company will hold?

   a. 1,300 units **b.** 1,400 units **c.** 1,500 units   **d.** 1,600 units **e.** 1,700 units

©1992 The Dryden Press
All rights reserved.

15. What is the average inventory the company will hold?

    a. 600 units   **b.** 850 units   **c.** 1,100 units   **d.** 1,200 units   **e.** 1,700 units

16. How often will the company order?

    a. Every 2.0 days   **b.** Every 3.60 days
    c. Every 5.25 days   **d.** Every 2 weeks
    e. Continually

17. What are the firm's annual total inventory costs disregarding the safety stock?

    a. $50,000   **b.** $120,000   **c.** $150,000   **d.** $170,000   **e.** $200,000

18. What are the annual total inventory costs including the safety stock?

    a. $50,000   **b.** $120,000   **c.** $150,000   **d.** $170,000   **e.** $200,000

ANSWERS TO SELF-TEST QUESTIONS

1. Accounts receivable
2. volume; sales; collections
3. credit policy
4. sales
5. marginal; profits
6. period; cash discount
7. sales; accounts receivable
8. Collection
9. aging schedules; days sales outstanding (DSO)
10. carrying
11. Credit associations
12. open account

13. promissory note
14. raw materials; work-in-process; finished goods
15. lowest cost
16. increase; carrying
17. inversely
18. economic ordering
19. reorder point
20. Safety stocks; usage
21. stock-out
22. just-in-time
23. range

24. b. No new customers are being generated. The current customers pay either on Day 10 or Day 30. The increase in trade discount will induce some customers who are now paying on Day 30 to pay on Day 10. Thus, the days sales outstanding is shortened which, in turn, will cause a decline in accounts receivable.

25. b. The aging schedule breaks down accounts receivable according to how long they have been outstanding.

26. e. The goal of credit policy is to maximize overall profits. This is achieved when the marginal profits equal the marginal costs.

©1992 The Dryden Press
All rights reserved.

27. b. Receivables are based on sales price which presumably includes some profit. Only the actual cash outlays associated with receivables must be financed. The remainder, or profit, appears on the balance sheet as an increase in retained earnings.

28. c. Depreciation and obsolescence are inventory carrying costs.

29. b. The total cost, or sum of ordering and carrying costs, is minimized, but neither of the component costs is minimized. For example, to minimize carrying costs, no inventory would be kept on hand at all.

30. b. The addition of a safety stock increases the reorder point by the amount of the safety stock.

SOLUTIONS TO SELF-TEST PROBLEMS

1. d. 0.3(10 days) + 0.4(30 days) + 0.3(40 days) = 27 days.

2. e. Receivables = (DSO)(Sales/360) = 27($1,200,000/360) = $90,000.

3. d. New days sales outstanding = 0.3(10) + 0.7(30) = 24 days.

Sales per day = $1,200,000/360 = $3,333.33.

Receivables = $3,333.33(24 days) = $80,000.00.

Thus, the average receivables would drop from $90,000 to $80,000. Furthermore, sales may decline as a result of the tighter credit and reduce receivables even more. Also, some additional customers may now take discounts, which would further reduce receivables.

4. c. The incremental receivable investment is calculated as follows:

$$\text{Old credit policy: } \text{DSO} \times \frac{\text{Sales}}{\text{per day}} \times \frac{\text{Variable}}{\text{cost ratio}} =$$

$$(30)\left(\frac{\$1,000,000}{360}\right)(0.4) = \$33,333.$$

$$\text{New credit policy: } \text{DSO} \times \frac{\text{Sales}}{\text{per day}} \times \frac{\text{Variable}}{\text{cost ratio}} =$$

©1992 The Dryden Press
All rights reserved.

$$(45)\left(\frac{\$1,100,000}{360}\right)(0.4) = \$55,000.$$

The incremental investment in receivables is $55,000 - $33,333 = $21,667.

5. b. The incremental cost of carrying receivables would be calculated as follows:

Old credit policy: $\text{DSO} \times \dfrac{\text{Sales}}{\text{per day}} \times \dfrac{\text{Variable}}{\text{cost ratio}} \times \dfrac{\text{Cost of}}{\text{funds}}$.

$$(30)\left(\frac{\$1,000,000}{360}\right)(0.4)(0.15) = \$5,000.$$

or $\qquad\qquad$ $\$33,333(0.15) = \$5,000.$

New credit policy: $\text{DSO} \times \dfrac{\text{Sales}}{\text{per day}} \times \dfrac{\text{Variable}}{\text{cost ratio}} \times \dfrac{\text{Cost of}}{\text{funds}}$.

$$(45)\left(\frac{\$1,100,000}{360}\right)(0.4)(0.15) = \$8,250.$$

or $\qquad\qquad$ $\$55,000(0.15) = \$8,250.$

Thus, the incremental cost is $8,250 - $5,000 = $3,250.

6. a.

	Income Statement Under Current Policy	Effect of Change	Income Statement Under New Policy
Gross sales	$1,000,000	$100,000	$1,100,000
Less discounts	0	0	0
Net sales	$1,000,000	$100,000	$1,100,000
Productions costs	400,000	40,000	440,000
Profit before credit costs and taxes	$ 600,000	$ 60,000	$ 660,000
Credit related costs:			
Cost of carrying receivables	5,000	3,250	8,250
Collection expenses			
Bad debt losses	10,000	3,000	13,000
Profit before taxes	$ 585,000	$ 53,750	$ 638,750
Taxes (40%)	234,000	21,500	255,500
Net income	$ 351,000	$ 32,250	$ 383,250

7. d. The incremental change in receivable investment would be calculated as follows:

©1992 The Dryden Press
All rights reserved.

Old credit policy: $\text{DSO} \times \dfrac{\text{Sales}}{\text{per day}} \times \dfrac{\text{Variable}}{\text{cost ratio}} =$

$$(40)\left(\frac{\$2,000,000}{360}\right)(0.6) = \$133,333.$$

New credit policy: $\text{DSO} \times \dfrac{\text{Sales}}{\text{per day}} \times \dfrac{\text{Variable}}{\text{cost ratio}} =$

$$(30)\left(\frac{\$1,750,000}{360}\right)(0.6) = \$87,500.$$

The incremental change in receivables is $87,500 - $133,333 = -$45,833.

8. b.

	Income Statement Under Current Policy	Effect of Change	Income Statement Under New Policy
Sales	$2,000,000	($250,000)	$1,750,000
Less discounts	0	0	0
Net sales	$2,000,000	$250,000	$1,750,000
Productions costs	1,200,000	150,000	1,050,000
Profit before credit costs and taxes	$ 800,000	($100,000)	$ 700,000
Credit related costs:			
Cost of carrying receivables	16,000	5,500	10,500
Collection expenses			
Bad debt losses	100,000	65,000	35,000
Profit before taxes	$ 684,000	($ 29,500)	$ 654,500
Taxes (40%)	273,600	(11,800)	261,800
Net income	$ 410,400	($ 17,700)	$ 392,700

9. d. $\text{EOQ} = \sqrt{\dfrac{2(F)(S)}{(C)(P)}} = \sqrt{\dfrac{2(\$25)(16,200)}{0.20(\$5)}} = \sqrt{\dfrac{\$810,000}{\$1.00}} = 900 \text{ bags}.$

10. c. $\dfrac{16,200 \text{ bags per year}}{900 \text{ bags per order}} = 18 \text{ orders per year}.$

11. b. Daily rate of use = 16,200/360 = 45 bags.
Reorder point = 300 + 5(45) = 525 bags.

©1992 The Dryden Press
All rights reserved.

Thus, South Florida Lawn Supply Company will have 1,200 bags on hand immediately after a shipment is received, will use 45 bags per day, will reorder when the stock is down to 525 bags (which is 5 days' requirement, plus the safety stock), and will be down to 300 bags just before a shipment arrives.

12. a. Average inventory level = EOQ/2 + Safety stock = 900/2 + 300 = 750 bags. Note that the inventory fluctuates between 1,200 and 300 bags.

13. d. $EOQ = \sqrt{\dfrac{2(F)(S)}{(C)(P)}} = \sqrt{\dfrac{2(\$600)(120,000)}{0.20(\$500)}} = \sqrt{\dfrac{\$144,000,000}{\$100}} = 1,200$ units.

14. e. Maximum inventory = EOQ + Safety stock = 1,200 + 500 = 1,700 units.

15. c. Average inventory = EOQ/2 + Safety stock = 600 + 500 = 1,100 units.

16. b. $\dfrac{120,000 \text{ units per year}}{1,200 \text{ units per order}} = 100$ orders per year.

$\dfrac{360 \text{ days per year}}{100 \text{ orders per year}} = 3.60$ days.

The firm must place one order every 3.60 days.

17. b. $TIC = (C)(P)(Q/2) + (F)\left(\dfrac{S}{Q}\right)$

$= 0.2(\$500)(1,200/2) + \$600\left(\dfrac{120,000}{1,200}\right)$

$= \$60,000 + \$60,000 = \$120,000.$

Note that total carrying cost equals total ordering cost at the EOQ.

18. d. Now, the average inventory is EOQ/2 + Safety stock = 1,100 units rather than EOQ/2 = 600 units.

$TIC = 0.2(\$500)(1,100) + \$600\left(\dfrac{120,000}{1,200}\right)$

$= \$110,000 + \$60,000 = \$170,000.$

Another way of looking at this is TIC = Cost of working inventory + Cost of safety stock = $120,000 + 0.2($500)(500) = $120,000 + $50,000 = $170,000.

©1992 The Dryden Press
All rights reserved.

CHAPTER 20
MERGERS, DIVESTITURES,
HOLDING COMPANIES, AND LBOs

OVERVIEW

A merger involves the consolidation of two or more firms. Mergers can provide economic benefits through economies of scale, but they also have the potential for reducing competition; and, for this reason, mergers are carefully regulated by governmental agencies. Of the several rationales for mergers, perhaps the most common is the existence of synergy. When synergy is present, the value of the combined enterprise is greater than the sum of the values of the separate firms. Merger analysis may be regarded as a specialized form of capital budgeting analysis, with the most difficult part of the analysis being the estimation of the incremental cash flows that would result from the merger. Investment banking firms have specialists who can assist both the acquiring firm and the target firm in the valuation process. Divestitures, the opposite of mergers, also occur frequently. The reasons for divestiture are varied, and they range from the need for cash to governmental insistence (antitrust reasons). Holding companies are firms whose sole purpose is to own operating interests in the stock of other firms. The holding company structure has both advantages and disadvantages over the conventional divisional structure.

OUTLINE

I. **Several reasons have been proposed to justify corporate mergers.**

   A. The primary goal of most mergers is to increase the value of the combined enterprise.
      1. If Companies A and B merge to form Company C and if C's value exceeds that of A and B taken separately, then *synergy* is said to exist.
      2. Synergism can arise from four sources: operating economies of scale, financial economies, differential management efficiency, and increased market power.
      3. Operating and financial economies, as well as increases in managerial efficiency, are socially desirable. However, mergers to increase market power are both undesirable and illegal.

   B. Tax considerations have stimulated a number of mergers.
      1. A highly profitable firm might merge with a firm which has accumulated tax losses so as to put these losses to immediate use.
      2. A firm with excess cash and a shortage of internal investment opportunities might seek a merger rather than pay the cash out as dividends, which would result in the shareholders paying immediate taxes on the distribution.

©1992 The Dryden Press
All rights reserved.

C. Sometimes a firm will become an acquisition candidate because the replacement value of its assets is considerably higher than its market value.

D. Diversification is often cited by managers as a rationale for mergers. Although diversification may bring some real benefits to the firm, stockholders can generally diversify more easily and efficiently than can firms by simply holding portfolios of stocks.

E. The ability for management to maintain control has caused defensive mergers, which are designed to make a company less vulnerable to a takeover.

II. **There are four primary types of mergers: horizontal, vertical, congeneric, and conglomerate.**

A. A *horizontal merger* occurs when one firm combines with another in its same line of business.

B. A *vertical merger* exists when firms combine in a producer-supplier relationship.

C. A *congeneric merger* involves related enterprises but not producers of the same product (horizontal) or firms in a producer-supplier relationship.

D. A *conglomerate merger* occurs when completely unrelated enterprises combine.

III. **The high level of merger activity in the 1980s has been sparked by several factors.**

A. The depressed level of the dollar relative to Japanese and European currencies, which made U.S. companies look cheap to foreign buyers.

B. The unprecedented level of inflation that existed during the 1970s and early 1980s, which increased the replacement value of firms' assets.

C. The Reagan and Bush administrations' view that "bigness is not necessarily badness," which resulted in a more tolerant attitude toward large mergers.

D. The general belief among the major natural resource companies that it is cheaper to "buy reserves on Wall Street" than to explore and find them in the field.

E. Attempts to ward off raiders by use of defensive mergers.

F. The development of the junk bond market, which made it possible to use far more debt in acquisitions than had been possible earlier.

G. The increased globalization of business.

©1992 The Dryden Press
All rights reserved.

IV. **In most mergers, one company, the target company, is acquired by another, the acquiring company.**

    A. In a *friendly merger*, the management of the target company approves the merger and recommends it to their stockholders.
        1. Under these circumstances, a suitable price is determined and the acquiring company will simply buy the target company's shares.
        2. Payment will be made either in cash or in shares of the acquiring company.

    B. A *hostile merger* is one in which the target firm's management resists the takeover. The target firm's management either believes the price offered is too low, or it may simply want to remain independent.
        1. Under these circumstances, the acquiring company may make a *tender offer* for the target company's shares. This is a direct appeal to the target firm's stockholders asking them to exchange their shares for cash, for bonds, or for stock in the acquiring firm.
        2. The number of tender offers has increased greatly during the past several years.

V. **While merger analysis may appear simple, there are a number of complex issues involved.**

    A. The acquiring firm must perform a capital budgeting analysis. If it appears that the target firm can be purchased for less than its intrinsic value, then the offer should be made. However, the target firm's shareholders must believe that a "fair" price is being offered. Otherwise, they will not tender their shares.

    B. From a financial standpoint, there are two basic types of mergers:
        1. An *operating merger* is one in which the operations of two companies are integrated in hopes of synergistic gains.
        2. A *financial merger* is one in which the merged companies will not be operated as a single unit and from which no significant operating economies are expected.

    C. In a financial merger, the postmerger cash flows are simply the sum of the expected cash flows of the two companies if they continued to operate independently. However, if they are to be integrated, then accurate estimates of future cash flows are essential. In planning operating mergers, the development of accurate pro forma cash flows is the single most important aspect of the analysis.

    D. The terms of a merger include two important elements:
        1. *Postmerger control* is of great interest to managers due to their concern for their jobs.
        2. The *price paid* determines whether the shareholders of the acquiring company or the shareholders of the target company reap the greater benefits from the merger.

©1992 The Dryden Press
All rights reserved.

VI. **The valuation of the target firm involves two key items: (1) a set of pro forma financial statements and (2) a discount rate to apply to the projected cash flows.**

    A. In a complete merger evaluation, just as in a capital budgeting analysis, the component cash flow probability distributions would be specified, and sensitivity, scenario, and simulation analyses would be conducted.

    B. Merger cash flows should be discounted at the target company's cost of equity rather than at the overall cost of capital. The Security Market Line can be used to determine the approximate postmerger cost of equity.

    C. The present value of the incremental merger cash flows is the maximum price that the acquiring firm should pay for the target company.

VII. **Investment bankers play an important role in merger activities.**

    A. The major investment banking firms have merger and acquisition (M&A) departments which help to match merger partners.

    B. These same investment bankers can also help a firm fend off an unwanted suitor.
        1. Sometimes a *white knight* will be lined up to acquire a firm that is trying to avoid being taken over by an unfriendly suitor.
        2. Investment bankers can also recommend *poison pills,* which are actions that effectively destroy the value of the firm in the event of merger, and hence drive off unwanted suitors.

    C. Finally, investment bankers are used to help establish the offering price. Generally, both acquiring and target firms will use investment bankers to help establish a price and also to participate in the negotiations.

VIII. **Mergers are not the only ways in which resources of two firms can be combined. In fact, many companies are striking cooperative deals, corporate alliances, which fall far short of merging. One form of corporate alliance is the joint venture, which involves the joining together of parts of companies to accomplish specific, limited objectives. Joint ventures are controlled by a combined management team formed from the parent companies, and are operated independently from the parent companies.**

IX. **Although corporations do more buying than selling of productive assets, selling, or divestiture, does take place.**

    A. There are four primary types of divestitures:
        1. A division may be sold intact to another firm. This is the most common form of divestiture.
        2. A division may be sold to its managers. Such a managerial buyout results in the owners-managers reorganizing into a closely held firm.

©1992 The Dryden Press
All rights reserved.

3. A division may be set up as a corporation with the parent firm's stockholders then being given stock in the new corporation on a pro rata basis. This type of divestiture is called a spin-off.
4. Sometimes, when a firm cannot find a buyer for an entire division, the division's assets must be sold off piecemeal. This is a liquidation.

B. There are a variety of reasons cited for divestitures:
1. Sometimes the market does not appear to properly recognize the value of a firm's assets when they are held as part of a conglomerate. Thus, divestiture can occur to enhance firm value.
2. Often, firms will need to raise large amounts of cash to finance expansion in their core business or to reduce an onerous debt burden, and divestitures can raise the needed cash.
3. Sometimes, assets are just no longer profitable and must be liquidated.

X. **A holding company is a firm that holds large blocks of stock in other companies and exercises control over those firms. The holding company is often called the parent company, and the controlled companies are known as subsidiaries or operating companies. Holding companies may be used to obtain some of the same benefits that could be achieved through mergers and acquisitions.**

A. Advantages of holding companies include the following:
1. *Control with fractional ownership.* Effective control of a company may be achieved with far less than 50 percent ownership of the common stock.
2. *Isolation of risks.* Claims on one unit of the holding company may not be liabilities to the other units. Each element of the holding company organization is a separate legal entity.
3. *Legal separation.* Certain regulated companies such as utilities and banks find it easier to operate as holding companies in order to separate those assets under the control of regulators from those not subject to regulation.

B. Disadvantages of holding companies include the following:
1. *Partial multiple taxation.* Consolidated tax returns may be filed only if the holding company owns 80 percent or more of the voting stock of the subsidiary. Otherwise, intercorporate dividends will be taxed. Note, though, that 70 percent of the dividends received by the holding company may be deducted from taxable income.
2. *Ease of enforced dissolution.* It is much easier for the Justice Department to require disposal of a stock position than to demand the separation of an integrated business operation.

C. The holding company vehicle can be used to control large amounts of assets with a relatively small equity investment. The substantial leverage involved in such an operation may result in high returns, but it also involves a high degree of risk.

20-5

©1992 The Dryden Press
All rights reserved.

XI. The 1980s witnessed a huge increase in the number and size of leveraged buyouts, or LBOs. This development occurred for the same reasons that mergers and divestitures occurred—the existence of potential bargains, situations in which companies were using insufficient leverage, and the development of the junk bond market. Generally, the newly formed company will have at least 80 percent debt, so the term "leveraged" is most appropriate.

SELF-TEST QUESTIONS

Definitional

1. If the value of two firms, in combination, is greater than the sum of their separate values, then _____ is said to exist.

2. Synergistic effects may result from either _____ economies or _____ economies.

3. The Justice Department may be concerned about the _____ implications of a proposed merger.

4. A _____ merger takes place when two firms in the same line of business combine, while the combination of a steel company with a coal company would be an example of a _____ merger.

5. A _____ merger is the merger of two completely unrelated enterprises.

6. An _____ company is a firm which seeks to take over another company, while the firm it seeks to acquire is referred to as the _____ company.

7. A merger may be described as "friendly" or "hostile," depending upon the attitude of the _____ of the target company.

8. A _____ _____ is a request by the acquiring company to the target company's _____ to submit their shares in exchange for a specified price or specified number of shares of stock.

9. An _____ merger combines the business activity of the two firms with the expectation of _____ benefits.

10. _____ mergers do not combine the business operations of two firms, and no operating economies are expected.

11. Merger analysis is very similar to _____ _____ analysis.

©1992 The Dryden Press
All rights reserved.

12. In valuing the target firm, the analysis focuses on the cash flows that accrue to the stockholders of the _____ firm.

13. A _____ _____ occurs when two firms combine parts of their companies to accomplish specific, limited objectives.

14. A pro rata distribution of stock in a new firm which was formerly a subsidiary is called a _____-_____.

15. Unless a holding company owns at least ___ percent of the voting stock of a subsidiary, it may be subject to multiple _____ on a portion of any intercorporate _____.

Conceptual

16. In a financial merger, the expected post-merger cash flows are generally the sum of the cash flows of the separate companies.

    a. True   b. False

17. Interest expense must be explicitly included in an incremental merger cash flow analysis.

    a. True   b. False

18. The holding company device can be used to take advantage of the principle of financial leverage. Thus, the holding company can control a great deal of assets with a limited amount of top-tier equity.

    a. True   b. False

SELF-TEST PROBLEMS

(The following data apply to the next four Self-Test Problems.)

TransCorp, a large conglomerate, is evaluating the possible acquisition of the Chip Company, a transistor manufacturer. TransCorp's analyst projects the following post-merger incremental cash flows (in millions of dollars):

©1992 The Dryden Press
All rights reserved.

	1992	1993	1994	1995
Net sales	$200	$230	$250	$270
Cost of goods sold	130	140	145	150
Selling/administrative expense	20	25	30	32
EBIT	$ 50	$ 65	$ 75	$ 88
Interest	10	12	13	14
EBT	$ 40	$ 53	$ 62	$ 74
Taxes (40%)	16	21	25	30
Net income	$ 24	$ 32	$ 37	$ 44
Retained earnings	12	13	14	15
Cash available to stockholders	$ 12	$ 19	$ 23	$ 29
Terminal value				400
Net CF	$ 12	$ 19	$ 23	$429

The acquisition, if made, would occur on January 1, 1992. All cash flows above are assumed to occur at the end of the year. Chip currently has a market value capital structure of 10 percent debt, but TransCorp would increase the debt to 50 percent if the acquisition were made. Chip, if independent, pays taxes at 30 percent, but its income would be taxed at 40 percent if consolidated. Chip's current market-determined beta is 1.80. Its estimated post-merger beta is 2.67.

The cash flows above include the additional interest payments due to increased leverage and asset expansion, and the full taxes paid by TransCorp on the Chip income stream. Depreciation-generated funds would be used to replace worn-out equipment, so they would not be available to TransCorp's shareholders. Retained earnings would be used, in addition to new debt, to finance required asset expansion. Thus, the net cash flows are the flows that would accrue to TransCorp's stockholders. The risk-free rate is 10 percent and the market risk premium is 5 percent.

1. What is the appropriate discount rate for valuing the acquisition?

   a. 10.00%   b. 15.00%   c. 19.00%   d. 21.75%   e. 23.35%

2. What is the value of the Chip Company to TransCorp?

   a. $197.73 million   b. $206.42 million   c. $219.78 million
   d. $322.85 million   e. $429.00 million

3. Chip has 5 million shares outstanding. Chip's current market price is $32.50. What is the maximum price per share that TransCorp should offer?

   a. $32.50   b. $37.50   c. $41.37   d. $43.96   e. $46.93

4. TransCorp should offer Chip's stockholders $32.625 per share.

   a. True   b. False

©1992 The Dryden Press
All rights reserved.

ANSWERS TO SELF-TEST QUESTIONS

1. synergy
2. operating; financial
3. antitrust
4. horizontal; vertical
5. conglomerate
6. acquiring; target
7. management
8. tender offer; stockholders
9. operating; synergistic
10. Financial
11. capital budgeting
12. acquiring
13. joint venture
14. spin-off
15. 80; taxation; dividends

16. a. In a financial merger, no synergistic effects are anticipated.

17. a. The target firm generally has embedded debt that is being assumed by the acquiring firm. Since these costs are not marginal, they must be specifically included in the analysis.

18. a. This statement is true.

SOLUTIONS TO SELF-TEST PROBLEMS

1. e. $k_s = 10\% + (5\%)2.67 = 23.35\%$.

2. c. $V = \dfrac{\$12 \text{ million}}{(1.2335)^1} + \dfrac{\$19 \text{ million}}{(1.2335)^2} + \dfrac{\$23 \text{ million}}{(1.2335)^3} + \dfrac{\$429 \text{ million}}{(1.2335)^4}$
   $= \$219.78$ million.

3. d. $219.78 million/5 million = $43.96.

4. b. It does not make sense to offer Chip's shareholders just a little above the current market price. Enough shares would not be tendered to gain control, the expenses would be for nought, and other firms could be induced to make competing bids.

©1992 The Dryden Press
All rights reserved.

CHAPTER 21
MULTINATIONAL FINANCIAL MANAGEMENT

OVERVIEW

As the world economy becomes more integrated, the role of multinational firms is increasing. Although the same basic principles of financial management apply to multinational corporations as well as to domestic ones, the financial managers of multinational firms face a much more complex task. The primary problem, from a financial standpoint, is the fact that the cash flows must cross national boundaries. These flows may be constrained in various ways, and, equally important, their values in dollars may rise or fall depending on exchange rate fluctuations. This means that the multinational financial manager must be constantly aware of the many complex interactions among national economies and their effects on international operations.

OUTLINE

I. **A multinational corporation is one that operates in two or more countries. The growth of multinationals has greatly increased the degree of worldwide economic and political interdependence.**

   A. Companies, both U.S. and foreign, go "international" for five primary reasons:
       1. After a company has saturated its home market, growth opportunities are often better in foreign markets.
       2. Many of the present multinational firms began their international operations because raw materials were located abroad.
       3. Because no single nation holds a commanding advantage in all technologies, companies are scouring the globe for leading scientific and design ideas.
       4. Still other firms have moved their manufacturing facilities overseas to take advantage of cheaper production costs in low-cost countries.
       5. Finally, firms can avoid political and regulatory hurdles by moving production to other countries.

   B. The past decade has seen an increasing amount of investment in the U.S. by foreign corporations. This "reverse" investment has been growing at a higher rate than U.S. investment abroad. These developments suggest an increasing degree of mutual influence and interdependence among business enterprises and nations.

II. **In theory, financial concepts and procedures are valid for both domestic and multinational operations. However, there are several factors which distinguish financial management as practiced by firms operating entirely within a single country from management by firms that operate in several different countries.**

©1992 The Dryden Press
All rights reserved.

A. Cash flows will be denominated in different currencies, making exchange rate analysis necessary for all types of financial decisions.

B. Economic and legal differences among countries can cause significant problems when the corporation tries to coordinate and control world-wide operations of its subsidiaries.

C. The ability to communicate is critical in all business transactions. U.S. citizens are often at a disadvantage because we are generally fluent only in English.

D. Values and the role of business in society reflect the cultural differences that may vary dramatically from one country to the next.

E. Financial models based on the traditional assumption of a competitive market-place must often be modified to include political (governmental) and other non-economic facets of the decision.

F. Political risk, which is seldom negotiable, and may be as extreme as expropriation, must be explicitly addressed in financial analysis.

III. **An exchange rate specifies the number of units of a given currency than can be purchased for one unit of another currency.**

A. An exchange rate listed as the number of U.S. dollars required to purchase one unit of foreign currency is called a *direct quotation*. The number of units of foreign currency that can be purchased for one U.S. dollar is called an *indirect quotation*. Normal practice in the U.S. is to use indirect quotations for all currencies other than British pounds, for which direct quotations are given.

B. Converting from one foreign currency to another foreign currency requires the use of cross rates. For example, if the direct quotation between pounds and dollars is $1.7875, and the indirect quotation between francs and dollars is FF5.6344, the cross rate between pounds and francs can be calculated as follows:

$$\text{Cross rate} = \frac{\text{Dollars}}{\text{Pound}} \times \frac{\text{Francs}}{\text{Dollar}} = \frac{\text{Francs}}{\text{Pound}}$$

= 1.7875 dollars per pound × 5.6344 francs per dollar

= 10.0715 francs per pound.

IV. **The International Monetary Fund (IMF) was the center of a fixed exchange rate system that operated for 25 years after World War II.**

A. Under this system the U.S. dollar, which was linked to gold by a fixed price of $35 per ounce, was the base currency, and the relative values of all other currencies to the dollar were controlled within narrow limits, but then adjusted periodically.

©1992 The Dryden Press
All rights reserved.

1. Currency fluctuations depend on supply and demand, capital movements, and the activities of international speculators. However, these fluctuations were kept within limits by the actions of the various central banks, which bought or sold currency to maintain specific prices.
2. If a country devalued its currency, then fewer units of another currency would be required to buy one unit of the devalued currency. Its "price" would be reduced, making the country's goods cheaper and thus stimulating exports and discouraging imports. A country could devalue its currency only with the approval of the IMF.

B. In 1971, the fixed exchange rate system was replaced by a system under which the U.S. dollar was permitted to "float."
1. A floating exchange rate system is one under which currency prices are allowed to reach their own levels without much governmental intervention.
2. The present managed floating system permits currency rates to move without any specific limits, but central banks do buy and sell currencies to smooth out exchange rate fluctuations.

C. The inherent volatility of exchange rates under a floating system increases the uncertainty of the cash flows for a multinational corporation. This uncertainty is known as *exchange rate risk*, and it is a major factor differentiating the multinational corporation from a purely domestic one.

D. Not all currencies are *convertible*. A currency is convertible when the issuing nation allows it to be traded in the currency markets and is willing to redeem the currency at market rates.

V. **Importers, exporters, and tourists, as well as governments, buy and sell currencies in the foreign exchange market, which consists of a network of brokers and banks based in New York, London, Tokyo, and other financial centers.**

A. The rate paid for delivery of currency two days after the day of trade is called the *spot rate*.

B. When currency is bought or sold and is to be delivered at some agreed-upon future date, usually 30, 90, or 180 days into the future, a *forward exchange rate* is used.
1. If one can obtain more of the foreign currency for a dollar in the forward market than in the spot market, then the forward currency is less valuable than the spot currency, and the forward currency is said to be selling at a *discount*.
2. If a dollar will buy fewer units of a currency in the forward market than in the spot market, then the forward currency is worth more dollars than the spot currency and the forward currency is said to be selling at a *premium*.

C. Individuals and firms buy or sell forward currencies to hedge against unwanted changes in exchange rates.

©1992 The Dryden Press
All rights reserved.

VI. Relative inflation rates have many implications for multinational financial decisions. Equally important, they have a dominant influence on relative interest rates as well as exchange rates.

   A. A foreign currency on average will depreciate at a percentage rate approximately equal to the amount by which its country's inflation rate exceeds the U.S. inflation rate. Conversely, foreign currencies in countries with less inflation than the U.S. will, on average, appreciate relative to the U.S. dollar.

   B. Countries experiencing higher rates of inflation tend to have higher interest rates.

   C. Gains from borrowing in countries with low interest rates can be offset by losses from currency appreciation in those countries.

VII. There exists a well developed system of international capital markets.

   A. Americans can invest in world markets by investing in the stock of U.S. multi-national corporations, or by buying the bonds and stocks of large corporations (or governments) headquartered outside the United States.
   1. Investment by U.S. firms in foreign operating assets is called direct investment.
   2. Investment in foreign stocks and bonds is called portfolio investment.

   B. The Eurodollar market is essentially a short-term market for handling dollar-denominated loans and deposits made outside the United States.
   1. A Eurodollar is a U.S. dollar placed on deposit in a foreign (normally European) bank, including foreign branches of U.S. banks.
   2. The major difference between a dollar on deposit in Chicago and a dollar on deposit in London is the geographic location. The deposits do not involve different currencies, so exchange rate considerations do not apply.
   3. If rates in the United States are above Eurodollar rates, these funds will be sent back and invested in the United States, while if Eurodollar deposit rates are significantly above U.S. rates, more dollars will be sent out of the United States.

   C. Two international bond markets have developed which trade in long-term funds.
   1. Foreign bonds are bonds sold by a foreign borrower but denominated in the currency of the country in which the issue is sold.
   2. Eurobonds are bonds sold in a country other than the one in whose currency the issue is denominated.

VIII. There are several important differences in capital budgeting analysis of foreign versus domestic operations.

   A. Cash flow analysis is much more complex for overseas investments.
   1. Usually a firm will organize a separate subsidiary in each foreign country in which it operates.

©1992 The Dryden Press
All rights reserved.

2. Any dividends or royalties repatriated by the subsidiary must be converted to the currency of the parent company, and thus are subject to exchange rate fluctuations.
3. Dividends and royalties received are normally taxed by both foreign and domestic governments.
4. Some governments place restrictions, or exchange controls, on the amount of cash that may be remitted to the parent company in order to encourage re-investment of earnings in the foreign country.
5. The only relevant cash flows for analysis of an international investment are the financial cash flows that the subsidiary can legally send back to the parent.

B. The cost of capital may be higher for foreign investments because they may be riskier than domestic investments.
1. Exchange risk refers to the fact that exchange rates may fluctuate, increasing the uncertainty about cash flows to the parent company.
2. Political risk refers to the possibility of expropriation and to restrictions on cash flows to the parent company.

IX. **Significant differences have been observed in the capital structures of U.S. corporations in comparison to their German and Japanese counterparts. An analysis of both bankruptcy and equity reporting costs leads to the conclusion that U.S. firms use more equity and less debt than firms in Japan and Germany.**

X. **The objectives of working capital management in the multinational corporation are similar to those in the domestic firm but the task is more complex.**

A. The objectives of cash management in the multinational corporation are to speed up collections and to slow disbursements, to shift cash rapidly from those parts of the business that do not need it to those parts that do, and to obtain the highest possible risk-adjusted rate of return on temporary cash balances.

B. The same general procedures are used by multinational firms as those used by domestic firms, but because of longer distances and more serious mail delays, lockbox systems and electronic funds transfers are especially important.

C. Granting credit is more risky in an international context because, in addition to the normal risks of default, the multinational corporation must also worry about exchange rate changes between the time a sale is made and the time a receivable is collected. Credit policy is generally more important for a multinational firm than for a domestic firm.
1. Much of the U.S.'s trade is with poorer, less-developed countries; thus, granting credit is generally a necessary condition for doing business.
2. Nations whose economic health depends upon exports often help their manufacturing firms compete internationally by granting credit to foreign countries.

21-5

©1992 The Dryden Press
All rights reserved.

D. The physical location of inventories is a complex consideration for the multinational firm. The multinational firm must weigh a strategy of keeping inventory concentrated in a few areas from which they can be shipped, and thus minimize the total amount of inventory needed to operate the global business, with the possibility of delays in getting goods from central locations to user locations around the world. Exchange rates, import/export quotas, the threat of expropriation, and taxes all influence inventory policy.

SELF-TEST QUESTIONS

Definitional

1. The _____ _____ determines the number of units of one currency that can be exchanged for another.

2. International financial transactions were carried out under a _____ _____ _____ system from the end of World War II until 1971.

3. The organization which controlled the fixed exchange rate system was the _____ _____ _____, which served as a world central bank.

4. Under the fixed rate system, the relative values of various currencies were based on the _____ _____ _____.

5. Countries with export surpluses and a strong currency might have to _____ their currencies upward.

6. In 1971, the _____ rate system was replaced by one that permitted the U.S. dollar to _____ against other currencies.

7. Evaluation of foreign investments involves the analysis of dividend and royalty cash flows that are _____ to the parent company.

8. Some foreign governments restrict, or block, the amount of income that can be repatriated to encourage _____ in the foreign country.

9. _____ risk refers to the possibility of restrictions on cash flows or the outright _____ of property by a foreign government.

10. A dollar deposited in a non-U.S. bank is often called a _____.

11. Firms can hedge against exchange rate movements by buying or selling _____ or _____ contracts.

21-6

©1992 The Dryden Press
All rights reserved.

12. Investment by U.S. firms in foreign operations is called _____ investment, while the purchase of foreign bonds and stock by U.S. citizens or firms is called _____ investment.

13. _____ bonds are bonds sold by a foreign borrower but denominated in the currency of the country in which the issue is sold.

Conceptual

14. Financial analysis is not able to take into account political risk.

   a. True   b. False

15. When a central bank of a country buys and sells its currency to smooth out fluctuations in the exchange rate, the system is referred to as a managed floating system.

   a. True   b. False

16. A foreign currency will, on average, appreciate at a percentage rate approximately equal to the amount by which its inflation rate exceeds the inflation rate in the United States.

   a. True   b. False

17. Which of the following statements concerning multinational cash flow analysis is <u>not</u> correct?

   a. The relevant cash flows are the dividends and royalties repatriated to the parent company.
   b. The cash flows must be converted to the currency of the parent company and, thus, are subject to future exchange rate changes.
   c. Dividends and royalties received are normally taxed only by the government of the country in which the subsidiary is located.
   d. Foreign governments may restrict the amount of the cash flows that may be repatriated.
   e. All of the above statements are correct.

18. The cost of capital is generally lower for a foreign project than for an equivalent domestic project since the possibility of exchange gains exists.

   a. True   b. False

©1992 The Dryden Press
All rights reserved.

SELF-TEST PROBLEMS

1. The "spot rate" for Greek drachmas is 0.0313 U.S. dollars per drachma. What would the exchange rate be expressed in drachmas per dollar?

   a. 0.0313 drachmas per dollar   **b.** 3.1300 drachmas per dollar
   c. 31.9489 drachmas per dollar   **d.** 319.4890 drachmas per dollar
   e. 400.0000 drachmas per dollar

2. The U.S. dollar can be exchanged for 942.1432 Italian lire today. The Italian currency is expected to appreciate by 10 percent tomorrow. What is the expected exchange rate tomorrow expressed in lire per dollar?

   a. 836.1935 lire per dollar   **b.** 841.3167 lire per dollar
   c. 847.9289 lire per dollar   **d.** 958.2334 lire per dollar
   e. 965.9813 lire per dollar

3. You are considering the purchase of a block of stock in Galic Steel, a French steel producer. Galic just paid a dividend of 10 francs per share; that is, D_0 = 10 francs. You expect the dividend to grow indefinitely at a rate of 15 percent per year, but because of a higher expected rate of inflation in France than in the United States, you expect the franc to depreciate against the dollar at a rate of 5 percent per year. The exchange rate is currently 5 francs per U.S. dollar, but this ratio will change as the franc depreciates. For a stock with this degree of risk, including exchange rate risk, you feel that a 20 percent rate of return is required. What is the most, in dollars, that you should pay for the stock?

   a. $20.90   **b.** $31.70   **c.** $46.00   **d.** $53.60   **e.** $60.34

4. Refer to the previous question. Now assume that the franc is expected to appreciate against the dollar at the rate of 1 percent per year. All other facts are unchanged. Under these conditions, what should you be willing to pay for the stock?

   a. $20.90   **b.** $31.70   **c.** $46.00   **d.** $53.60   **e.** $60.34

ANSWERS TO SELF-TEST QUESTIONS

1. exchange rate
2. fixed exchange rate
3. International Monetary Fund (IMF)
4. U.S. dollar
5. revalue
6. fixed; "float"
7. repatriated
8. reinvestment
9. Political; expropriation
10. Eurodollar
11. forward; futures
12. direct; portfolio
13. Foreign

©1992 The Dryden Press
All rights reserved.

14. b. Political risk must be explicitly addressed by international financial managers.

15. a. This statement is correct.

16. b. The foreign currency will depreciate if its inflation rate is higher than that of the United States.

17. c. Dividends and royalties received will generally also be taxed by the U.S. government, but the total taxes paid to both governments will not exceed that which would be paid had the earnings occurred in the United States.

18. b. The cost of capital is generally higher because of exchange risk and political risk.

SOLUTIONS TO SELF-TEST PROBLEMS

1. c. The exchange rate for drachmas per dollar would be the reciprocal of the exchange rate of dollars per drachma: 1/(0.0313 dollars per drachma) = 31.9489 drachmas per dollar.

2. c. 942.1432(0.90)/$1.00 = 847.9289 lire per dollar.

3. a. First, the valuation equation must be modified to convert the expected dividend stream to dollars:

$$D_t = D_0(1 + g)(ER),$$

where ER = exchange ratio. ER = 1/5 today, but if francs depreciate at a rate of 5 percent, it will take more francs to buy a dollar in the future. The value of ER at some future time (t) will be

$$ER_t = \frac{\text{Dollars}}{\text{Francs}} = \frac{1}{5(1.05)^t}.$$

Therefore, D_t in dollars may be calculated as follows:
Thus, if the dividend in francs is expected to grow at a rate of 15 percent per year, but the franc is expected to depreciate at a rate of 5 percent per year against the dollar, then the growth rate, in dollars, of dividends received will be 9.52 percent. We can now calculate the value of the stock in dollars:

©1992 The Dryden Press
All rights reserved.

$$D_t \text{ (in dollars)} = (10 \text{ francs})(1 + g)^t(ER_t)$$

$$= \frac{\$10(1.15)^t}{5(1.05)^t}$$

$$= \frac{\$2(1.15)^t}{(1.05)^t}$$

$$= \$2\left(\frac{1.15}{1.05}\right)^t$$

$$= \$2(1.0952)^t.$$

$$\hat{P}_0 = \frac{D_1}{k_s - g} = \frac{\$2(1.0952)}{0.20 - 0.0952} = \frac{\$2.1904}{0.1048} = \$20.90.$$

4. e. Solve the problem as above: $ER_t = 1(1.01)^t/5$.

$$D_t \text{ (in dollars)} = (10 \text{ francs})(1 + g)^t\left[\frac{(1.01)^t}{5}\right]$$

$$= (\$10/5)(1.15)^t(1.01)^t$$

$$= \$2(1.1615)^t.$$

Thus, the franc dividend is expected to increase at a rate of 15 percent per year, and the value of these francs is expected to rise at the rate of 1 percent per year, so the expected annual growth rate of the dollar dividend is 16.15 percent. We can now calculate the stock price:

$$\hat{P}_0 = \frac{D_1}{k_s - g} = \frac{\$2(1.1615)}{0.20 - 0.1615} = \frac{\$2.3230}{0.0385} = \$60.34.$$

©1992 The Dryden Press
All rights reserved.